D0458189

9.45
110

STUDIES IN EUROPEAN HISTORY

IX

# THE RESTORED
# HOUSE OF LORDS

*by*

## MAXWELL P. SCHOENFELD

*Wisconsin State University, Eau Claire*

1967

## MOUTON & CO.

THE HAGUE · PARIS

UNIVERSITY OF VICTORIA
LIBRARY
Victoria, B. C.

© Copyright 1967 by Mouton & Co., Publishers, The Hague, The Netherlands

*No part of this book may be translated or reproduced in any form, by print, photoprint, microfilm, or any other means, without written permission from the publishers*

Printed in the Netherlands by Mouton & Co., Printers, The Hague

*To my Mother*

# PREFACE

In his monumental study of the peerage, *The Crisis of the Aristocracy 1558-1641*, Professor Lawrence Stone concluded that the abolition of the house of lords in 1649 "was not a mere by-product of the dynamics of war; it was the culmination of a crisis of confidence which had been maturing for well over half a century". Indeed it would be hard to doubt that the aristocracy had suffered a severe, perhaps even fatal blow when their house fell shortly after the death of Charles I. Yet the house of lords was to be revived in 1660, and was to show great endurance, as Mrs. C. C. Weston has demonstrated in her *English Constitutional Theory and the House of Lords 1556-1832*. It has been my hope to illuminate to some degree the period of crisis for the aristocracy, from the abolition of their house of parliament to the return of Charles II, and to trace their actions in the critical early days of the restoration period.

As the bulk of the sources consulted for this work have been drawn from materials well known to students of seventeenth century England, I have chosen not to include yet another select bibliography. I would, however, wish to mention a source of materials less frequently consulted, the collections available in the House of Lords Record Office. While much material deposited in Westminster Palace has been adequately calendared in the appendices to the *Reports* of the Historical Manuscripts Commission, there are some further manuscript materials which Mr. Maurice Bond and his staff will readily make available to any interested scholar. For the pamphlets cited in this work I have included the current British Museum press marks as some titles of quite different pamphlets are deceptively similar.

In the course of researching and writing this book, I have benefited from the generous assistance of many persons. I wish to acknowledge the co-operation provided me by library and archival staffs on both sides of the Atlantic. While it is not possible to acknowledge my gratitude to all such persons by name, I am particularly in the debt of Miss Janet Schmidt, who rendered assistance much beyond her duty. Professor F. G. Marcham of Cornell University read an early draft of this volume, which has gained much from his thoughtful advice and valuable suggestions. I am indebted to Professor Howard Lutz of Wisconsin State University-Eau Claire, who graciously found time to give a careful reading to and improve upon several chapters of the final draft of this work. The manuscript has also benefited from a meticulous examination by Mr. John O. Stark, of the Department of English, and the many suggestions he made for its improvement. Miss Catherine Yancey, of the University staff, cheerfully performed the exacting task of preparing the manuscript for printing. The shortcomings of the work are, of course, entirely my own.

Eau Claire, Wisconsin                                                    M.P.S.
July, 1965

# CONTENTS

# LIST OF ABBREVIATIONS

*Acts and Ordinances:* Acts and Ordinances of the Interregnum, 1642-1660, ed.,
C. H. Firth and R. S. Rait, 3 vols. (London, 1911).

*Add. Mss.:* British Museum, *Additional Manuscripts.*

*Baker's Chronicle:* A Chronicle of the Kings of England. From the Time of the
Romans Government, unto the Death of King James. Whereunto is added,
The Reign of King Charles the First, and the first Thirteen Years of his
Sacred Majesty, King Charles the Second, by Sir Richard Baker, Knight,
ed., E. Phillips (London, 1674).

B. M.: British Museum.

Bodley.: Bodleian Library, Oxford University.

*Braye Mss.:* House of Lords Record Office, *Braye Manuscripts.*

*Burton's Diary:* Thomas Burton, *Diary,* ed., John Towill Rutt, 4 vols. (London,
1828).

*Cal. Tr. Bks.:* Calendar of Treasury Books, 1660-1667, ed., W. A. Shaw (London,
1904).

*Carte Mss.:* Bodleian Library, *Carte Manuscripts.*

*C.C.A.M.:* Calendar of the Proceedings of the Committee for Advance of Money,
ed., M. A. E. Green, 3 vols. (London, 1888).

*C.C.C.:* Calendar of the Committee for Compounding, ed., M. A. E. Green, 5
vols. (London, 1889-1892).

*C.C.S.P.:* The Calendar of Clarendon State Papers preserved in the Bodleian
Library, vol. IV, ed., F. J. Routledge, 1932.

*C.J.:* Journals of the House of Commons.

*Clarendon Mss.:* Bodleian Library, *Clarendon Manuscripts.*

Clarendon's *Life:* The Life of Edward Earl of Clarendon, Lord High Chancellor
of England, and Chancellor of the University of Oxford, in which is included a Continuation of his History of the Grand Rebellion, Oxford,
Clarendon Printing House, 1759.

*Clarendon S. P.:* State Papers collected by Edward, Earl of Clarendon, vol. III,
ed., Thomas Monkhouse, 1786.

Clarendon's *Rebellion:* Edward Hyde, first earl of Clarendon, *The History of the
Rebellion and Civil Wars in England . . .* (Oxford, 1843).

*C.S.P.D.:* Calendar of State Papers, Domestic Series, 1657-1662, ed., M. A. E.
Green (London, 1861-1886).

*C.S.P.V.:* Calendar of State Papers and Manuscripts, relating to English Affairs
existing in the Archives and Collections of Venice, 1657-1664, 3 vols., ed.,
A. B. Hinds (1931-1932).

*Egerton Mss.:* British Museum, *Egerton Manuscripts.*

*E.H.R.:* English Historical Review.

*G.E.C.:* The Complete Peerage of England, Scotland, Ireland, Great Britain, and the United Kingdom, ed., G. E. Cockayne, *et. al.,* 14 vols. 2nd edition (1910-1959).

*Hargrave Mss.:* British Museum, *Hargrave Manuscripts.*

*Harleian Mss.:* British Museum, *Harleian Manuscripts.*

*H.L.R.O.:* House of Lords Record Office, Westminster Palace.

*H. Mss. C.: Historical Manuscripts Commission.*

*Kennet's History:* White Kennet, *A Complete History of England: with the Lives of all the Kings and Queens thereof: from the earliest Account of Time, to the Death of His Late Majesty King William III,* 3 vols., (2nd edition, London, 1719).

*Kennet's Register:* White Kennet, *A Register and Chronicle Ecclesiastical and Civil: containing Matters of Fact, delivered in the Words of the most authentic Books, Papers, and Records; digested in Exact Order of Time* (London, 1728).

*Lansdowne Mss.:* British Museum, *Lansdowne Manuscripts.*

*L.J.: Journals of the House of Lords.*

Ludlow's *Memoirs:* Edmund Ludlow, *Memoirs,* ed., Charles Harding Firth, 2 vols., (Oxford, 1894).

*New Parliamentary History: Cobbett's Parliamentary History of England from the Norman Conquest, in 1066, to the year 1803,* 36 vols. (1806-1820).

*Old Parliamentary History: The Parliamentary or Constitutional History of England; from the Earliest Times to the Dissolution of the Convention Parliament that restored King Charles II,* 24 vols. (1759-1760).

*Pepys' Diary:* Samuel Pepys, *The Diary of Samuel Pepys,* ed., Henry B. Wheatley, 6 vols. (London, 1896).

*Rawl. Mss:* Bodleian Library, *Rawlinson Manuscripts.*

*Somers Tracts: A Collection of Scarce and Valuable Tracts . . . of the late Lord Sommers,* ed., Sir Walter Scott. First Collection, 1748; Second Collection, 1750, Second Edition (London, 1812).

*S.R.: Statutes of the Realm,* ed., T. E. Tomlins, *et. al.,* 18 vols (1810-1824).

*Steele: Bibliotheca Lindesiana. A Bibliography of Royal Proclamations of the Tudor and Stuart Sovereigns and of Others published under Authority 1485-1714,* ed., Robert Reynolds Steele, 2 vols. (Oxford, 1910).

*Stowe Mss.:* British Museum, *Stowe Manuscripts.*

*Thurloe S. P.: A Collection of the State Papers of John Thurloe, Esq.,* ed., Thomas Birch, 7 vols. (1742).

*T.R.H.S.: Transactions of the Royal Historical Society.*

Whitelocke's *Memorials:* Bulstrode Whitelocke, *Memorials of the English Affairs: or, an Historical Account of what passed from the Beginning of the Reign of King Charles the First, to King Charles the Second His Happy Restoration* (London, 1682).

# INTRODUCTION

The History of England in the seventeenth century is dominated by the disruption of government which occupied the middle years of that era. Men who lived through the vivid and often violent events which characterized that upheaval not unnaturally sought for reasons to explain why their time was so troubled. Several men, such as John Lilburne and James Harrington, pointed to the changing condition of the house of lords, and particularly to the declining influence of the peerage, as most important in those causes which produced upheaval in their lives. Through their works, and recorded by several others, there runs a general thread of agreement: the house of lords had lost power, and this loss of power had serious and upsetting effect upon the stability of the government of the realm. This decline was as recent in its origins as Tudor times.

Throughout the Middle Ages the baronage had been a power in English political life. They had struggled against the authority of the crown and occasionally for the crown itself. Through the time of troubles of the mid-fifteenth century their military activity had come to dominate the political scene and made all other considerations secondary to the resolution of the chaos they had unleashed upon the country. In their dependence upon the political force represented by livery and maintenance, the baronage largely abandoned the institution of parliament, save as a hastily convened and dismissed rubber stamp. The house of lords, ancient agency of noble advice and consent, was neglected. The membership overshadowed the institution.

The violence of conflicts among the nobles produced a demand for an end to such lack of governance and from the war of the roses emerged a new royal family able to offer a remedy. The policies of Henry Tudor transformed the battle of Bosworth Field from another baronial burying ground into a landmark in English History and the resting place of the ambitions of the noble king-makers. The nobility had aided Henry VII in his task by decimating their own ranks in the

war of the roses. Henry did the rest. He removed by means judicial
and non-judicial his most formidable opponents in the baronage. He
granted new honors sparingly, and those few went to his own servants, largely new men, called by the old baronage men raised from
the dust. His son and famous grand-daughter continued his policy.[1]

While all three great Tudors carefully reduced the peerage to a
position clearly beneath that of the crown, all three needed the assistance of parliament for the successful execution of their policies.
Having thus expelled the military influence of the nobility by the
front door, they admitted the constitutional influence of the house
of lords by the back door, and in so doing, the Tudors made the
institution of the house of lords rival the territorial prominence of
its privileged members. In the Tudor parliaments the house of lords
was acknowledged superior to the house of commons, but it was
from the commons that the Tudors most desired approbation of their
policies and to the commons that they increasingly turned for support.
This period also saw a growing relationship between the membership of the lower house and the most talented and successful members
of the gentry and professional classes. The Tudors could create peerages and execute individual peers; they could not create members of
the house of commons or alienate these necessary allies of their policy
of a secure monarchy and nation in an insecure century. At the end
of Elizabeth's reign Essex's rising was met by the headman's axe, but
to the demands of the house of commons the best Elizabeth could
offer were alternate threats for better manners and the touching
flattery of a golden speech.

The romance of Elizabeth I with the commons was not continued
by James I. He and his unfortunate son rode the twin rails of divine
right monarchy and episcopal authority over the precipice of constitutional compromise and into the chasm of political revolution. While
*en route* to the destruction of their monarchy both James I and
Charles I found time to add substantially to the small body of peers
of Tudor and pre-Tudor creation. When Elizabeth died, the number
of temporal peers was fifty-nine, only eight of her creation. From 1603
to 1640, the first two Stuarts had added some ninety peers to this
number; Charles also called up eight eldest sons of peers to sit in
their own right in the house of lords.[2]

---

[1]  Edward Jenks, *The Constitutional Experiments of the Commonwealth* (Cambridge, 1890), pp. 8-9.
[2]  Godfrey Davies, *The Early Stuarts*, 2d ed. (Oxford, 1959), p. 226.

This house, still feeling the effects of Tudor and early Stuart policies, was particularly vulnerable to the new forces and ideas of the great English revolution which dominated the middle years of the seventeenth century. The Puritan Revolution altered constitutional thinking by a process of addition much more than of subtraction or even of substitution. The old justifications and theories of government lived on and even enjoyed revivals of popularity after the civil wars. But new justifications, new explanations, were necessary to the men whose strongest claim to govern was in fact victory on the field of battle. The Long Parliament and its successor bodies during the Protectorate seized upon the concept of representation in the constitution and the corresponding right to rule based upon their representation in the wealth of England. The commons had earlier offered this proposition in slightly different form in their Apology, characterizing themselves as the flower and power of England. This doctrine expanded steadily until it found its leading spokesman in James Harrington.

In their Apology, the commons had qualified their claim, "the higher nobility excepted". From 1649 to 1660, they abolished the qualification with the lords' house, and expanded their argument to justify the abolition. Harrington explained the apparent decline of the peerage and the disappearance of their representation in the constitution as a consequence of the decline of their proportion in the wealth of England, and particularly their shrinking stake in the soil.

When the appearance of the old constitution was patched together in 1660, this concept of representation as a right of wealth remained popular. But its popularity was greatest with those it had recently been used against — the occupants of the house of lords. In fact, the wealth of the peerage was still substantial, had not suffered beyond point of recovery in the civil wars, and was to improve notably. The peerage used the house of lords as the instrument to secure and extend their economic position during the restoration, when no other group had available and was able to exploit such a formidable tool. The subsequent promotion of wealth into the upper house in the late seventeenth and the eighteenth centuries, and the new wealth that sprang from old lands in the nineteenth century, bastioned the house of lords in its powers until the opening years of the present century. The argument of the revolutionary house of commons was the lords' justification. The system that emerged when the houses of parliament went into alliance in 1689 ruled England as a political aristocracy for several generations. The senior partner in this constitutional coalition secured its right to membership at the very time the junior partner was most offensive toward it. The house of lords survived abolition in the seventeenth century and it took the house of commons from 1832 until 1911 properly to subdue it again. The first struggle is the topic of this volume.

# I

## FROM THE ACCESSION OF JAMES I TO
## THE ABOLITION OF THE HOUSE OF LORDS

James I substantially inflated the peerage with his creations. This inflation had one advantage; it prevented the house of lords from becoming a house based solely on blue blood and old estates and opened the path to honors for the new men of talent or wealth. Overbalancing this advantage was James's choice of nobles. He was infatuated with favorites, men like Robert Carr, who as Viscount Rochester was the first Scotsman to sit in the house of lords, and George Villiers, first duke of Buckingham. The raising of these favorites of the court incited opposition from the old nobility, and added another complaint to the cause of the group coming to be called the country peers. Buckingham inflamed this opposition to a new height by encouraging James to sell honors. A barony sold for £ 10,000 and viscounties went at £ 15,000. An earldom could be purchased for £ 20,000. This practice created opposition not only from the old peers, but in the house of commons, and weakened the respect of that body for the upper house, with serious consequences later. The commons early expressed their attitude toward this practice. One of the charges at Buckingham's impeachment was that he frightened a man into paying £ 10,000 for a barony.[1]

In the eyes of some observers, the peerage was seen as having lost ground economically, when measured against the wealth represented by the house of commons. In 1601, Thomas Wilson the younger

---

[1] G. Davies, *Early Stuarts*, pp. 16-25, 30, 263, 267; A. S. Turberville, *The House of Lords in the Reign of William III* in *Oxford Historical and Literary Studies*, 3 vols. (Oxford, 1913), p. 227; Luke Owen Pike, *Constitutional History of the House of Lords* (London, 1894), pp. 274, 355; Charles Harding Firth, *The House of Lords during the Civil War* (London, 1910), pp. 11-20. To summon a son to the house of lords in a father's barony, while the father is sitting by a higher title, only hastens the descent of the lesser dignity and temporarily adds to the number of peers. It has no permanent effect, as upon the death of either father or son in the life of the other, the survivor absorbs the title of the deceased.

estimated that the income of 16,000 families of the gentry was three times greater than the income of the nobility, bishops, deans and chapters, and richer yeomen combined. In 1628, men said that the house of commons could buy the house of lords three times over.[2]

Inflation of honors, favorites, selling privileges, loss of power to the commons — all struck at the house of lords. So did the increasing complexity of government. The Tudors had largely excluded the natural born counsellors of the realm from the government administration. Only a favored few held prominent places of power in the erratic but increasingly bureaucratic administration of James I and his son.

The reign of Charles I saw the weaknesses of his father's peerage intensified. In the first years of his reign sales of peerages continued. All told, between 1615 and 1628 at least eighteen persons had purchased English peerages. The older peers attempted to strengthen themselves, and in 1629 petitioned the king on behalf of the twentieth earl of Oxford, an impecunious officer in Flanders, that he might be preferred in service above those of meaner birth and aided in gaining a landed estate. The Stuart peerage was viewed as deficient in those three qualifications thought vital to their order: "virtue and meritorious service, ancient family, and broad acres".[3] Much debate has raged around the issue of broad acres, and virtue and meritorious service are often found wanting when measured by critical observers. But the English peerage was unique among aristocracies in the possession of a particular political power as peers of parliament. Accordingly, how the house of lords acted, in its corporate sense, could have substantial effect upon the fate of individual peers, and upon the peerage altogether.

As conflict between Charles and the leaders of parliament deepened, the position of the house of lords was not at all clear. The upper house had on occasion treated Charles roughly. By limiting the number of proxies a peer might hold to two, it deprived Buckingham of

---

[2] C. H. Firth, *House of Lords*, p. 5; H. E. Chesney, "The Transference of Lands in England, 1640-1660", *T.R.H.S.*, 4th Series, XV (London, 1932), p. 208; R. H. Tawney, "Harrington's Interpretation of His Age", *Proceedings of the British Academy* (London, 1942), p. 217. For a discussion of Tawney's interpretation of Harrington's interpretation, see J. H. Hexter, *Reappraisals in History* (Evanston, Ill., 1961), pp. 117-162.
[3] G. Davies, *Early Stuarts*, pp. 266-276; C. H. Firth, *House of Lords*, pp. 20, 28, 31; A. S. Turberville, "Lords in the Reign of William III", pp. 62-63; David Ogg, *England in the Reign of Charles II*, 2d ed. (Oxford, 1955), I, p. 136; C. R. Mayes, "The Sale of Peerages in Early Stuart England", *Journal of Modern History* (Chicago), 1957, p. 34.

eleven of the thirteen he held. When Charles wished to impeach the earl of Bristol for his revelations of the Madrid fiasco, the lords accepted Bristol's charges against Buckingham. Charles could not depend upon the house of lords to check the house of commons' proceedings against his favorite and had to dissolve parliament. Actually the upper house was not particularly opposed to Charles. Much more they were attempting to exert an independence firmly checked by the Tudors. They acquiesced in the Petition of Right, but by 1640 refused to condemn Strafford by process of impeachment. As king and commons drifted further apart, the lords attempted to mediate, to find a middle way. This newly conceived role came too late. They were too much compromised and too deficient in influence to be successful. From 1628 to 1642 members of the house of lords sought a constitutional resolution to England's difficulties. Their failure lay largely in the discovery by the commons that they could proceed successfully without regard for the lords. Sir John Eliot had already said: "Should the lords desert us, we should yet continue flourishing and green." Until the passage of the Petition of Right the two houses had proceeded together; after its passage the rising democratic spirit of the house of commons, led by Eliot, found the conciliatory spirit of the house of lords irksome. In the Short Parliament the two houses closed ranks, viewing parliament as "the soul of the body politic"; but they parted ways when the lords, by 61 to 25, agreed with Charles that supply should precede grievances. When the Long Parliament opened, a good half of the peerage openly supported Charles. About a quarter favored the parliamentarians, while the remainder were disqualified from an active role by age, health, or in some other way. Charles could reasonably expect substantial support from a house where forty-four peers of his own creation and thirty-eight of his father's creation sat, as opposed to only forty-six of more ancient patent. At first he could hope that the house of lords' insistence upon judicial processes in Strafford's trial would save his servant. But the house of commons saw the issue as political, and when the legal process moved too slowly they pressed upon the lords a bill of attainder. Harried by the London mob, the house of lords passed the measure on May 8, 1641. Four days later one of the most able of their number was beheaded.[4]

[4]  G. Davies, *Early Stuarts*, pp. 36-37, 41; R. W. Perceval, "The Origins and Development of the House of Lords", *Parliamentary Affairs*, VII, 1 (London, 1953), p. 40; C. H. Firth, *House of Lords*, pp. 75, 80, 88-89, 115.

Dissatisfied with the upper house's behavior in the Strafford affair, and aware of Charles's natural majority in it, the commons' leaders determined to strike down this possible support of the royal cause. On December 1, 1641, the Grand Remonstrance of the house of commons proclaimed that by the sale of honors the "common justice of the kingdom hath been much endangered" and "bribery, extortion, partiality" fostered. They further protested, with an ominous note for the future, "But what can we the Commons, without the conjunction of the House of Lords, and what conjunction can we expect there, when the Bishops and recusant lords are so numerous and prevalent that they are able to cross and interrupt our best endeavours for reformation, and by that means give advantage to this malignant party to traduce our proceedings?" The claims the Grand Remonstrance foreshadowed were swift in materializing. Within a few days the house of commons appointed a committee to review bills the house of lords had rejected, and to ask why they had done so. The instructions to the committee observed that the commons were representatives of the whole kingdom, while the lords were only particular persons coming to parliament in a particular capacity. The parliamentarians now centered their attack upon the bishops, who were for some days prevented from sitting by the threat of violence. Charles unwisely urged the bishops to protest that everything done in their absence was illegal, successfully driving his enemies in the house of lords closer to the lower house. When he then attempted to proceed against the five members and Mandeville, parliament closed ranks against him.[5]

This unity was short-lived, and it was the parliamentarians who precipitated the split when, in early 1642, they renewed their assault upon the bishops, determined to strip them of their temporal jurisdiction and amputate them from the house of lords. With the mob at its back, the commons thrust the exclusion bill upon an unhappy upper house, which turned to Charles for leadership, or some expression of policy which would hold forth the hope of pacifying the sharpening crisis without doing violence to the constitution of the house of lords. Charles, at his most unsteady, failed to respond and his disappointed peers conducted themselves without distinction. On Feb-

[5] Samuel Rawson Gardiner, ed., *Constitutional Documents of the Puritan Revolution* (Oxford, 1889), pp. 138, 151; George Peabody Gooch, *English Democratic Ideas in the Seventeenth Century*, 2d ed. (New York, 1959), pp. 90-91; G. Davies, *Early Stuarts*, pp. 122-123; C. H. Firth, *House of Lords*, pp. 92-93, 111.

ruary 5, 1642, the exclusion bill passed the upper house by a reputed vote of thirty-six to twenty-three. Eight days later the king signified his approval. The prestige of the house of lords sank to yet a new low.[6]

The lords were a depressed body in the spring of 1642. Many royalist peers had given up the struggle and ceased to attend parliament. Through April attendance averaged little better than thirty. So far the lords had suffered mutilation at other hands. In the summer of 1642 they proceeded to turn the scalpel upon themselves. In May a substantial number, led by the duke of Richmond, the marquess of Hertford, the earls of Lindsey, Southampton, and Northampton, and Baron Capel, responded to Charles's summons to his council at York. These prominent royalists abandoned the house to the parliamentary party headed by the earls of Essex, Warwick, and Bolingbroke, Viscount Say and Sele, and barons Brooke, Mandeville, and Howard of Escrick. On June 1 these latter joined with the commons in the Nineteen Propositions. Two of the propositions struck at the house of lords. The seventh requested that the votes of the Roman Catholic peers should be taken away, thus fulfilling the intent of the Grand Remonstrance. The last proposition called for a law restraining any peers thereafter created from sitting and voting in parliament without the consent of both houses. Even the pretence of lordly independence thus would be dispelled.[7]

The parliamentary peers now turned upon their royalist brethren at York. They summoned back from the North the earls of Northampton, Devonshire, Dover, and Monmouth, and the barons Howard of Charlton, Rich, Grey of Ruthyn, Coventry, and Capel. When the nine failed to obey the summons the house of lords barred them from ever sitting again as peers of parliament and their corresponding

---

[6]  S. R. Gardiner, *History of England from the Accession of James I to the Outbreak of the Civil War*, 10 vols. (London, 1884), X, p. 163; C. H. Firth, *House of Lords*, p. 111; S. R. Gardiner, ed., *Constitutional Documents*, p. 163. The Act for Disabling all Persons in Holy Orders to Exercise any Temporal Jurisdiction or Authority (16 Car. I, *cap.* 27) reads: "Be it enacted, that no Archbishop or Bishop or any other person that now is or hereafter shall be in Holy Orders, shall at any time after the fifteenth day of February ... have any power or place, suffrage or voice, or use, or execute any power or authority in the Parliaments of this realm. ..." *Statutes of the Realm*, ed. T. E. Tomlins, *et. al.*, 18 vols. (1810-1824), V, p. 138.

[7]  S. R. Gardiner, *History of England*, X, p. 185; Thomas May, "A Breviary of the History of the Parliament of England", in Francis, Baron Maserès, *Select Tracts Relating to the Civil War in England* (London, 1815), I, p. 46; C. H. Firth, *House of Lords*, p. 115; S. R. Gardiner, *Constitutional Documents*, pp. 173-174.

privileges were declared forfeit. As pressure built toward war the lords further divided. Many noble families did not present an united front, among them the Leicester-Sidney connection, the earl of Warwick and his son, Baron Rich, and the families of the earls of Kingston and Dover, and Baron Herbert of Cherbury. Yet within these divisions both parliamentary and royalist peers realized that a clear split between king and parliament would seriously injure their own house. Hence they struggled for compromise without closing their own ranks, until Charles raised his standard at Nottingham and exposed the futility of their haphazard proceedings. Ranke best described the unhappy position in which the peers now found themselves: "The contest was not between absolute power and a democratic republic, though these ideas at times appeared in the background. The one party in fact desired Parliament not without the King, the other the King not without Parliament: but the one sought to maintain the autonomy of the throne and of the Church, and the estates of the realm as hitherto constituted, the other would shake the foundations of the Church, and subject the crown unconditionally to Parliament. On this question a dispute broke out within the legislative body itself: part broke loose from the rest, and joined the king." In this disruption, the house of lords could not but suffer. When all parties abandoned the constitution to seek resolution in arms, they abandoned the institutions of the constitution as well. The fate of their house, along with the rest of England, now waited upon the outcome of battle. The house of lords was not abolished until 1649, but it was a matter of burying a body seven years dead.[8]

So the peers went off to war for king and country, leaving behind the corpse of their house, the immediate victim of their action. Of the 135 temporal peers of England living when Charles raised his standard on August 22, 1642, about half actively backed the royal cause with military service or contributions. It is not surprising that this majority flowed to the royal standard, while only about thirty peers could be numbered in the opposition. The earl of Newcastle spoke for the majority that "the nobility cannot fall if the King be victorious, nor can they keep up their dignities, if the king be overcome". Yet many peers of the most ancient patent were not royalist,

---

[8]  T. May, "Breviary", I, p. 47; Paul H. Hardacre, *The Royalists during the Puritan Revolution* (The Hague, 1956), pp. 10-11; C. H. Firth, *House of Lords*, pp. 120, 132; Leopold von Ranke, *A History of England principally in the Seventeenth Century*, 6 vols. (Oxford, 1875), II, p. 357.

the price of earlier Stuart policy. Of the marquesses and earls of pre-Stuart creation, only Hertford, Winchester, Bath, Cumberland, Huntingdon, Shrewsbury, Southampton, and Worcester were royalists, while Bedford, Essex, Lincoln, Northumberland, Nottingham, Pembroke and Rutland opposed the king. Arundell was abroad, Oxford a minor, and Kent, Sussex, and Derby were in their eighties, although Derby's successor was to die for the royal cause. This earl in 1642 mustered an estimated 60,000 men for the crown in Lancashire and Cheshire, one of the last great displays by an English lord of the feudal ability to raise retainers and friends. He was equalled by Lord Herbert of Raglan, later earl of Glamorgan and marquess of Worcester, who in June and July of 1642 poured no less than £ 122,500 into Charles's treasury from his and his father's estates. The contribution of the earl of Newcastle, in raising both men and money, was also very great, and earned him promotion to marquess by Charles I and to duke by Charles II. The Cavalier lords as a group fought bravely for the crown, but were not all disciplined soldiers. Eight died in the field. Lord Aubigny and the earl of Lindsey fell at Edgehill; the earls of Carnarvon and Sunderland at Newbury. Hopton Heath claimed the earl of Northampton. The earls of Denbigh and Kingston also fell in 1643. The earl of Lichfield was killed at Rowton Heath. Four more peers, the earls of Holland, Cambridge, Derby and Baron Capel, were executed for their efforts in the royal cause.[9]

The gaps left by death were more than filled by Charles's creations during the war. He bestowed peerages from the two motives of financial necessity and rewards for valiant service. Even under such necessity Clarendon claims that Charles was reluctant to use this much criticized practice. But to Richard Newport and John Lucas went baronies at £ 6,000. The earl of Worcester earned a marquisate for £ 10,000. In all, there were thirty-eight additions and promotions in

[9]   P. H. Hardacre, Royalists, pp. 4-5, 10, 10 n.; G. Davies, Early Stuarts, p. 127; L. von Ranke, History of England, II, p. 358; S. R. Gardiner, History of England, X, p. 207; The Complete Peerage of England, Scotland, Ireland, Great Britain, and the United Kingdom, ed., G. E. Cokayne, et. al., 2nd ed., 14 vols. (1910-1959), II, pp. 515-526; The account of Northampton's death indicates the royalist peer's concept of his duty. He was surrounded on the field but managed to kill several of his opponents with his sword. His armor was so good that he held his own until his helmet was struck off. When summoned then to surrender he answered that he scorned to take quarter "from such base rogues as you are" and was slain. A. H. Burne and Peter Young, The Great Civil War (London, 1959), p. 69; Margaret, duchess of Newcastle, The Life of the First Duke of Newcastle (London, 1667), p. 120.

the English peerage from the outbreak of war to the close of 1645. One promised promotion Charles was not able to carry out. He offered an earldom to Baron Brudenell for £ 1,000 to facilitate an escape from Carisbrooke Castle in 1648. Brudenell raised and sent the money to Charles, and in 1661 Charles II honored his father's pledge. The parliamentary party refused to recognize these creations and promotions, and both the Propositions of Uxbridge and the Propositions of Newcastle provided that all such honors bestowed after May 21, 1642, without consent of parliament, should be null and void, and no such peers should sit and vote at Westminster without consent of both houses. In these same propositions the parliamentarians struck against their most prominent enemies, and provided to exclude from pardon such eminent royalists as the marquess of Newcastle, the earls of Derby and Bristol, barons Cottington, Poulett and Digby, and the recently created earl of Norwich, and barons Byron and Langdale, all listed in the Propositions of Uxbridge. The Propositions of Newcastle excluded all recusants in arms against parliament, particularly the marquesses of Winchester and Worcester, Lord Herbert of Raglan, and barons Brudenell, Audley, and Arundell of Wardour. The Four Bills reiterated these exceptions in 1647. The excepted peers represented the most militant of Charles's partisans.[10]

Opposed to them stood an equally dedicated group of peers. Of the parliamentary lords, the most important at first were the earls of Essex and Northumberland. In Essex the cause gained its first military leader, the bearer of a famous and popular name. Northumberland went to war in defence of past rights and liberties, which he strove to safeguard. As his rearward vision became less and less a reality, he steadily moved away from the parliamentary cause. While Northumberland's disillusionment grew, more zealous newcomers crowded forward: barons Wharton, Robartes, Grey of Warke, and Willoughby. In addition to Essex, five other peers led troops for the parliament: the earls of Bedford, Manchester, and Stamford, and barons Brooke and Hastings. The earl of Warwick commanded the fleet. Thus the nation witnessed its peerage playing a prominent role in the first civil war.[11]

[10]  C. H. Firth, House of Lords, pp. 25, 27; P. H. Hardacre, Royalists, p. 13; S. R. Gardiner, Constitutional Documents, pp. 197, 201, 214-216, 256.
[11]  L. von Ranke, History of England, II, p. 359; C. H. Firth, House of Lords, pp. 116, 118-119; A. H. Woolrych, "Penruddock's Rising, 1655", The Historical Association, Pamphlet: General Series, G. 29 (London, 1955), p. 8; G.E.C., IV, p. 573, Appendix B.

In the years from 1642 to 1648 new attitudes appeared toward the peerage and the institution of the house of lords. As the struggle between king and parliament deepened, moderate opinions lost favor, and radical solutions were advocated. At first only the judicial power of the upper house was criticized, then its role in legislation was challenged, finally its very existence threatened. That several peers had played a prominent role in reducing Charles's power was forgotten, or disregarded. In 1646 an ordinance of parliament was passed to bar all recent creations from sitting. The next year the Four Bills provided for an extension of this disability to their heirs. Even at this date the house of commons thought in terms of a bicameral legislature. The army, however, was now moving distinctly apart from their parliamentary allies. When the army set down the Presbyterians in 1647, the peers divided, nine for the army and eight for the London Presbyterians. Seven of the eight moderates, the earls of Middlesex, Lincoln, and Suffolk, and barons Willoughby, Hunsdon, Maynard and Berkeley, were charged with treason and ceased to attend at Westminster. This brush did not prove fatal to the house. Under the moderating influence of Ireton and Cromwell, the army council, in the Heads of the Proposals in 1647, accepted the continued existence of the house of lords, and concerned itself with the question of how the house could be reconciled with the public safety and with the practical supremacy of the representatives of the people. Thus the Puritan Revolution skirted the edge of outright social struggle, inevitably fatal to the peerage.[12]

At this time of crisis, the lords gained support from an unexpected quarter. Among the men in England most imbued with principle was William Prynne. His fanatic devotion to the Presbyterian faith had made him the scourge of the Laudians in the 1630's, and had cost him his ears and other penalties. This man, filled with legalisms, utterly without discretion, now became the unlikely ally of the house of lords; this erstwhile leader of lost causes adopted the peers' as his own, and for the rest of his career as a pamphleteer he defended them through thick and thin. His arguments were often historically accurate, and his claims for an independent peerage largely admirable, but they ill fitted the sorry remnant of the great feudal order which now

---

[12] C. H. Firth, *House of Lords*, pp. 156, 162, 166-171, 173-182; *Acts and Ordinances of the Interregnum, 1642-1660*, ed. C. H. Firth and R. S. Rait, 3 vols. (London, 1911), I, pp. 884-885; S. R. Gardiner, ed., *Constitutional Documents*, p. 253; P. H. Hardacre, *Royalists*, Introduction, n. p.

depended upon the tolerance of the house of commons, and faced the army's ill will. Fortunate for the house of lords, their self-appointed champion has never been accused of submitting to the evidence of reality. On February 21, 1648, his first pamphlet in the lords' behalf appeared. Its title is the best gauge of its author: "The Levellers Levelled to the very Ground wherein this dangerous Seditious Opinion and design of some of them; That it is necessary, decent, and expedient, now to reduce the House of Peeres, and to bring down the Lords into the Commons House, to sit and Vote together with them, as one House. And the false absurd, grounds whereon they build this Paradox, are briefly examined, refuted, and laid in the dust." Prynne proposed to "wholly address" himself to the unwisdom, or to him illegality, of unicameral government. But in declaiming his intention he first loosed a salvo for the Presbyterian lords, Essex, Brooke, and Willoughby, as well as for the "ancient and undoubted power and right of Judicature in civill and criminall cases of Commoners as well as Peers". In his defence he summoned up the *Modus Tenendi Parliamentum* to support his contention that anciently parliaments were held without a house of commons, but never without a house of lords. He then advanced legal arguments against the process of abolishing the upper house, which he maintained would require the dissolution of parliament, and thus contravene the solemn leagues sworn to defend and obey both houses of parliament. One certain observation he did make, to bring down the house of lords was to assure the republicans of the determined opposition of virtually all the nobility. He then passed on to his conclusion, the exposure of "this whole design" as a "subversion of the Law and Custome of Parliaments, a device to destroy both Houses, under pretext of reducing them into one; an engine to dissolve this present, and all future Parliaments; to alter the fundamental Laws and Government of this Kingdom, ... yea, a project to extirpate Monarchy and Nobility, and set up a popular Anarchy and Polarchy: And therefore whoever hath plotted and fomented it, is more guilty of high Treason than Strafford, Canterbury, or the Gunpowder Traitors...." [13]

Prynne was opposed by a man of similar intensity, John Lilburne. Lilburne, the great leveller, had already directed his pen against the lords' judicial power. Spurred by Prynne's assault upon him, he extended his attack in "A Whip for the Present House of Lords". He

---

[13] C. H. Firth, *House of Lords*, pp. 190, 193-194; William Prynne, "The Levellers Levelled. ...", British Museum, E. 428 (7).

represented the present powers of the upper house as being entirely *de facto*, and without legal justification. He then boldly directed his new charge against the battered house, which in "exercising their pretended Legislative power, is destructive to the Libertie and Freedomes of England, it alone having been the chiefe cause of all the late warrs and bloodshed in England". Lilburne then paused to assault the "petty fogging" Prynne as deficient in "parts, abilities, courage, and mettell" before returning to "lay the guilt of all the blood" lost in recent conflict "at the House of Lords doore".[14]

While the pamphleteers exchanged paper lances the more immediately weighty metal of the army was cast into the scales of debate, with predictable effect. For the moment the lower house was the army's objective, and on December 6, 1648, Thomas Pride and a troop of soldiers purged the house of commons of the dissidents to the army's policy. The wiser of the remaining peers realized that the purge was among other things a victory for the opponents of the house of lords; only the most sanguine or opportunist among them hoped that submission would prolong their existence. On December 23, 1648, the house of lords itself deemed only twenty-eight peers still eligible to sit, and of this number only about half appeared at Westminster in the last days. In December the highest number sitting was fifteen on the fifth; by midmonth a low of three was reached. Four of the remainder, Pembroke, Salisbury, Denbigh, and North, made one last attempt to mediate with the king. Charles did not see Denbigh, who bore their address, and sterner methods intervened.[15]

On January 1, 1649, the house of commons passed the ordinance for the king's trial and a resolution setting up a court of commissioners; on the next day the measures were sent up to a house of twelve peers. Not one of them had a word to speak in favor of the ordinance. Pembroke alone remained silent. Northumberland saw no evidence of treason on the king's part. Denbigh said he would rather be torn to pieces than sit in such a judgment. Mulgrave, Rutland,

---

[14]  C. H. Firth, *House of Lords*, pp. 156-161; J. Lilburne, "A Whip for the Present House of Lords", B.M. E. 431 (1).

[15]  C. H. Firth, *House of Lords*, pp. 194, 206; *Journals of the House of Lords*, X, p. 637. Those peers deemed eligible to sit in the House of Lords on December 23, 1648, were: The earls of Warwick, Oxford, Northumberland, Kent, Rutland, Pembroke, Lincoln, Nottingham, Suffolk, Salisbury, Denbigh, Middlesex, Manchester, Mulgrave, and Stamford; viscounts Say and Hereford; barons DeLaWarr, Berkeley, Dacre, Wharton, North, Hunsdon, Montagu, Grey of Warke, Maynard, Howard of Escrick, and Bruce. S. R. Gardiner, *History of the Great Civil War*, 4 vols. (London, 1893), IV, pp. 284-286.

Kent, and Manchester; North, Hunsdon, Maynard, Berkeley, and Dacre joined the others in throwing out the ordinance. They then adjourned for a week, in the futile hope that the house of commons could not proceed without them. The house of commons did proceed. The lords' last gesture was a brave one, which condemned their house most certainly. But it mattered little, the house had been long doomed; at least they could be proud of their actions which finally brought their sentence into execution. On January 4, 1649, the house of commons responded to the upper house. They resolved:

That the Commons of England, in Parliament assembled, do Declare, That the People are, under God, the Original of all just Power:
  And do also Declare, that the Commons of England, in Parliament assembled, being chosen by, and representing the People, have the Supreme Power in this Nation:
  And do also Declare, That whatsoever is enacted, or declared for Law, by the Commons, in Parliament assembled, hath the Force of Law; and all the People of this Nation are concluded thereby, although the Consent and Concurrence of King, or House of Peers, be not had thereunto.

The house ordered the resolution printed on the same day Charles was beheaded. While neither kingship nor upper house was yet officially abolished, the resolution rendered that a formality, by striking down cause for their continued existence.[16]

On February 2, 1649, the house of lords, again sitting, sent messengers to the commons to ask for a joint committee to discuss the future government of the kingdom. The messengers were denied admittance, and the house of commons resolved to "take into Consideration and Debate the House of Lords...". On February 5 a motion to preserve the house of lords as a purely consultative body was rejected by forty-four votes to twenty-nine. On the 6th, the lords proceeded to nominate their own commissioners to consider the government of the kingdom. At the same moment the lower house was resolving "That the House of Peers in Parliament is useless and dangerous, and ought to be abolished: And that an Act be brought in, to that Purpose." On March 5, 1649, the bill was read for the first time. Two days later the bill passed its second reading and was sent to a committee instructed to bring in an additional act making the persons of peers, as well as their estates, liable for the payment of debts.

[16] C. H. Firth, *House of Lords*, pp. 207-208; S. R. Gardiner, *History of the Great Civil War*, IV, pp. 288-290; *L.J.*, X, pp. 641-642; G. Davies, *Early Stuarts*, p. 156; *Journals of the House of Commons*, VI, pp. 111, 126; L. von Ranke, *History of England*, I, pp. 540-542.

The doctrine of the dependence of peers' privileges upon their status as lords of parliament was thus recognized by the commons. On March 19, 1649:

The Commons of England, assembled in Parliament, finding by too long experience, that the House of Lords is useless and dangerous to be continued, have thought it fit to Ordain and Enact, and be it Ordained and Enacted by this present Parliament, and by the Authority of the same, That from henceforth the House of Lords in Parliament, shall be and is wholly abolished and taken away; And that the Lords from henceforth shall not meet or sit in the said House called the Lords House, or in any other House or Place whatsoever, as a House of Lords, nor shall Sit, Vote, Advise, Adjudge, or Determine of any matter or thing whatsoever, as a House of Lords in Parliament.

The privileges of peers were also abolished with the house of lords.

And be it further ordained and enacted . . . that no Peer of this land . . . shall claim, have, or make use of any privilege of Parliament, either in relation to his person, quality, or estate, any law, usage, or custom to the contrary notwithstanding.

The abolition of the house of lords was a natural conclusion of a successful revolution which based its justification upon the ultimate authority of the commons of England. Before this doctrine, the house of lords vanished with hardly a trace. There was no outcry at its abolition. Its power, and that of its members, had not been distinctive for a long time. Now the peers were left without the house of lords, to confront a future of uncertainty, which few of them could have faced hopefully. Remarkably enough, the house of lords emerged from the civil wars to enjoy renewed power. This potential gain was not evident in the period 1649 to 1660, and almost certainly no peer suspected it. Nevertheless, the fate of the peerage in their eleven years' exile determined that sufficient strength was preserved to enable the lords, when they again assembled at Westminster, to reassert their own authority and that of their house.[17]

[17]  C.J., VI, pp. 129, 132, 157-158, 168; S. R. Gardiner, History of the Commonwealth and Protectorate, 4 vols. (London, 1894), I, p. 3; Clarendon's Rebellion, p. 692. Clarendon is mistaken in his assertion that the lords found the doors padlocked against them when they returned from the week's adjournment. L.J., X, p. 650. The nominated were: the earls of Denbigh, Northumberland, Kent, Pembroke, Salisbury, and Nottingham. C. H. Firth, House of Lords, p. 213; G. Davies, Early Stuarts, p. 160; Acts and Ordinances, II, p. 24; S. R. Gardiner, ed., Constitutional Documents, pp. 296-297; T. A. Spalding, The House of Lords (London, 1894), p. 55; E. Jenks, Constitutional Experiments of the Commonwealth, pp. 8-9; A Chronicle of the Kings of England from the Time of the Romans Government, unto the Death of King James . . . by Sir Richard Baker, Knight, ed. E. Phillips (1674), p. 606.

## II

## THE PEERAGE WITHOUT THE HOUSE OF LORDS

The army had opposed existence of the lords for many years; the Rump had abolished the upper house. The period that followed was a time of the nobility's greatest degradation. No longer leaders of English society, they were the objects of both scorn and ridicule. In some areas they were treated as outcasts from the social pale of their country.[1] The saddest group of all were those not only outcast from the social pale of England, but who were in fact exiles from their native land. With the Queen Mother and her sons they fled to the continent, there to hope and plot for the day of restoration. They carried their old antagonisms with them; divisions grown up as far back as the 1630's and brought into sharp relief during the civil wars. Three parties established themselves; the oldest and closest to France was the Louvre party, led by the indefatigable daughter of France, Henrietta Maria. Lords Jermain (later earl of St. Albans) and Percy were her closest allies. In often bitter opposition was the Old Royalist party, intensely loyal to the Anglican communion and composed of the immediate servants and advisors of the young Charles II. The marquess of Ormond was their titular leader, though in fact Sir Edward Hyde, later Baron Hyde of Hindon and earl of Clarendon, and Edward Nicholas discharged the heaviest duties. The last group were known as the swordsmen, led by James, duke of York, and Prince Rupert. Lords Gerard and Wentworth were their closest companions. The swordsmen, hot for an invasion of England, spent their time fighting in continental conflicts while agitating for such leaders as Marshal Turenne to take an army across the Channel. Turenne promised to help, without his government's knowledge, but never was able to do so. His master, Mazarin, from policy opposed Turenne's inclination. Thus the swordsmen could offer no solution to their monarch, nor could the Louvre party, hopelessly compromised in

[1] A. S. Turberville, *House of Lords*, p. 227.

English eyes by its deep Roman Catholic flavor. The only exile party which could reasonably, though hardly with optimism, be expected to aid the royal and noble cause was the Old Royalist group. Yet the intrigues among the exiles were so strong that Thurloe's agent in Paris, Colonel Bampfylde, could steadily pass information to the Protectorate even after Hyde had discovered him. In Paris Henrietta, Lord Gerard, and Sir John Berkeley tried to discredit Hyde, the royalists' wisest leader. Baron Gerard went so far as to press the charge against Hyde of reviling the king. Hyde also had to fend off Louvre attempts to parcel out the spoils and offices of a restoration not accomplished and indeed of slim possibility.[2] Not only was the regaining of England improbable but the continued survival of the exiles called for serious efforts. Hyde wrote on January 6, 1650, "All our money is gone, and let me never prosper if I know or can imagine how we can get bread for a month longer." Although the French and Spanish governments extended a dole from time to time, and funds dribbled in from sympathizers in England, relatively little relief was gained. In 1652 Hyde was writing, "At this time I have neither clothes nor fire to preserve me from the sharpness of the season." Matters did not improve with time and as shortly before the restoration as February 4, 1659, Lord Wentworth from Antwerp wrote Hyde that his credit for meat and beer had run out and if not speedily relieved he saw no remedy but direct starvation. But against these accounts must be balanced the condition of the marquess of Newcastle, who managed to keep a full stable of horses in his exile. Indeed Charles II is reputed to have said that Newcastle's credit could procure better meat than his own.[3]

While the royalist leadership struggled abroad, the lords' champion continued the struggle at home. Prynne addressed two "Pleas for the Lords" in defence of the right of the peers to exist as a house of parliament. In his first plea he went back to the laws of God as the foundation of his case. After a rambling discussion of the Mosaic law and government, Prynne rounded on the "paradox" of the levellers "touching the peoples choice and call to inable Peers to sit

[2] David Underdown, *Royalist Conspiracy in England, 1649-1660* (New Haven, 1960), pp. 10-11; *Baker's Chronicle*, p. 647; A. H. Woolrych, "Penruddock's Rising", p. 6; *Clarendon's Rebellion*, pp. 808-809; John, Lord Campbell, *The Lives of the Lord Chancellors*, 7 vols. (Philadelphia, 1847), III, p. 147.
[3] J. Campbell, *Lives of the Lord Chancellors*, III, pp. 145, 150; *C.C.S.P.*, IV, p. 143; Margaret, duchess of Newcastle, *Life of the First Duke of Newcastle*, p. 83.

in Parliament".[4] To this proposal that peers might sit in the commons he answered, "that a particular, explicit actuall choice and election by the people, of any to be ... Peers of Members of Parliament, is neither necessary nor convenient to make them just and lawful". Rather he insisted, "the ancient Lawes, Statutes, & Customs of the Kingdom enable all Lords who are Peers or Barons of the Realm to sit in Parliament whenever summoned to sit by the King's Writ, without any election of the people". In the first part of the pamphlet, Prynne's narrow concern with the leveller proposals continually obscures his concern with the greater issue of the very existence of the upper house. In the second part he faces the greater constitutional question fortified by the *Modus Tenendi Parliamentum* and a mass of parliament rolls and statute books. "By, and in the very primitive constitution of our English Parliaments, it was unanimously agreed by the Kingdomes and peoples generall consents, that our Parliaments should be constituted and made up, not of Knights and Burgisses onely ... but likewise of the King ... and by the Lords, Peers, Barons, (ecclesiasticall and civill) and great Officers of the Realme, who ought of right to sit, vote, make Lawes, and give Judgement in Parliament by vertue of their Peerage; Baronies and Offices." Lastly he offered the unusual for him, but increasingly popular economic justification for the lords' existence, that their great holdings and wealth give them a great concern in the state of the nation's affairs. His second plea was a five hundred page effort, providing detailed citations to support the contentions of the first plea.[5]

Prynne's pen again appeared to be overweighted by events. On February 3, 1649, a new court of justice was summoned to try the duke of Hamilton (earl of Cambridge in the English peerage), the earls of Holland and Norwich, and Baron Capel. Three days later all were sentenced to death. Holland's brother, the earl of Warwick, a person entitled to the consideration of parliament, appealed for his life but the motion of mercy was rejected in the commons. The petitions of Hamilton and Capel were rejected without a division. Only Norwich escaped death, and he by the casting vote of the Speaker. Two years later the earl of Derby was executed for leading the Lancashire rising. These actions did much to cool noble ardor

---

[4] *Vide infra.*

[5] William Prynne, "A Plea for the Lords, ...", B.M., E. 430 (8), pp. (4), (6)-(8), 1-5, 7-12, 13-15, 17-18, 25-32; "A Plea for the Lords, and House of Peers. ...", B.M., E. 749.

for forceful restoration. More than this, the nobility was struck by these executions as deeply as by the abolition of the house of lords. Hobbes recorded in his *Behemoth* that "This affrighted divers of the Kings Party out of the Land; for not only they, but all that had borne Arms for the King, were at that time in very great danger of their lives." [6]

Despite such stern measures the deliberate intent of the leaders of the Long Parliament never was to drive all the peerage from public life. The act of abolition had contained a reservation stating this, by expressing the hope that some of the peers would sit with the commons if duly elected, and in time this happened. The earl of Pembroke was elected, somewhat incongruously, as a knight of the shire from Berkshire. The new burgess from Lynn was the earl of Salisbury. Baron Howard of Escrick was chosen as a representative of Carlisle. However in 1651 he was fined £ 10,000 and expelled from the house, to take up residence in the Tower for accepting bribes from royalists who hoped to gain modifications of their fines. [7] The council of state set up in 1649 also had noble representatives. Of the forty-one nominated five were peers, and all five were approved by the house of commons. These were the earls of Denbigh and Mulgrave, the two new "commoners", Pembroke and Salisbury, and Baron Grey of Warke. At the council's first meeting Grey refused to sign anything emanating from one house only and was excluded. The earl of Mulgrave never took his seat on the council. This constituted virtually all the lords' participation in government from 1649 to 1658. [8]

The peers' social decline during the Commonwealth was nearly as sharp as the slump in their political fortunes. They were no longer immune from arrest, or entitled to trial by peers; all privileges were gone, "either in relation to person, quality, or estate". A particular grievance to some of them concerned their titles of honor. The peers created since 1642 were not allowed to bear their titles. In 1646 an ordinance had declared such patents null and void and an act of

[6]   S. R. Gardiner, *History of Commonwealth and Protectorate*, I, pp. 11-12, 462-463; D. Underdown, *Royalist Conspiracy*, p. 13; Thomas Hobbes, *Behemoth: The History of the Civil War of England* (n.p., 1680), pp. 224-225.

[7]   C. H. Firth, *House of Lords*, p. 221; John Oldmixon, *The History of England during the Reigns of the Royal House of Stuart* (London, 1730), p. 372; S. R. Gardiner, *History of the Commonwealth and Protectorate*, I, p. 472; C.J., VI, p. 91.

[8]   S. R. Gardiner, *History of the Commonwealth and Protectorate*, I, pp. 4, 6-8; J. Oldmixon, *History of England*, p. 372.

1652 directed that all such patents should be surrendered into the court of chancery. Although fines were provided for disobedience, evidently no determined effort was made to gain these patents. The status of the peerage was altered in many ways after the spring of 1649; the most serious changes concerned the lords' wealth. Though their effects were to be limited by the restoration, the financial levies upon the peerage were no less serious when they occurred.[9]

Clarendon recorded that the nobility "could scarse breathe under the insupportable burdens which were laid upon them". While it is difficult to estimate the full effects of this economic depression upon the nobility, some observations may be made. As the majority fought for the losing side, their estates as well as their persons were at the mercy of their conquerors. Some peers were completely ruined, at least temporarily, as will be related below, and none escaped some degree of impoverishment. Their influence declined with their wealth until their state approached that of a baronet whose epitaph read:

> Here lies the noble knight, Sir Robert,
> Laid forth by fate beneath this culvert,
> Who while'st he'd breath and he could stand,
> And other senses could command,
> Was a companion excellent.
> But now he is mortgaged and lent,
> By cruel fate to death's sad door;
> Till twelve hours' time did pay death's score.
> Thus I'll say more; here doth he lie,
> Whose daily task is thus to die.
> For none on earth can living be,
> And be more mortgaged than he.[10]

In many ways the peers were better off than such lesser royalists. Until the house of lords fell, its members showed favor to their royalist brethren and allowed them to make advantageous arrangements concerning their lands. The royalist lords were also protected in all parliamentary privileges except sitting and voting. Things were more difficult after 1649, but often with greater resources to start with, the peer had a better chance at saving some of his wealth than did his own dependents who had gone to war with him. Many noble families received allowances and grants that their mode of life be

---

[9] C. H. Firth, *House of Lords*, pp. 232-233, 234; P. H. Hardacre, *Royalists*, p. 121; G. Davies, *Early Stuarts*, p. 623.

[10] Clarendon's *Rebellion*, p. 745; G. Davies, *Early Stuarts*, p. 271; C. H. Firth, *House of Lords*, p. 237; B.M., *Add. Ms.* 34,217 fo. 68.

not utterly destroyed. The tenant farmer received no such consideration.[11]

Notwithstanding such favors, the peerage found times hard enough.
The attack upon their property took several forms; the most drastic
was total confiscation. This ultimate course was reserved for those
who by the highness of their royalist pretensions, the excess of their
zeal, or simply the threat posed by their ability appeared most
dangerous to the parliamentarians. About seventy individuals suffered this fate, the majority being peers and members of their families. The erratic second duke of Buckingham headed this list. Such
royalists as the earls of Berkshire, Bristol, Chesterfield, and Derby,
and barons Hopton, Byron, and Langdale forfeited all. Such notorious
characters as the earl of Cleveland, his son Baron Wentworth, and
Lord Wilmot were included. Hardest hit were the Roman Catholic
peers. Among them, the marquesses of Winchester and Worcester,
and barons Arundell of Wardour, Herbert of Raglan, and Morley were
stripped of their lands. Barons Digby, Vaughan, Craven, Eure, and
Howard of Escrick also suffered confiscations. Many of these had
gone into exile, for fear their lives would be forfeited with their
estates. Now many found their position reduced to that of beggars;
all their income was lost. Yet the term confiscation may be decep-
tive; there is evidence that several peers, while ostensibly suffering
such a fate, had in fact managed by various devices to protect and
preserve portions of their lands from the confiscators. The exceptions
to the flight abroad were the Roman Catholic peers, who usually
remained in England and survived with their lives but little else.
They lived largely upon the generosity of their coreligionists, by now
well used to oppression.[12] Although confiscations had begun five
years earlier, no sales of lands took place until 1651. The parliamentarians were never fully decided on how far to move against the peerage; they were on the whole cautious of how deeply they stirred the
social order while relatively more careless of the political structure.[13]

This social conservatism is seen in the second financial levy upon
the delinquents, the defeated royalists. This was the system of com-

---

[11]  P. H. Hardacre, *Royalists*, p. 28; G. Davies, *Early Stuarts*, p. 272.
[12]  C. H. Firth, *House of Lords*, p. 276; Mable Geraldine Woodruff Peacock,
*An Index of the Names of the Royalists Whose Estates were Confiscated during
the Commonwealth* (London, 1879), pp. 70-111.
[13]  Joan Thirsk, "The Sale of Royalist Land during the Interregnum", *Economic
History Review*, 2d Series, V, No. 2 (Cambridge, 1952), p. 188; G. Davies,
*Early Stuarts*, pp. 271-272.

pounding and sequestration. The latter came first. A sequestration committee was set up in London with subordinate committees in every shire where parliamentary authority extended, reaching ultimately to all England. Sequestration had the effect of placing the title of the land in suspension and caused the revenues of the land to flow not to the owner but to the government. Further, if not promptly compounded for, sequestrated land could be sold, the title actually transferred, although it was not usual for this to occur. Thus at a single stroke the income of the nobility declined while that of the government rose, and the title of delinquents to their lands came under threat. Such pressure made the delinquent understandably anxious to secure his title. This he accomplished by the process of compounding, for which purpose a parliamentary committee was set up in London in August of 1644, and eventually committees in the shires operated under it. Its purpose was to afford the delinquent an agency through which he could come to terms with the authorities, by sacrificing part of his estate through fines to secure the remainder.[14] To regain title two things were necessary: the delinquent must promise his submission and good behavior for the future; he must pay at least a moiety of his fine. In 1645 the rule governing fines was set at two years' value or what was normally reckoned as one tenth of the total (though usually not the salable) value of the whole estate, based on an estimated value before the war. This value differed from the present value more or less according to the ravages of war, but in almost all cases the land was yielding less profit in the late 1640's and early 1650's than at the outbreak of war. Thus with total value estimated as a factor of so many years' revenue, the estates were uniformly over-valued in post-civil war terms, and the fines correspondingly became more burdensome. The commons had threatened much more severe measures in 1646, but the house of lords rejected them at that time. Not until the end of the civil wars did the government introduce several rates which depended upon the degree of delinquency of the particular individual. The five standard rates for compounding were the one tenth mentioned, and one sixth, one third, one half, and two thirds for the most notable offenders, although other rates sometimes obtained. Obviously, if a delinquent was so unfortunate as to be required to compound at a rate as high as two thirds the value of his estate, he ended forfeiting the bulk of his estate to save a

---

[14] D. Underdown, *Royalist Conspiracy*, p. 7; *Calendar of the Committee for Compounding*, ed. M. A. E. Green, 5 vols. (1889-1892), I, p. vi.

remnant. But in practice the higher rates were not as severe as first appears, although not at all easy. The one tenth was based upon twenty years' purchase, or two years' value of the estate, but those fined at one sixth paid at a rate based on eighteen years' purchase, those at one third or one half paid at fifteen years' purchase, and those fined at two thirds paid at only twelve years' purchase, and there was individual variation. Thus in the case of Lord Belasyse his fine at two thirds, £ 10,360, and later reduced to one third or £ 5,180, was based on an estimated value of £ 15,540 for his estate. When his fine was reduced to one tenth at £ 2,073, the committee for compounding estimated the value of his estate at £ 20,732. This committee had discharged the bulk of its work by 1652 and was largely dormant until 1659, when Booth's rising caused its revival.[15]

The richer peers in England were among the first to take advantage of this committee. The earl of Westmorland approached the house of lords on January 30, 1644, and applied for permission to take the Covenant and to compound for his delinquency. His fine was a mild £ 2,000, later reduced to £ 1,000. The earl of Thanet was admitted to composition for £ 9,000, a much more substantial fine, but not the greatest. Viscount Campden was fined £ 14,000 and Baron Newport £ 10,000. In fact the earl of Thanet had managed to obtain a mitigation of his fine to £ 9,000 only by pleading his sufferings during the war. These were impressive, but only characteristic of what was happening to the nobility at this time. He had already paid to parliament a fine of £ 2,000 in 1643. He had lost in the war, he said, 6,000 ounces of plate, horses and sheep worth £ 2,000, a house which cost £ 32,000, woods and timber worth £ 20,000, besides his parks and deer which were destroyed. Also lost were all the household possessions of his Windsor, Heathfield, and London residences. With such a case he managed to reduce his fine from the £ 20,000 parliament was threatening to levy. Other peers gained reductions, such as Lord Poulett, whom Fairfax aided in gaining a reduction from £ 10,432 to £ 2,743. In fact, reductions in fines were common among the nobility, largely because the rates were vastly too high, and parliament was more interested in revenue to run the government and pay the

---

[15] *C.C.C.*, I, pp. vii, xi; V, pp. x, xxxv-xxxvi; Edith L. Klotz and Godfrey Davies, "The Wealth of Royalist Peers and Baronets During the Puritan Revolution", *E.H.R.*, LVIII (London, 1943), p. 218. Calculations of income by the Committee for Compounding for purposes of fines were based, it should be noted, on what we would probably call net income, that is, after all allowable deductions had been made.

army than in the impoverishment of the nobility as a matter of policy. The parliamentary records for forty-one peers who compounded and whose accounts are complete enough for evaluation give some picture of their wealth at this time. The forty-one had estates with a total estimated value of £ 1,241,900 or an average of £ 30,290. Sixteen of the peers were above average, led by the earls of Thanet and Westmorland at £ 150,000 and £ 90,000 respectively. Poorest were the earls of Norwich and Marlborough at £ 3,300 and £ 340.[16]

Confiscation and sequestration were but two revenue tools of the government which pressed upon the wealthy royalist. Other methods were employed as well. The committee for compounding handled only the discharge back to owners of lands sequestrated but compounded for. But there was another side to sequestration proceedings. Not until April, 1651, was a distinction clearly made between seizing or securing an estate and sequestrating it. In the former case the rents of the real estate were stayed in the tenants' hands, and the suspected delinquent was allowed to enjoy his personal estate on security of double its value, in case he should be convicted of delinquency. In other words, he lost only part of his income, and that only temporarily, if he were innocent. As most of the peerage were "notorious delinquents", few fell into this category. In the case of sequestration the whole property was placed in the hands of county commissioners, the estate let, and the goods sold. This was the fate of those who did not compound. There were some who did not. Their indignation toward the usurping power was so great that they refused in any way to acknowledge its authority and thus forfeited everything but the fifth (or third, if recusant and not also delinquent) reserved for the support of their families. The government rapidly accumulated substantial holdings in its hands. The lands of the earl of Arundel required the attention of 24 separate shire committees. In 1654 Arundel's sequestrated estates produced a revenue of £ 11,540. At that time the value of his estates was placed at £ 230,000. All this was lost for the duration of republican rule. Nor was recovery always complete. By 1667 the marquess of Newcastle had not managed to recover lands in direct possession which had

---

[16]   P. H. Hardacre, *Royalists*, p. 21; *C.C.C.*, V, pp. xi, xviii; E. L. Klotz and G. Davies, "The Wealth of Royalist Peers", p. 219. In fact these figures are of limited value, as rates of years' purchase varied from estate to estate, and all rates bore an inflated relationship to actual land values at the time. They are given only as general indicators.

yielded £ 2,015 a year and lands in reversion which had yielded £ 3,214 each year.[17]

As time passed, parliament found a sizable amount of property in the hands of its committees as the result of confiscation and sequestration proceedings where compounding was not entered into. In July of 1651 the government decided to sell the lands of seventy prominent royalists for the benefit of the Commonwealth, and appointed the Drury House trustees to accomplish this. By this and two subsequent acts of sale in 1651 and 1652 lands of the duke of Buckingham, the marquesses of Newcastle, Winchester, and Worcester, and the earls of Derby, Cleveland, and Chesterfield were sold. Many lesser royalists were also hard hit, but not to the extent of the peerage, though with more lasting effects.[18]

Confiscation, sequestration, and sales were supplemented by certain assessments levied at first irrespective of party, but later only upon royalists. The committee for advance of money was established to collect a rate of about one twentieth on real estate and of one fifth on personal property. Given the conditions at the time, as well as the ambitious rates of the levy, few assessments were paid in full. Further, the committee granted respites to individuals engaged in sequestration proceedings. As time passed, the assessments were by order of parliament pressed more and more directly upon delinquents, who had to bear this new burden when already pushed to the limit to remain solvent.[19]

Confiscation, sequestration, sales, and assessments fell upon the prominent royalists; yet this was not the end of their economic misfortunes. Assessments totaling £ 331,300 had been levied against the peerage, whose finances were already so weak that several were discharged for poverty; others had assessments of only £ 200, as did Lord Stourton. But some peers were still unbowed. Assessments of £ 10,000 each were laid on the marquesses of Hertford, Newcastle, and Worcester, and Baron Cottington. For Newcastle and Worcester this was swallowed up in the confiscation and sale of their estates.

---

[17] *Calendar of the Proceedings of the Committee for Advance of Money*, ed. M. A. E. Green, 3 vols. (1888), I, p. xii; *C.C.C.*, I, pp. 114-115, IV, pp. 2461-2480, V, p. xii; Margaret, duchess of Newcastle, *Life of the First Duke of Newcastle*, p. 103.

[18] J. Thirsk, "Sales of Royalist Lands", p. 190; C. H. Firth, "The Royalists under the Protectorate", *E.H.R.*, LII (London, 1937), p. 639; D. Underdown, *Royalist Conspiracy*, pp. 57-58.

[19] *C.C.A.M.*, I, pp. vii, x-xi.

Even with this the royalists had managed a rising in the West in 1655. Cromwell retaliated with the decimation tax, set at one tenth the value of real estate and one fifteenth of personal possessions. This tax did not fall widely, and as the peerage were relatively inactive at the time, they largely escaped its force. But not all avoided it. The young earl of Lindsey paid £ 1,200 to save his estate. Because the decimation was closely tied to the establishment of the major generals its effects were perhaps more psychological than economic; nevertheless it was an added strain upon an already overburdened nobility.[20]

The delinquent noble was not entirely passive to the government's levies. Sequestration officers suffered broken heads and other sorts of violence. More often bribery was used to get estates undervalued, not difficult to do as the sequestration officers were salaried and usually long unpaid. As Margaret, duchess of Newcastle later put it: "under-officers do not usually refuse bribes." Nobles with vast and widespread estates could conceal parts without undue difficulty. The bulk of the peerage eventually came to terms with the government, took the Engagement or the Covenant, compounded, and set about preserving their estates and their necks. But most never gave their loyalty. Even some who had stood with parliament in the 1640's, like the earl of Lincoln, were sending money to Charles II in the 1650's.[21]

The Commonwealth and Protectorate levies had forced some of the nobility to place their lands on sale. More often just the opposite occurred; the sequestrated royalists were buying back their own lands. However burdensome their debts, and in several cases these debts antedated the war, the great nobles seemed determined to preserve their estates and mortgaged themselves and their heirs to retain their lands intact. Consequently there grew up a firm check upon social change at the shire level, for the great landowners of old still sat upon their lands in the 1650's. Like Hyde at Breda they may have lacked clothes and fire to preserve them against the season but they were in possession of their own. This tenacity assured them of a base of power on the land which would be allied with the power of a restored house of lords to preserve their position in society for future

---

[20]   P. H. Hardacre, *Royalists*, p. 29; G. Davies, *Early Stuarts*, p. 269; *C.C.C.*, V, pp. xxxiv-xxxv; *Baker's Chronicle*, p. 644.
[21]   H. E. Chesney, "The Transference of Land", p. 182; D. Underdown, *Royalist Conspiracy*, p. 15; *H. Mss. C., Bath Mss.*, II, p. 134; Margaret, duchess of Newcastle, *Life of the First Duke of Newcastle*, p. 101.

years.[22] Only one peer who had the opportunity to repurchase his lands failed to do so. Lord Craven was unique in trying to recoup his loss by appeal to parliament. The bill for the sale of his property had passed the commons in 1652 by a small majority after it had been several times rejected. Although parliament twice reconsidered the case upon his petition, Craven's lands were not restored to him until Charles had returned to England.[23]

Most of the peerage preferred not to rely upon any parliamentary mitigation of their lot but to concentrate upon methods of repurchase. A common way was to employ royalists in London, who were familiar with the committees' proceedings, to act as agents for the peer, who became owner again, but silent partner in the transaction. In these dealings the peerage had the immense advantage of social prestige — and in some cases the financial reserves as well — to command the credit necessary at the moment of repurchase. This success in regaining their lands placed the peerage in contradistinction to the lesser royalists who were unable to save themselves.[24]

Royalist repurchases were carried out with the tacit approval of the authorities. Goffe complained to Thurloe that the marquess of Winchester was not only regaining his estates but placing the land in forms of trust to protect it from future government attacks. Thurloe himself commented on the large sums of money borrowed to finance the transactions. The marquess, despite Goffe's displeasure, was successful in his venture. Of fifteen estates in Hampshire and Berkshire, only two eluded his purchase. One, Englefield Manor in Berkshire, had been granted to a distant relative of the marquess, and was in his hands in 1655. The second property was Halshott farm in Hampshire, in which the marquess possessed only a life interest, and apparently he did not regain it. Lord Arundell recovered his estates in Oxfordshire under the eyes of the government, and Ludlow charged Cromwell with intervening with the Drury House trustees to discharge substantial sums owing from Arundell. Peers as much in the government's disfavor as the marquess of Newcastle and Lord Morley were also succesful repurchasers. Although some of the republi-

---

[22] H. E. Chesney, "The Transference of Land", pp. 188-189; Joan Thirsk, "The Restoration Land Settlement", *Journal of Modern History*, XXVI, 4 (Chicago, 1954), p. 327; "Sale of Royalist Lands", p. 203.

[23] C. H. Firth, "Royalists under the Protectorate", p. 639; J. Thirsk, "Sale of Royalist Lands", p. 193.

[24] H. E. Chesney, "The Transference of Land", p. 191; J. Thirsk, "Sale of Royalist Lands", pp. 192-193.

cans objected to the government's position, neither Commonwealth nor Protectorate attempted to conduct a program of land redistribution outside of the royal and ecclesiastical estates, but remained respectful of private property even where such respect benefited their obvious enemies. Similarly the vigor of the peerage in retaining and regaining their lands was the significant first step on their road to regaining power. At a high cost they preserved their base on the land. Subsequent events were fully to repay the cost.[25]

While most of the nobility were intent upon securing their lands, a minority appeared equally intent upon losing theirs. These were the conspirators, the men who led the royalist plans for a recovery of England by internal armed risings. The record of the conspirators is a particularly poor one. Their natural leader, Charles II, was never with them after 1651, but from abroad he encouraged even their wildest ventures, to Hyde's despair, although the loyal royalist historian faithfully left a picture of a patient and considerate king tempering the rashness of his agents in England. The conspirators also lacked wide support among the peerage, who, wisely aware of the government's vigilance, sat at home and deprived the risings of much hope of effective organization and force. The closest the cavaliers ever came to possessing an organization was the "sealed knot", the most conservative of their groups. Of its six members, two, Belasyse and Loughborough, were peers and two, Sir William Compton and Colonel John Russell, were of noble families, but they never succeeded in rallying significant support to their cause. The fact that a fifth member, Sir Richard Willys, informed Thurloe of their plans assured that the knot itself would never become a significant body. The secrecy of the knot was in fact greater to many royalists than it was to the government; exacerbated relations among the royalists also weakened their own cause.[26]

The knot was at least designed with the purpose of making use of the territorial influence of the peerage. This failed because of the social dislocation of the times as well as through the reluctance of many nobles to engage. But it was a plan; most of the other conspiracies could hardly be dignified with that title. When the old royalists and their new allies — conservatives variously dissatisfied

[25] *Thurloe S.P.*, IV, p. 444; J. Thirsk, "Sale of Royalist Lands", pp. 192-193; Ludlow's *Memoirs*, II, p. 155.
[26] A. H. Woolrych, "Penruddock's Rising", pp. 4-5; D. Underdown, *Royalist Conspiracy*, pp. 22, 76; *Baker's Chronicle*, p. 647.

with the extent to which change had occurred in England — attempted to rally against Cromwell in 1654, he swiftly committed to the Tower the earl of Lindsey and barons Willoughby, Newport, Maynard, Lucas and Petre. All six were active spirits but so guileless that they were soon released. Their amateur efforts were followed in 1655 by the wild schemes of the undisciplined earl of Rochester. A man of erratic temperament, he was notorious equally as a hard fighter and a hard drinker. He was commended only by his assurance and Charles's favor. Neither was sufficient, and the rising that followed failed dramatically when Sir Marmaduke Langdale, later Baron Langdale of Holme, who disliked Rochester, did not raise Yorkshire as planned. Sir George Booth, a Presbyterian ally later to rise, was unsuccessful in his organization, but an unfortunate squire named Penruddock did lead out a futile band. He was repaid by the decimation tax and the major generals, which dimmed the ardor of even the highest royalists. Throughout these undertakings the bulk of the nobility had kept distant and cursed the misfortunes their less restrained members brought upon them.[27] Although hopeless when pitted against Cromwell's arms and Thurloe's spies, their cause was gaining strength. The constitutional thinking of the Puritan Revolution was growing conservative in the 1650's. There was a revival of interest in ordered government and in the old system.

It was in these years that James Harrington presented his views on the order of government. He had much to say about the position of a nobility in the state. Harrington's judgments closely concerned the peerage and their historical share in the wealth, government, and society of the nation. At the foundation of his analysis was the theory that institutions are not accidental, or arbitrary, or easily mutable, but rather are the consequences of causes which can be discovered and examined. Thus to Harrington it was not the civil wars which had destroyed the old order, but the ebbing of the foundations of the old order which had led to the civil wars. When Harrington came to examine the state of England in 1656, he concluded that a king governing in England by parliament would find the nobility of no effect at all. This he attributed to a change in the distribution of landed property.[28]

[27] D. Underdown, *Royalist Conspiracy*, pp. 85-86; *Baker's Chronicle*, p. 643; A. H. Woolrych, "Penruddock's Rising", pp. 10, 15, 17, 23.
[28] R. H. Tawney, "Harrington's Interpretation of His Own Age", pp. 205, 212; A. S. Turberville, "House of Lords under Charles II", *E.H.R.*, XLIV, XLV (London, 1929-1930), XLV, p. 60; C. H. Firth, *House of Lords*, p. 28.

Harrington's basis for government was that:

EMPIRE is of two kinds, Domestic and National . . ..
DOMESTIC Empire is founded upon Dominion.
DOMINION is Property real or personal, that is to say, in Lands, or in
Mony and Goods.
LANDS, or the parts and parcels of a Territory, are held by the Proprietor
or Proprietors, Lord or Lords of it, in som proportion; and such . . . as
is the proportion or balance of Dominion or Property in Land, such is
the nature of the Empire.[29]

Applying this measure to the nobility and clergy, he found that until
the opening of the Tudor period their holdings "cannot be esteem'd
to have overbalanc'd those held by the People less than four to one.
Wheras in our days, the Clergy being destroy'd, the Lands in possession of the people overbalance those held by the Nobility, at least,
nine in ten." To Tudor policy Harrington attributed the present
misfortunes of the nobility and crown alike. To him, Henry VII "first
began to open those Sluces that have since overwhelm'd not the King
only, but the Throne. For wheras a Nobility strikes not at the Throne
without which they cannot subsist, but at som King that they do not
like, popular power strikes thro the King at the Throne, as that which
is incompatible with it." He saw the nobility as the first, but not the
last victims of the emergence of a new order of society, and in the
allies of the Tudors he saw the masters of the Stuarts. To Harrington,
the fatal flaw in monarchy the Tudor system could not repair:

AND for a Monarchy by a Nobility, as of late in *Oceana* . . ., it was not in
the power or wit of Man to cure it of that dangerous flaw, that the nobility
had frequent interest and perpetual power by their Retainers and Tenants
to raise Sedition, . . . wherfore Monarchy by a Nobility is no perfect Government.

The inefficacy of the Tudor remedy, he said, became evident when
the Stuarts inherited the throne, and finally ended in armed conflict.

But a Monarchy, devested of its Nobility, has no refuge under Heaven but
an Army. Wherfore the dissolution of this Government caus'd the War, not
the War the dissolution of this Government.

This dissolution had its origins in the legislation of Henry VII, "by
those several Statutes that were made in his Reign, as that for Population, those against Retainers, and that for Alienations".[30]

---

[29] John Toland, ed., *The Oceana and Other Works of James Harrington.* . . .
(London, 1747), p. 39.
[30] *Ibid.*, pp. 53, 69-70, 388; R. H. Tawney, "Harrington's Interpretation of
His Own Age", pp. 211-212; An account of Henry VII's policy toward the

In proposing his ideal form of government, Harrington spoke of retaining a nobility. He agreed with Machiavelli "that a Nobility..., overbalancing a popular Government, is the utter bane and destruction of it; so I shall shew in another, that a Nobility or Gentry, in a popular Government not overbalancing it, is the very life and soul of it". Though Harrington spoke of a nobility or gentry, in fact by the standards of his time it was a gentry he meant to have in his government, for he proposed a rigid agrarian law that would eventually bar to anyone the holding of estates producing a revenue exceeding £ 2,000 a year. His very definition of nobility, he admitted, embraced the gentry. He thus spoke of "the Nobility; in which stile, to avoid farther repitition, I shall understand the Gentry also, as the *French* do by the word *Noblesse*".[31]

With this qualification, Harrington proposed to see his "nobility" active in the two house system of government he advocated. His observations fell naturally into his times. He wrote in the hope that a balanced and stable government would be erected in England in his time. Indeed the years from 1656 to 1660 were a period of search and discussion in politics. Not surprisingly, there was among this discussion a revival of interest in the traditional structure of parliament, with a house of lords. Among those concerned with this question was included the lord protector. Certainly Oliver Cromwell considered his house of lords, the "Other House", a buttress to stable government and to his government.

---

nobility may be found in Thomas Pitt Taswell-Langmead, *English Constitutional History from the Teutonic Conquest to the Present Time*, ed. A. L. Poole, 9th ed. (Boston, 1929). See also W. S. Holdsworth, *History of English Law*, 9 vols. (London, 1922-1927), III, pp. 113-120. Taswell-Langmead points out the dependence of 4 Hen. VII, *cap.* 24 upon 19 Hen. VIII and 32 Hen. VIII, *cap.* 36 to accomplish the intended restriction of alienations.

[31] W. S. Holdsworth, *History of English Law*, VI, p. 150; J. Toland, ed., *Harrington's Works*, pp. 42, 72, 102, 134.

## III

## CROMWELL'S LORDS: THE OTHER HOUSE

The protectoral house was not in order in 1657. Since the death of Charles I England had been exposed to a series of governmental arrangements, none of which were satisfactory to all the elements concerned. A succession of suggestions had been produced in this eight year interval. There had been offered the Proposals of the Army, the Agreement of the People, and the Instrument of Government. None of these led to a satisfactory balance, either between the army and parliament, or later, between the protector and parliament. There were now also signs of strain between Cromwell and the army. As 1657 opened, the army leaders were anxious that individual liberties should be better protected from the self-appointed political and religious orthodoxy of the parliamentarians. The politicians were uneasy about the power of the army and its officers in politics, and were willing to agree to some system of checks which would encourage military withdrawal from the political arena. Above all, Cromwell was dissatisfied with the irresponsible behavings of his first and second parliaments; and in particular with parliament's vicious onslaught upon the erratic Quaker, James Naylor.[1]

It was the case of Naylor that Cromwell put to the army officers. Burton recorded him as saying, "That it is time to come to a settlement, and lay aside arbitrary proceedings, so unacceptable to the nation. And by the proceedings of this Parliament, you see they stand in need of a check, a balancing power ... for the case of James Naylor might happen to be your own case. By their judicial power they fall upon life and member, and doth the Instrument enable me to control it?"[2] Cromwell clearly had a remedy in mind, and a traditional solution to the commons' use of power. About the same

[1]  C. H. Firth, *Last Years of the Protectorate, 1656-1658*, 2 vols. (London, 1909), I, pp. 103-104.
[2]  Burton's *Diary*, I, pp. 384-385.

time he spoke to the army officers, renewed attention to the nobility appeared in the *Mercurius Politicus* and the *Public Intelligencer*, the two official newspapers of the Protectorate. Books concerning peerage and the house of lords were offered for sale. These contained information concerning not only the old peers but those of Cromwell's creation as well. In 1657 the protector had exercised the royal prerogative of granting honors by creating Charles Howard Baron Dacres of Gilsland and Viscount Howard of Morpeth. Cromwell's cousin, Edmund Dunch, became baron of Barnell. Cromwell's interest in the peerage was not limited to creations; he sufficiently esteemed the nobility to give the hand of one daughter in marriage to the grandson and heir of the earl of Warwick, and another to the young Viscount Fauconberg. Thus it is not surprising that the protector should entertain ideas of a second, and noble, chamber as an ideal check upon the commons.[3]

What perhaps was surprising was the initial lack of opposition to the proposed revival of the house of lords. A great outcry was expected in the commons. However, the protector's allies in parliament saw a second chamber as a step toward a Cromwellian dynasty which had seemed thwarted by the army's opposition to Oliver assuming the title of king. His enemies saw it evidently as a point of weakness and bided their time. Neither party expected the creation of a second chamber to be a final adjustment to the constitution-making of the period.[4]

In February of 1657, Christopher Pack, London alderman and Cromwellian, had risen on the floor of the commons to offer a Humble Petition and Remonstrance which provided for both kingship and house of lords. While the royal provision vanished upon Cromwell's rejection of the title, the idea of the "other house" remained. Early in March the house of commons carried without a division "That his Highness will, for the future, be pleased to call a Parliament, consisting of two Houses...". On the eleventh, they resolved that the other

---

[3]  G. Davies, *Restoration of Charles II* (San Marino, 1955), pp. 118-119; *Mercurius Politicus*, Nov. 5-12, 1657 (#389), p. (93); P. H. Hardacre, *Royalists*, p. 121; John Lingard, *History of England from the First Invasion of the Romans to the Accession of William and Mary*, 5th ed., 10 vols. (London, 1849), VIII, pp. 568, 568 n.; Clarendon's *Rebellion*, pp. 842, 861; C. H. Firth, *House of Lords*, p. 240.

[4]  C. H. Firth, *Last Years of the Protectorate*, I, pp. 141-143; R. C. H. Catterall, "Failure of the Humble Petition and Advice", *A.H.R.*, IX (New York, 1903), p. 42.

house should consist of not more than seventy members nor less than
forty members, nominated by the protector and approved by the
house of commons. The other house's quorum was set at twenty-
one, after thirty-one was rejected by a 96-53 division. On April 24,
the house of commons decided that the protector should name suc-
cessors to "lords" who died, and the hereditary principle was rejected by implication, if not specifically. This ambivalence carried
over to the naming of the house. Whether it was in fact to be a house
of lords was not resolved by the commons, although there was newsletter opposition to such a title.[5]

As the Humble Petition and Advice left parliament on May 25,
1647, it referred to the second chamber only as the "other House",
and barred the use of proxies to its members, a clear blow to the
concept of hereditary councilors. The house of commons also defined
and restricted the other house's judicial powers. It was barred from
proceeding in civil cases except by writ of error from inferior courts,
petitions from proceedings in courts of equity, or in cases of privileges
of its own members. All criminal processes were barred to the other
house save its judicial role in impeachments. In fact, the house of
commons had been enjoying a considerable exercise of judicial power,
and was not desirous of yielding it up. Although its claims to this
power were somewhat weak — the argument that upon the dissolution
of the house of lords, all judicial power in parliament had been transferred to the house of commons — the house was none the less reluctant to part with it. The army, with the memory of Naylor still fresh,
wished they would be divested of it. But while the Humble Petition
and Advice did provide judicial powers to the other house it did not
provide for any specific renunciation of judicial power by the house
of commons, and as the other house was not declared to be a house
of lords, the general issue of judicial powers remained unsettled.
Equally ominous for the future, the legislative functions of the other
house were not defined at all. Evidently the Cromwellians in the
commons had framed the Humble Petition and Advice in the confidence that they would have a king, and the other house would then
be a house of lords, with that body's traditional functions. Without a

---

[5]  C. H. Firth, *House of Lords*, p. 247; Burton's *Diary*, I, pp. 385-386, II, pp.
21-23; *Calendar of State Papers and Manuscripts, relating to English Affairs
existing in the Archives and Collections of Venice, 1657-1664*, ed. A. B. Hinds,
3 vols. (1931-1932), 1657-1659, p. 71; C. H. Firth, ed., *The Clarke Papers*,
4 vols. (London, 1899-1901), III, p. 108.

king, this was not self-evident. Thus from its birth, the other house faced a precarious existence.[6]

Some slight changes followed the Humble Petition and Advice. In June the commons debated if they should approve the members nominated to the other house, as originally provided for. Some argued that many persons would be reticent if they would be "tossed up and down here, and their lives ripped up". Against this, others argued that if the commons relinquished their check, many of the old lords might return. The latter argument was overruled by 90 to 41, and the Humble Additional Explanatory Petition and Advice left nominations wholly in the hands of the protector. Ludlow claimed this was achieved by the direct intervention of Cromwell; it is also probable that it flowed from the desire of several of the commons to be elevated to the greater dignity without the scrutiny of their old colleagues.[7]

The outcome of the Humble Petition and Advice was a less, rather than a more stable government. The offer of the crown to Cromwell had injected a new note of rancor into the constitutional debates. His rejection of that crown had left the other house in a dubious constitutional position. Because it had first appeared with the offer of the crown, the other house was forever damned in the eyes of true commonwealthsmen, and toward it all opponents of the Protectorate turned their antagonism. Many republicans remembered that Oliver Cromwell had said that it would never be well, and they would never see good days, while there was one lord left in England, and until the earl of Manchester was called Mr. Mountagu.[8]

In the face of rumbles of opposition, the protector addressed himself to the selection of the members of the other house. Evidently the task gave him great difficulty. That Cromwell treated the selection as a matter of great importance is clear from Thurloe's letters to Henry Cromwell in Ireland. On November 10, 1657, he wrote, "A mistake here will be like that of waure and mariage; it admits noe repentance." He revealed some of the problems facing the protector

[6]   S. R. Gardiner, *Constitutional Documents*, pp. 336, 338-339; Burton's *Diary*, I, pp. 248-251, 387; C. H. Firth, *Last Years of the Protectorate*, I, pp. 90-91, II, p. 7; R. C. H. Catterall, "Failure of Humble Petition and Advice", pp. 41-42.
[7]   Burton's *Diary*, II, p. 301; R. C. H. Catterall, "Failure of the Humble Petition and Advice", 41 n.; S. R. Gardiner, *Constitutional Documents*, p. 347; C. H. Firth, ed., *Memoirs of Edmund Ludlow*, 2 vols. (Oxford, 1894), II, p. 22.
[8]   W. S. Holdsworth, *History of English Law*, VI, p. 198; G. Davies, *Early Stuarts*, p. 184; R. C. H. Catterall, "Failure of the Humble Petition and Advice", IX, p. 37; "A List of Names ... that sat in the other House ...", in *Harleian Miscellany* (London, 1809), III, p. 481.

on December 1, 1657: "The difficulty proves great betweene those, who are fitt and not willinge to serve, and those who are willinge, and expect it, and are not fitt." Thurloe added that on the first day of December not one man was yet fully resolved upon. Later in the month the Venetian resident informed the Doge and Senate that if the names were selected, they were still not public. Finally, on the tenth of the month, sixty-three writs were issued in the ancient form used by the kings of England to those they summoned to the house of lords. Only here the title of protector replaced that of king.[9]

Even while the summons were going out to call parliament together on January 20, 1658, the debate whirling about the other house began to focus upon the old peers, the creations of the kings of England. Whether some or all of them would either be summoned to sit or would attempt to sit of right remained uncertain. The opponents of nobility did not choose to wait upon the event, but with Sydenham as their spokesman denounced any house of lords on the basis that the old peers would be admitted, and if they did take their places, the Stuart restoration would follow. Opposing this group, many of the protectorians sought to strengthen the government by gaining over the peerage; thus they insisted that the house of commons should not pass on the members of the other house. They feared peers nominated would not accept if they had to be approved by commoners. Godfrey Davies was of the opinion that this anticipation of noble participation was so strong that had it been assumed that the other house was to consist only of men named by Cromwell, it would never have gained the recognition of the commons. The royalists, too, were concerned that the lords might sit, as Mordaunt's correspondence with Hyde demonstrates. Upon the presence of the old lords largely hung the question of whether the other house would be an upper house, or only an equal or even a lower house. The peers themselves had also considered the matter, and Viscount Say and Sele spoke for all but a few of them when he answered Lord Wharton's request for advice on obeying the protector's summons to the other house.

My Lord, . . . the Government of this Kingdome accordinge to the right constitution thearof . . . I think it to be the best in the worlde; beinge a mixture of the 3 lawfull governments in that manner that it have the qintissence of them all, and thearby alsoe the one is a boundary unto the other, whearby they are keapt from fallinge into the extreames which

---

[9] *Thurloe S. P.,* VI, pp. 609, 648; *C.S.P.V.,* 1657-1659, p. 142; C. H. Firth, *House of Lords,* p. 248; Ludlow's *Memoirs,* II, p. 31.

eather apart are apt to slippe into, Monarchy into Tyranny, and Aristocracy into Oligarchy, Democracy into Anarchy; now the chiefest remedie and prope to opholde this frame and building and keape it standinge and steady is, and experience hath shewed it to be, the Peeres of England, and theyr power and priviledges in the House of Lords, they have bin as the beame keepinge both scales, Kinge and people, in an even posture, without incroachments one uppon another to the hurt and damage of both. . . . . This beinge soe, will it not be as most unjust, soe most dishonourable, and most unworthy, for any antient Peere of England to make himself a *felo de see* both to the Nobilyty of England and to just and rightly constituted Government of the Kingdome by beinge made a partye and indeed a stalking horse and vizard to carry on the designe of overthrowinge the House of Peeres, and in place thearof to bringe in and sett up a House chosen att the pleasure of him that hath taken power into his hands to due what he will, and by this House that must be carryed on as picked out for that pourpose, and altered and newe chosen as tyme and occasion shall require, some 5 or six Lords called to sitt with them whoe may give some countenance to the designe, which for my part I am resolved neaver to doe, nor be guilty of seeminge to allow thearof, but rather to professe and bare witnes agaynst it: a barbones Parliament, as they call it, without choyce of the people att all is not worse than this, which is layinge asyde the Peeres of England whoe by byrth are to sitt, and pickinge out a company to make another House of in theyr places at the pleasure of him that will rule and with all call a few Lords thearby causinge them to disowne theyr own rights and the rights of all the Nobylyty of England, dawbinge over the business in this manner to theyr perpetual shame whoe shall yealde thearunto . . . .[10]

Forty-two men answered the sixty-three writs of summons issued by Cromwell and assembled at Westminster when parliament opened on January 20, 1658. Of the summons, seven were addressed to peers of England, one each to a Scottish and an Irish peer, and five to the sons of peers. Cromwell's intention apparently was to build his house around a nucleus of hereditary lords supported by a larger number of peers for life. The Irish peer summoned was Roger Boyle, first Lord Broghill, who duly took his place. From Scotland, Cromwell had considered summoning the earls of Sutherland and Cassilis, but a writ was finally issued only to the latter, who did not come. The English peers nominated were the earls of Manchester, Mulgrave, and Warwick, viscounts Say and Fauconberg, and lords Eure and Wharton. Charles Howard, a viscount of Cromwell's own creation, was also

[10] R. C. H. Catterall, "Failure of the Humble Petition and Advice", IX, p. 43; C. H. Firth, *Last Years of the Protectorate*, II, pp. 8-9; Burton's *Diary*, II, pp. 298-300; G. Davies, *Restoration of Charles II*, p. 61; *Clarendon S. P.*, III, p. 432; C. H. Firth, ed., "A Letter from Lord Say and Sele to Lord Wharton", *E.H.R.*, X (London, 1895), pp. 106-107.

summoned, as was Philip Sidney, eldest son of the earl of Leicester, and styled Lord Viscount Lisle. Two sons of Viscount Say, Nathaniel and John Fiennes, were called. Of all these, it was the response of the seven English peers of the old nobility that was considered important. Their response was crushing to hopes for the other house. Although both his sons accepted, Say not only stayed away but was instrumental in Wharton's non-attendance. Mulgrave, old and ill, was to die in a few months and did not come. Manchester was absent, and also Warwick, who had been expected generally to attend. Ludlow attributed this abstention to Warwick's discovery that Hewson the cobbler and Pride the drayman were also to sit. More likely Warwick's motives were similar to Say's. In the event, only Cromwell's son-in-law, Fauconberg, and George Lord Eure, an impoverished nobleman of little note, attended. This thin showing of nobility impressed no one, least of all the peers of weight and influence, who forbore their attendance rather than acknowledge in the other house the final destruction of the house of lords.[11]

Joining the peers in abstaining were Gilbert Pickering, William Pierrepont, Alexander Popham, John Crewe, and Cromwell's arch-enemy, Arthur Haselrig. Their duties elsewhere prevented the attendance of Henry Cromwell, George Monck, Oliver St. John, William Steele, Francis Rous, Gilbert Gerrard, Archibald Johnston of Wariston, and Matthew Tomlinson. The result of these absences was a threefold blow to the other house. The absence of the peers deprived the house of reputation and weight. It also indicated that the breach in the Puritan party effected by the events of 1648 and 1649 was not healed. Haselrig's refusal to attend left Cromwell's sharpest critic able to create mischief in the house of commons from which the protector had withdrawn his most prominent supporters. The necessary absence of Henry Cromwell, George Monck, and the others by official duties deprived the other house of the ablest and most influential of the protectorians. The remainder were not distinguished for statesmanship, and possessed a clear military flavor. From the fleet there was Edward Montagu and from the army John Desborough, Phillip Skippon, Edward Whalley, Richard Ingoldsby, George

[11]   G. Davies, *Early Stuarts*, pp. 184-185; C. H. Firth, *Last Years of the Protectorate*, II, pp. 11, 12-15; J. D. Ogilvie, ed., *Diary of Sir Archibald Johnston of Wariston*, 3 vols. (Edinburgh, 1940) in Scottish Historical Society, Third Series, v. 34, III, pp. 87, 93; C. H. Firth, *House of Lords*, pp. 249-50; *G.E.C.*, IV, p. 574; G. Davies, *Restoration of Charles II*, p. 61; Ludlow's *Memoirs*, II, p. 32; *Harleian Miscellany*, III, p. 488.

Fleetwood, and William Goffe, among others. The civil side of this party was weakly represented by Nathaniel Fiennes, Bulstrode Whitelocke, and William Lenthall. These composed the better known of the new lords.[12]

This membership came immediately under attack. The Venetian resident reported that the members were popularly viewed as being selected solely on the basis of their subservience to the protector. Particular members were flayed in pamphlets. Richard Cromwell was described as "a person of great worth and merit, and well skilled in hawking, hunting, horse-racing, with other sports and pastimes; one whose undertakings, hazards, and services for the Cause cannot well be numbered or set forth, unless the drinking of King Charles's, or, as is so commonly spoken, his father's landlord's health". Whitelocke was "one who is guided more by policy than by conscience, and being on that account more fit for the Protector's service". John Fiennes, "not being redeemed much from the fear and favour of man, will, it is probable, follow his brother, who is, as it is thought, much steered by old Subtlety, his father, that lies in his den". Counterblasts, largely in vain, pointed out the Cravens and Cranfields of earlier days as deficient in blue blood. The membership of the other house was defamed even as it first met.[13]

The meetings were brief. The other house sat thirteen times from their first meeting to the dissolution of parliament on February 4, 1658. Attendance at these sessions averaged thirty-five. The record of business at the sessions is barren. Standing committees were appointed on January 21. Messages were sent to the house of commons on January 22 and February 3. That is all save for the consideration of prayer and fasting, and the examination of laws concerning drunkenness and profanity. The house managed to expend £ 200 for furnishings to support the dignity the protector bestowed upon it. From the first, he had treated it as a new house of lords. The Venetian resident recorded that the state proceedings in the other house followed the ancient custom of the house of lords. The ceremony did

---

[12] *H. Mss. C., House of Lords Mss.,* New Series, IV, *Journal of the Protectorate House of Lords* (London, 1908), pp. xliv, 503-506; C. H. Firth, *House of Lords,* pp. 251-252; *Last Years of the Protectorate,* II, p. 15; *G.E.C.,* IV, pp. 589-590; Bodley, *Rawlinson Ms.* A 74 fo. 440; *Thurloe S. P.,* VI, p. 668; *Mercurius Politicus,* Dec. 10-17, 1657 (#394), p. (165); *Harleian Miscellany,* III, pp. 475-476, 486.

[13] *C.S.P.V.,* 1657-1659, pp. 140, 149; *Harleian Miscellany,* III, pp. 475, 479-480, 486; J. Oldmixon, *History of England,* p. 419.

little good, for officially the house of commons ignored the other house's existence, and unofficially denounced that existence. The sending of messages to the house of commons only served to spur debate upon the role of the other house, and the messages went unanswered. The new lords did not aid their case by proposing in the second message that delinquents and priests should have to remove to twenty miles from London. Cries of noble aggression arose at once. Actually the commons needed no such excuse; they were already loud in their denunciations before the message.[14]

Even the most faithful Cromwellians in the commons had cause for complaint. The other house was accused of lacking interest in the land, or any other independent interest. It appeared too subservient to the protector to serve as an impartial judge of differences between him and the commons. Cromwell's enemies did not restrain themselves to these observations. Scot set their tone by opening, "The other house was justly cast out by their being clogs upon passing of many good laws." He moved that the second chamber be named the "other house", arguing that it was not a house of lords. Mr. Trevor opposed, stating, "We know what the House of Lords could do. We know not what this other House may do." Anthony Ashley Cooper concluded debate on the name of the other house with the lapidary observation: "Admit Lords, and admit all." Haselrig now joined the fray, having ignored the summons to the other house, taken the oath from some friends, and seated himself in the commons. He turned all his considerable parliamentary skills against the other house. He seized upon the observation of Colonel Matthews that there was an act of 1649 specifically abolishing the house of lords. Still his case would have had poor chance had not thirty of the ablest Cromwellians been removed from the commons into the other house. But out they were, and debate circled aimlessly, any device being offered by the republicans to block the acknowledgement of a house of lords, or a chamber with all the powers of a house of lords. In this objective they were successful. Unmoved by the argument that "If they be not a House of Lords, you cannot be a House of Commons", they kept the debate turning until a new issue was injected.[15]

---

[14] *H. Mss. C., Journal of the Protectorate House of Lords*, pp. xlix, 508-525; *Calendar of State Papers, Domestic Series, 1657-1662*, ed., M. A. E. Green (1861-1886), 1657-1658, p. 557; R. C. H. Catterall, "Failure of the Humble Petition and Advice", IX, p. 50; *C.S.P.V.*, 1657-1659, p. 157; Burton's *Diary*, II, pp. 339-334; L. von Ranke; *History of England*, III, pp. 197-198.

[15] C. H. Firth, *House of Lords*, pp. 252-254; Burton's *Diary*, II, pp. 347, 337-

The new issue was that of the old peers. Mr. Thistlewaite broached
the issue by asking, if you have a house of lords, how then can you
exclude the old peers? To this Anthony Ashley Cooper offered the
distinction: "There is nothing but a compliment to call a man Lord;
but if one call himself Lord of my manor, I shall be loth to give him the
title, lest he claim the manor." Discussion of manors led to a general
discussion of the land issue, and Harrington's observations upon
property were cited as evidence against the other house.[16] All arguments were cut short on February 4 when Cromwell suddenly
descended upon Westminster and with a withering blast dissolved
parliament. His speech betrayed his disappointment. For some reason he appeared not to have anticipated the storm latent in the resurrection of the second chamber, and when it was assaulted in the
commons he was unable to bring debate under control and had to
have recourse to a dissolution reminiscent of Charles I. Cromwell
told the house of commons that he had stated upon taking up the
government under the Humble Petition and Advice, "That I would
not undertake it, unless there might interpose between Me and the
House of Commons, who then had the Power to prevent tumultuary
and popular Spirits; and it was granted I should name any other
House; and I named it of Men who shall meet you wheresoever you
go, and shake hands with you, and tell you it is not Titles nor Lords,
nor Party that they value, but a Christian and an English Interest,
Men of your own Rank and Quality, who will not only be a Balance
unto you, but to themselves." The republicans did not wish to shake
hands with traitors to the ideal of the good old cause. To many commoners, the men of quality selected to interpose between them and
the protector appeared to mirror too much the image of Oliver Cromwell. Thus the institution Oliver had seized upon to relieve one
crisis touched off a new constitutional conflict. The commons' rejection
of the other house involved the rejection of the Protectorate, and the
Protectorate alone stood between the poles of restored monarchy and
extreme republican rule. Cromwell did not live to see the choice
made; this fate was reserved for his son.[17]

---

378, 382-394, 398-403, 404-424; *C.S.P.V.*, 1657-1659, p. 164; *C.S.P.D.*, 1657-
1658, pp. 273, 276; Ludlow's *Memoirs*, II, pp. 32-33; C. H. Firth, *Last Years of
the Protectorate*, II, pp. 19-20, G. Davies, *Early Stuarts*, p. 185.
[16] Burton's *Diary*, II, pp. 428-440; C. H. Firth, *Last Years of the Protectorate*,
II, p. 23.
[17] C. H. Firth, *House of Lords*, p. 255; Laurence Echard, *History of England*,
3 vols. (London, 1718), II, p. 814; *Baker's Chronicle*, pp. 649-650.

The succession of Richard Cromwell appeared so untroubled that Hyde speculated to his English agent, Mordaunt, that the new protector would assume the crown and dispense with the other house. The Venetian resident was more accurate in reporting that the council of state about Richard was divided on the wisdom of summoning the other house to sit in the new parliament. The center of this division was the imprecision of the Humble Petition and Advice, which did not provide Richard with the clear powers that his father had. Thus both the radical and moderate wings of the Puritan party contended for Richard's opinion. For the moderates, George Monck sent the new protector a letter from Scotland advocating that the other house be strengthened by summoning the most prudent of the old nobility, as well as some of the leading gentry, among whom he designated Sir George Booth. Monck and Booth were both prominent in the socially moderate wing of the Puritan party and both were to earn peerages for their roles in the restoration. At the beginning of 1659 they were still willing to gather at the protectoral half-way house, but if that house did not produce stable and ordered government they were ready to continue their trip toward a conservative solution. The radicals turned to pamphlets to assault the idea of any other house. Blasting its members as "a few inconsiderable Lords having not so much power and interest as five hundred Yeomen", the radicals argued against summoning the other house again. The course resolved upon settled nothing. Writs were issued to the members of the other house, as the Humble Petition and Advice provided, but that membership was not strengthened, as the Humble Petition gave Richard no power for new nominations. So the constitutional formula which had failed in 1658 was offered again in 1659. On January 24, the Venetian resident informed the Doge and Senate that, "When parliament meets, both the upper and lower chambers are to sit; but it is greatly to be feared that differences and disputes will arise between them in the first sessions, because the house of Commons seems indisposed to accept the house of Lords."[18]

Three days after the resident's letter parliament met. Conflict between the houses flared at once, with about half the house of com-

[18]    H. Mss. C., 10th Report, Appendix, Part VI, Mss. of Lord Bray (London, 1887), p. 194; C.S.P.V., 1657-1659, pp. 277-284; R. C. H. Catterall, "Failure of the Humble Petition and Advice", IX, pp. 43-44; G. Davies, Restoration of Charles II, p. 20; Baker's Chronicle, p. 654; "A Secret Word to the Wise: or, seventeen Queries, humbly proposed to the well-affected People of the Good Old Cause", B. M., E. 986 (6); Ludlow's Memoirs, II, pp. 48-49.

mons refusing to come up to the lords for the opening ceremonies. Burton recorded in his diary, "They say there were about 150 Members sitting in the House while his Highness was speaking in the other House, and that the Black Rod went for them, but they came not." On the other hand the keeper, Fiennes, had declared that the government considered the other house "the highest and last resort" of all "Courts of Judicature". The lords themselves knew what to expect now, and sent off no communications to the commons. From their first sitting until the dissolution of parliament on April 22 the other house met in 64 sessions and discussed substantive matters at 33 sessions. One bill passed three readings; no act was passed and the parliament left no law behind it. There was no communication between the houses until mid-April, shortly before parliament ended. Bordeaux represented this silence of the other house to Mazarin as a matter of policy, to avoid alienating any vote in the commons, where the government majority was precarious. This policy left time heavy on the lords' hands. They safely proceeded against Charles Stuart by bill, considered indemnities, favored the confirmation of sales, and debated their own poor attendance.[19]

The lords' caution was well-advised. Hyde's correspondents reported to him that the commons were expected to pick a quarrel with the other house. But this did not at once transpire. The debates of the commons until mid-February concerned mainly finance and control of the army and militia. Discussions of the government and constitution were general. Perhaps the members recalled as Anthony Ashley Cooper did: "I would not have things misrepresented to the House. I was here last Parliament, and the constitution of the other House was disputed all along, and their coordinate powers denied still, else we had not been so soon dissolved." [20]

However, the nature of the elections for the parliament of 1659 assured that the other house would come under discussion. The government had done very little to influence the elections, and censorship had generally ceased in the nation. For the first time in a decade

[19] J. Lingard, History of England, VIII, pp. 562-563; Burton's Diary, III, p. 2; Bulstrode Whitelocke, Memorials of the English Affairs. ... (London, 1682), p. 671; F. P. G. Guizot, History of Richard Cromwell and the Restoration of Charles II (London, 1956), I, p. 300; H. Mss. C., Journal of the Protectorate House of Lords, pp. 525-527, 529-537, 539-554, 557-567.
[20] The Calendar of Clarendon State Papers Preserved in the Bodleian Library, ed. F. J. Routledge (vol. IV, 1932), IV, p. 140; Burton's Diary, III, p. 1; W. D. Christie, ed., Memoirs, Letters, and Speeches of Anthony Ashley Cooper, First Earl of Shaftesbury (London, 1859), p. 189.

a high degree of unregulated political opinion was possible, and the complexion of the commons had changed. The Puritan party split from the last parliament not only continued, but also for the first time there was an influx of hardly disguised royalists. These joined so obviously with the commonwealthsmen to bring down the Protectorate that Serjeant Maynard protested that Charles Stuart had more friends in the house than the protector.[21]

On February 19, the other house became the topic of debate, and the general principle of a second chamber was accepted without a division. While the commons showed little disposition to agree on the powers of a second chamber, this first move was regarded hopefully by the protectorians. Fauconberg wrote to Henry Cromwell that he forsaw "a regular settlement". Such hopes were misplaced, as the second stage of the debate revealed. On the question of the limits and powers of the other house three opinions appeared. The radical wing of the Puritan party pointed out that the parliament of 1658 was determined, and it was to that body that the second chamber of the Humble Petition referred. The whole matter of a second house was to be renegotiated. In other words, the whole of the constitutional settlement must be opened up to discussion. A second group of uncertain alliance raised the question if the other house could have powers without its proper membership, and that membership the old peers. It is probable that royalists gathered behind both these proposals, seeking the same goal by both constructive and destructive methods. Their communications with the continent were uncertain at this time, and Hyde was unable to co-ordinate policy in response to their requests. Against these proposals the protectorians rallied about the Speaker's simple proposal to delay discussion of the issue of powers and his motion that the house of commons treat with the other house as with a house of parliament. The protectoral party was strong enough to defeat the first two proposals and carry the motion that the Speaker's proposal be discussed by a 177-113 vote.[22]

The vote, however, bore little relation to the proportion of debating skills in the house, and discussion became general and bitter. The heavy representation of military officers in the other house, over twenty, was brought up again. On this subject even loyal protec-

---

[21]  G. Davies, *Restoration of Charles II*, p. 59; *C.C.S.P.*, IV, p. 166.
[22]  G. Davies, *Restoration of Charles II*, pp. 59-60; *C.J.*, VII, p. 605; Burton's *Diary*, III, pp. 352-357; *Thurloe S.P.*, VII, p. 628; *C.C.S.P.*, IV, p. 144; *C.S.P.V.*, 1657-1659, p. 295.

torians were uneasy, and the swordsmen undoubtedly reduced the government's margins in the commons. But the parliamentarians were sowing the wind in their abuse of the soldiers. While they flayed the presence of the officers in parliament and sought to deny them legislative authority, the officers were preparing to sweep away the whole legislature.[23] Insensitive to this whirlwind on the horizon, the commons turned to the land question. Henry Neville upheld the commons' right to a predominant voice on the grounds of the shift in land holding. Ludlow solicitously observed what a better interest in land the old peers possessed than the new lords of the Protectorate. Captain Baynes favored two houses: "If we can find out such persons as have such properties as may balance this House by property, in any considerable number, it is fit we should have them; but if there be none such, I would have another House ... chosen ... by the people." Mr. Stephens observed that in any circumstances the larger share in the government should be the commons', as they had "obtained a larger interest in the land". Major General Kelsey dismissed the old lords as having "scarce a twelfth part" of the land of the nation.[24]

However, the old lords proved harder to dismiss than the new peers presently sitting. The debates turned to the rights of the old peers if the other house should be recognized as presently constituted. The government's supporters seemed hesitant to discuss this and at first opposed outright any consideration of the old peers. However, Bordeaux reported to Mazarin that the majority of the commons were shifting their opinion from fear that the other house would be too much an echo of the protector without the representation of an independent nobility. By early March a majority for the old peers was forming, Bordeaux felt. The arguments for their rights ran from the provisions of the triennial act to the nobles' defence of English liberties in Magna Carta. Even Haselrig allowed that he preferred the old lords to new swordsmen.[25]

If Haselrig was so willing to transgress republican principles, Scot was not. "If the old lords be not taken away, then I have no right to

[23] G. Davies, *Restoration of Charles II*, pp. 48, 60; *Baker's Chronicle*, pp. 656-657; *C.S.P.V.*, 1659-1661, p. 13.

[24] Burton's *Diary*, III, pp. 132-133, 336, 404, 408; Ludlow's *Memoirs*, II, pp. 58-59.

[25] *Clarendon S. P.*, III, p. 451; F. P. G. Guizot, *History of Richard Cromwell*, I, pp. 311, 315; D. Ogg, *Reign of Charles II*, I, p. 2; G. Davies, *Restoration of Charles II*, pp. 61-62.

sit here, by the writ of that person that summoned me; but by another person. The same argument makes the Duke of Gloucester King of England." Another member put the case against the old lords more bluntly: "Peerage will necessarily bring in regality, high and great enough." Upon this the royalists and republicans agreed. Hyde wrote that if the old lords, even only those who were not delinquents, should return, he looked for the ending of his misery. The moderates were less certain of the attitude to adopt toward the old peers. Anthony Ashley Cooper opposed their restoration for their own sake. "To bring in the old Lords upon the Petition and Advice, upon that foot, I should ever abhor them and myself for doing it. Upon this new foot, you cannot restore them; though I honour them as much as any man, and wish they were restored, but rather never see a Lord, than have them on such a foot." Cooper did not say upon what foot he would have them, but the republicans professed to know. Other of the moderates doubted that the lords would sit if called in now to join the new lords. The bulk of the moderates, their doubts notwithstanding, were prepared to proceed to the recognition of the other house with the salvo "That it is not intended to exclude such peers as have been faithful to the Parliament from their privileges of receiving a summons to the other house." [26]

The opponents of the other house were not prepared to give up the struggle without a last attempt. Cooper appealed to the moderates upon behalf of the old lords. "I have observed the fortune of the old Peers, that the saving of their rights is the asserting of the rights of these; which is the most destructive to them that can be. It is clearly a putting others in their place, and is setting up a thing that is quite contrary. The saving of their rights is the proscription of their rights." Henry Neville followed with a lengthy assault for the republicans. In particular, he raised the spectre of the military. "But give me leave to conclude with that which ... shows the confidence they have of themselves and us: after having many times trampled on the authority of the House of Commons, and no less than five times dissolved them, they hope, for those good services to the House of Commons, to be made a House of Lords." [27]

---

[26]   Burton's *Diary*, III, p. 525, IV, p. 34; *C.C.S.P.*, IV, p. 159; W. D. Christie, ed., *Memoirs of Shaftesbury*, p. 193; *C.S.P.V.*, 1657-1659, pp. 297-298; G. Davies, *Restoration of Charles II*, p. 62; *C.J.*, VII, pp. 611-612.

[27]   W. D. Christie, ed., *Memoirs of Shaftesbury*, pp. 201-205, 208-209, 212-214, 217; "A seasonable Speech, made by a worthy Member of Parliament in the House of Commons, concerning the other House", in *Harleian Miscellany*, III,

Neither all of Neville's considerable forensic skills, nor Cooper's parliamentary mastery was sufficient to block recognition of the other house. Nor did an attempt to challenge the right of the Irish and Scottish members of the commons to vote turn the majority aside from acknowledgment of the new lords. So, on March 28, 1659, the other house was accepted by the commons, although there was no admission of their claims to peerage, or of a negative voice, or of a right to sit in subsequent parliaments. The commons consented only to transact business with them, with a saving to the rights of the old peers. In the transaction of business no superiority was to be acknowledged, and messages would be received from the other house only if carried by the members themselves.[28]

The saving of the rights of the old peers had been the main block to this acknowledgment of the other house. Cooper had not prevailed aginst the moderates' formula, which Hyde took to mean that the Puritan peers were free to sit at their pleasure. Bordeaux attributed the passage of the salvo to the electoral influence of peers in the elections to the new parliament, and that many men indebted to them now sat in the commons. The Cromwellian party yielded to these independent members rather than lose their votes to the republicans. However, the margin was narrow for the old peers, 195 to 188, according to Burton. The royalists favored the old peers, at Hyde's direction, and Mr. Turner recommended Prynne's "Plea for the Lords" to the house.[29]

Of great significance was the commons' final resolution to recognize the other house. Early divisions on discussing the matter of recognition had given the protectorians about a forty vote margin. This rose to 73 votes, 198-125, on the key March 28 division to transact business with the other house as with another house of parliament. However, subsequent votes relating to the other house were 135-96 on April 5, 136-102 on April 8, and 144-100 on April 14. So the normal majority of the protectoral party remained about forty. In fact,

---

pp. 490, 492, 494. There is disagreement on the authorship of this speech. Christie attributes it to Cooper; Firth and L. F. Brown believe it is Neville's. The best case is Miss Brown's in her *First Earl of Shaftesbury,* p. 73. Burton lists both men as speakers on March 28, 1659, but does not give this speech.

[28] *Somers' Tracts,* 1st Collection, IV, pp. 529-531; J. Lingard, *History of England,* VIII, p. 566; *Thurloe S. P.,* VI, pp. 615-647; *Clarendon S. P.,* III, pp. 429-432.

[29] Burton's *Diary,* IV, pp. 68, 87, 284; Clarendon's *Rebellion,* p. 865; F. P. G. Guizot, *History of Richard Cromwell,* I, pp. 329-330, 335.

the majority of the house of commons were becoming anxious to have the association and support of the other house.[30]

The commons were becoming aware that their baiting of the army was imperiling their own existence. Realizing that the army leaders were exerting pressure on Richard to disband parliament, the commons hastened to align the other house with themselves. On April 18 they voted that during a parliamentary session the general council of the officers should meet only with the approval of protector and both houses of parliament. They also moved that no one should hold a military command who did not pledge himself not to interrupt the free meetings of parliament. These votes were sent up to the other house on the 19th, and there the commons met another setback. Confident that the other house would be grateful for the commons' acknowledgment, they were stunned that the motion to take their proposals under immediate consideration passed by only one vote. The swordsmen in the other house had already resolved upon another course of action. Giavarina, the Venetian resident, reported general pleasure in the army at this setback to the legislators. The rumor was already about that a new parliament would be called to replace the one sitting. Although Mordaunt reported to Hyde that Richard was being driven toward parliament by the army, just the opposite occurred. On April 22, 1659, he dissolved parliament at the bidding of the army officers. Broderick had correctly reported to Hyde that Desborough and his colleagues had been anxious to have done with the present parliament. Discussion of a new parliament included the old peers' right, but no more was heard of the Cromwellian creations.[31]

The protector did not long survive his parliament; Richard retired to private life and the army council replaced him. Giavarina reported on the other house: "The title of Protector having disappeared all the gentlemen and lords created by Oliver and Richard lose their rank and now only enjoy the titles they had before their elevation, which is stated openly to have been by usurpation and by indirect ways." No one spoke for the other house on its disappearance as Prynne had for the house of lords. Lacking such a voice, the testimony of one of

---

[30] F. P. G. Guizot, *History of Richard Cromwell,* I, p. 321; Burton's *Diary,* III, p. 578, IV, pp. 340-341, 375, 378, 427; Ludlow's *Memoirs,* II, pp. 60-61; *C.J.,* VII, pp. 605, 621; *Mercurius Politicus,* March 3-10, 1659 (#557), p. (288).
[31] G. Davies, *Restoration of Charles* II, pp. 73, 80, 82; *Baker's Chronicle,* p. 659; *C.S.P.V.,* 1659-1661, p. 11; *H. Mss. C., 6th Report,* Appendix, Part I, Mss. of Miss Ffarington (London, 1877), p. 442b; *C.C.S.P.,* IV, p. 176; *Clarendon S. P.,* III, p. 441.

its members, Archibald Johnston of Wariston, will have to serve to mark its passing. "Lord sanctifye to me the dounfall of my new lordship, pardon my vanity ... in a foolish, rash taking the new style and title of it to myself, in sending or receiving of letters and papers. I have maid little good use of the means I haive had from people by my place and the Protectors letter; justly may thou taik it from me, becaus we haive not been accurat in keeping our vows of wairing the teyth of our income upon pious uses." [32]

The Cromwellian lords had met the same fate as royalist peers. In the summer of 1659 the prospects of neither appeared good. Actually there was a great difference between them. Nothing can be more distinct than Say's letter to Wharton and Johnston of Wariston's confidence to his diary. Johnston put off the vanity of the moment; Say looked to and planned for the resumption of his proper place in the constitution. A year and three days from the dissolution of the protectoral house of lords the old peers were to enter into their own again. Before this, a year of great events was to intervene.

---

[32]  C.S.P.V., 1659-1661, p. 24; J. D. Ogilvie, ed., Diary of Sir Archibald Johnston of Wariston, III, p. 107.

# IV

# THE POLITICS OF RESTORATION

The army had pulled down the shell of the Protectorate. Its leaders now inherited the constitutional rubble that cluttered the site. The general council of officers attempted to initiate a five-fold formula of government. They proclaimed no kingship, no single person, no house of peers, and a separation of executive and legislature, the latter to be composed of a senate and lower chamber elected by duly qualified persons. In addition there were to be twenty-one conservators of liberty, whose duty was to preserve inviolate the fundamentals of the constitution. This program encountered immediate difficulties. The army had power but nothing approaching a popular majority. To operate any legislature above the character of a farce they needed allies. Since royalists were obviously barred, and the protectorians had just been levelled, only the republicans remained. The republicans, led by Harry Vane, Haselrig, and Ludlow, realized this and placed a high price upon their co-operation. Particularly, they balked at a select senate, and no proposed second chamber satisfied them. After several consultations, it was decided to recall the members of the Rump, and to give the government the aura of the good old cause.[1]

However, the good old cause had become a discredited cause, and the Rump was without honor in England. A strong conservative current was running, and into this stream the Cromwellian monarchists flowed in search of a king. Prominent among these was Charles Howard, whom Oliver had made a viscount. With great influence in the far north of England, he transferred his allegiance to the exiled Stuart and was to be paid with an earldom. He was closely followed by Cromwell's son-in-law, Viscount Fauconberg, with his not inconsiderable interest in Yorkshire. Edward Montagu promised to deliver

---

[1]  D. Ogg, *Reign of Charles II*, I, p. 15; *Mercurius Politicus*, (#598); *Steele*, I, 3141; G. Davies, *Restoration of Charles II*, pp. 88-89.

the navy to the exiled cause, and received the promise of an earldom and the Garter. Even so loyal a Cromwellian as Richard Ingoldsby made his peace with Charles II through the agency of the earl of Northampton. That Fauconberg and Northampton were peers, and Howard and Montagu were to be peers, was significant. The nobility were rising upon the conservative flood tide, and those who joined this tide had ambitions of attaining honor. As the fortunes of the monarchy rose, so did the prominence of the peerage.[2]

The Cromwellians were not alone in paying homage to Charles II. Among the Presbyterian wing of the Puritan party the old order of government was gaining favor. This was particularly true of the peers in that party. In 1659 the names of the earls of Manchester and Denbigh, Lord Willoughby and Lord Fairfax began to appear in royalist correspondence to the exiled court. Sir George Booth, Sir William Waller, Sir Anthony Ashley Cooper, and Sir Horatio Townshend — all but Waller to earn peerages — were also mentioned. This was not an unrestricted movement toward the old order; neither was the move completed in one jump. Manchester, with Arthur Annesley and Denzil Holles, began to communicate with the continent, but they talked of conditions. Nevertheless, the Presbyterians were organizing with the end in mind of seeing a king in England and a house of lords at Westminster. Royalist hopes in this movement were sufficiently high for the marquess of Ormond to have been dispatched to England to sound the leaders. He communicated with Viscount Say, who held out for the Treaty of the Isle of Wight. Denbigh was less restrained, but he had started his return to the old allegiance as early as 1653. Matters were still in flux, but there was a rising call for a second house, even if the king's name was not yet heard. But then Cooper had said, admit lords, admit all, and even in the army lords were being mentioned favorably.[3]

For the bolder of the cavaliers and Presbyterians talk was not enough. These spirits actively pushed for an armed rising to bring in the king. They achieved many pledges of support. Sir George Booth

[2] J. Oldmixon, *History of England*, pp. 433-434; F. R. Harris, *The Life of Edward Mountagu, K. G., First Earl of Sandwich* (London, 1912), I, p. 141; Bodley, *Clarendon Ms.* 61 fos. 291, 303, 335; Thomas Carte, ed., *Duke of Ormond's Papers* (London, 1739), II, pp. 333-334.

[3] T. H. Lister, *Life and Administration of Edward, First Earl of Clarendon* (London, 1837-1838), I, p. 456; J. Oldmixon, *History of England*, pp. 457-458; D. Underdown, *Royalist Conspiracy*, p. 218; C. H. Firth, *House of Lords*, pp. 129, 261.

would raise Lancashire and Cheshire. Sir Thomas Middleton would bring out Shropshire and Flintshire. The earl of Stamford pledged for Leicestershire; Lord Willoughby for Suffolk. Lord Herbert of Raglan promised to lead Gloucestershire and Sir William Compton Hertfordshire. Horatio Townshend was to secure Lynn. Though a good body of the nobility and gentry were pledged, the only significant rising was in Cheshire, where the Presbyterian magnate, Sir George Booth, and the cavalier earl of Derby co-operated. The whole rising foundered and Booth was imprisoned. In Surrey lords Mordaunt and Lichfield, both royalists, fled in the night. Their Presbyterian colleagues, lords Stamford, DeLaWarr, and Willoughby were imprisoned, as were the royalist duke of Buckingham and earl of Oxford. The earl of Northampton and marquess of Worcester, Lord Belasyse, Lord Falkland, and Charles Howard were also jailed. To check the rising the government had felt impelled to imprison a sizable proportion of the peerage.[4]

Although they suffered most from the rising's failure, the lords were blamed for that failure. Hyde had warned against reliance upon the great peers. While he held them valiant, he thought them unwilling to hazard their sorely-tried fortunes. He believed the years of alternate hope and depression had damped their spirits. Nevertheless he had the honor to praise them for their efforts while others did not and in particular he admitted that all royalist efforts were at a stop, "most of the nobility being at present in custody". Giavarina reported that confiscations were expected to follow the arrests.[5]

It was in fact rumored that Booth's rising was to be made the occasion finally to bring the peers to the ground. Giavarina wrote the Doge and Senate, "Gentlemen of rank are being arrested every day so that at present all the nobility of the realm is in prison, and those who are not found are summoned to present themselves. ... By thus destroying all rich and noble persons they deprive the king of whatever hopes were left of returning to this kingdom." Gumble claimed that he himself saw a list of "many of the best Estated-men in England, both in City and Countrey" who were to be stripped of their holdings, and that this arbitrary action roused his master, George

---

[4]  *Baker's Chronicle*, pp. 667-668; J. Oldmixon, *History of England*, pp. 438-439.
[5]  D. Underdown, *Royalist Conspiracy*, p. 288; P. H. Hardacre, *Royalists*, p. 135; *C.C.S.P.*, IV, p. 462; Clarendon's *Rebellion*, pp. 868, 871-872; *C.S.P.V.*, 1659-1661, pp. 62-63.

Monck, against the government. Such reports never gained substance. There was no effective government operating with general support in the population and if such a program were planned, it was never carried out. Just the opposite occurred, if anything. By November, the earl of Northampton, marquess of Worcester, and lords Belasyse, Herbert, Howard, and Falkland were free upon security to live peaceably. Whitelocke attributed this to an effort "to ingratiate with the Cavaliers" on the part of many purported republicans. Booth himself was also freed, and sequestration proceedings against his estates suspended. Although his rising had failed, it had not checked the rising popularity of a conservative solution after eleven years of experiment.[6]

The royalists did not leave this outcome to chance. In 1658 the volatile but able and totally dedicated young John Mordaunt had begun to emerge as Hyde's most consistent and effective agent in England. In May of that year Charles II recognized his services "to restore that which belongs to me...". Those services were important. Mordaunt labored to check the intention of his republican connections to attack the nobility, upon whom the royalists depended as the base of their interest in England. Among the nobility his main achievement was in finally committing the great Presbyterian magnates, Manchester and Northumberland, to the restoration cause. This alone merited him the kind words of Charles, "I have information enough how much I am beholding to you", and the viscounty that accompanied them in 1659. Mordaunt's efforts were complemented by the untiring Prynne. This time the pamphleteer produced a "Brief Register" of the peerage, which gave the historical case for summoning the lords temporal and spiritual to parliament. By now even the bishops, his enemies of times past, were restored to the old warrior's favor. He justly claimed: "I have ... more fully vindicated the just, antient Privileges and Hereditary right of the Lords and Barons of this Realm, to sit, vote, judge in all English Parliaments, than any others have done in former ages...." As was his usual fate, Prynne stirred a flurry of pamphlet literature, the majority of which Davies judged to favor a single chamber to two. Men found it still hard to read the future in the summer of 1659.[7]

[6]  C.S.P.V., 1659-1661, pp. 68-69, 90; Thomas Gumble, *The Life of George Monck, Duke of Albemarle* (London, 1671), pp. 218-219; Whitelocke's *Memorials,* p. 688; *Mercurius Politicus,* Feb. 16-23, 1660, (#608), p. (1125).
[7]  H. *Mss. C.,* 10th *Report,* Appendix, Part VI, Mss. of Lord Bray, pp. 188-190;

In the British Isles were some set on reading that future, if not shaping it. Most notable of these was George Monck, a Devonshire man by birth and a soldier by profession. He had served in several armies, including that of Charles I, before his capture by the parliamentary forces. He had gained the good opinion of Cromwell and had commanded troops under him. For his able services the protector entrusted him with the responsibility of order in Scotland. This he discharged with ability, and Scotland was as quiet as England was tumultuous. With the Protectorate gone, his loyalty was unclaimed, and if he were ambitious, his ambition did not reach as high as Cromwell's. Clarendon later wrote that if Monck did anything toward the restoration, circumstances forced him to move so. However, the case for restoration was bound to be strong in him. A soldier not a politician, he respected the order of society and ordered society. He had once served the Stuarts, and as Charles II wrote to John Grenville, "I am confident that George Monck can have no Malice in his Heart against Me; nor hath he done any thing against Me which I cannot easily pardon." This letter was meant for Monck's eyes, for Grenville, a Devonshire man, was a royalist agent to Scotland. To Grenville's voice was added that of Thomas Clarges, a relative of Monck and a royalist. Further, Monck's remarkable wife was outspoken for Charles Stuart. Bordeaux had reported to France that Monck was solicitious not only of the crown, but also of the interest of the nobility.[8]

In London, another man of many parts was taking the wind's gauge. Anthony Ashley Cooper was solidifying his influence with both parliamentarians and military. He had put himself in opposition to the republicans, Vane and Haselrig, and was corresponding with Lawson and Montagu in the fleet to block the republican interest, a policy that was to carry him into the service of the crown. In May of 1659 neither man had come into the open, and the good old cause was enjoying its last hour in the sun.[9]

On May 7, the Rump returned to Westminster, but not without contest. The Presbyterian members of the Long Parliament who had been secluded by the army in 1648 felt they had as good a claim to

M. Coate, ed., *The Letter-Book of John Viscount Mordaunt* (= Camden Society, 3d Series, vol. 69) (London, 1945), p. 67; L. von Ranke, *History of England*, III, p. 282; William Prynne, "The First Part of a Brief Register. . . ." (London, 1659), pp. 101-120, 194-241; G. Davies, *Restoration of Charles II*, p. 92.

[8] Clarendon's *Rebellion*, p. 883; F. P. G. Guizot, *History of Richard Cromwell*, II, p. 361; *Baker's Chronicle*, p. 669.

[9] J. Oldmixon, *History of England*, p. 450; Clarendon's *Rebellion*, p. 884.

resume sitting as did the rumpers expelled by Cromwell. One hundred ninety-four of this first group were still alive, and about eighty resided in or near London. They were predominently royalists, and attached to monarchical government by the provisions of the Treaty of the Isle of Wight. As their London contingent alone could outvote the rumpers, these republicans would not permit their return. A deputation of fourteen, led by Booth, Prynne, and Annesley, attempted to force the issue, going down to Westminster to seek admittance. The doors were closed in their faces, a troop of soldiers filled the lobby, and the Rump rushed through a resolution that no former member who had not subscribed to a republican engagement should sit until further order. Prynne returned on the ninth, and somehow gained entry into the house. There he maintained his right against the whole house until dinner time. Upon trying to re-enter, he was stopped by some army officers. The house was shaken by Prynne's boldness, which he followed up with "Loyalty Banished", describing his experiences, to the chagrin of the commons.[10]

The Rump continued to sit until the events which culminated in Monck's arrival in London rendered its position untenable. As the conservatives gained an army to support them the secluded members made good their return to the commons. The Presbyterians entered into a brief ascendancy. They had majorities in both parliament and the council of state. The Presbyterian peers were prominent in the direction of affairs, but no lords gathered to sit at Westminster. By the doctrine of the secluded members they were a house of commons only. Without the house of lords their legislative actings were by their own standards illegal. However, Monck now controlled the army, and Monck was inflexible. He said the army would not support the return of the house of lords, so the commons had to justify their unitary proceedings by the extraordinary circumstances of the times.[11]

If the commons could not have the lords, they could act generously toward them. The two sequestration acts which had followed Booth's rising were repealed. The duke of Buckingham was freed upon the word and bond of Fairfax. The commons also dropped the proceedings the Rump had initiated concerning the earl of Arundel. The earl, a Protestant, had been living in Padua for twelve years in ill

---

[10] D. Ogg, Reign of Charles II, I, p. 3; J. Lingard, History of England, VIII, pp. 573-574, 574 n.; Baker's Chronicle, p. 662.
[11] Clarendon S. P., III, p. 696; C. H. Firth, House of Lords, p. 269; J. Lingard, History of England, VIII, p. 607.

health, while his brother, a Roman Catholic like most of the Howard
family, actually controlled the affairs of this great house in England.
The earl was neither recusant nor delinquent, but the Rump found
intolerable the sight of both these kinds sheltering behind the vast
influence he represented. The Rump and council of state had determined to bring the earl, allegedly detained by his brother, to England
and to place his estates in the hands of trustees of their own
choosing. However, plans for moving the earl cooled upon report
that he was indeed an "incurable maniac", quite unable to travel.
By this time the rumpers were flooded by the secluded members
and the matter was dropped.[12]

Such half-measures did not fit the plans of the Presbyterian magnates. Led by Manchester, their goal remained a constitutional settlement according to the Treaty of the Isle of Wight and the return of
the peers of 1648 they considered essential to securing this result.
They were thwarted in their design by Monck. Manchester entered
into negotiations with him, arguing that two houses were legally
necessary and that the army would be gainers by the peers' return.
The land transfers to soldiers could then be confirmed. Monck took
the stronger position that legally parliament was determined by the
death of Charles I and the present sitting, even with peers, had no
real legality, but was justified only by necessity. When the lords then
attempted to enter their house and thus deliver a *fait accompli*, Monck
charged adjutant-general Miller to block them. A letter to Edward
Nicholas reported that a double guard was maintained on the doors
of the upper chamber to secure the situation. Thomas Lutterall wrote
Ormond that the lords were "in a great indignation", particularly
as the secluded members, who had promised the lords' return with
their own, now passed the matter by. They might well be indignant;
Monck's decision increased considerably the chances of an unconditional restoration, so unpalatable to the Presbyterian magnates.
Ludlow accused Monck of acting with this goal in mind, but the
general's concern over the army was sufficient public explanation of
his decision. In any event, this parliament, elected twenty years
before, was shortly to disband.[13]

---

[12] *Acts and Ordinances*, II, p. 1423; B.M., *Add. Ms.* 29,550 fo. 368; *C.S.P.V.*,
1659-1661, pp. 73, 76, 83, 88.
[13] G. Davies, *Early Stuarts*, p. 258; C. H. Firth, *House of Lords*, pp. 271-272;
*Baker's Chronicle*, p. 714; John Price, "The Mystery and Method of His Majesty's
Happy Restauration, laid open to Publick View", (London, 1680), in Maserès,

The dissolution was a confused one. Hyde described the difficulties
to Bennet. "The lawyers make great difficulties how to dissolve this,
except the Lords may be admitted to sit in their House to join in the
act of dissolution; and if they shall be once suffered to sit again,
besides that it destroys the fundamentals of their Republic, they cannot tell whether they will be willing to dissolve, or what other acts
they may be ready to perform." Now the lords would not sit anyway,
as Nicholas's correspondent reported, on grounds "it would make
them incapable of sitting ye next intended Parliament". In the end
necessity prevailed over legality, but not before Prynne had further
confused matters. On March 8 he moved not to dissolve, and for an
hour contended for the immediate acknowledgment of king and house
of lords. Annesley tacked around him, called his arguments un-
answerable, but moved for the necessity of adjournment.[14]

Before the commons went, they transacted some final business
concerning the peers. The confiscation of Lord Craven's lands was
terminated. Sales of his estates were stopped, although no redress
was offered. The whole matter of the house of lords was taken up on
March 13. "Ordered, That it be referred to a Committee to consider
what hath been done in this House concerning the Lords House, who
are to state the whole matter of fact, and report it to the Parliament...." Pepys recorded for the date that all proceedings against
the house of lords by the Rump were declared void. On March 16
the bill for dissolving the parliament called in November of 1640
contained the qualification, "Provided alwayes, and be it declared that
the single Actings of this House, enforced by the pressing necessities of
the present times, are not intended in the least to infringe, much lesse
take away, the Ancient native right which the House of Peers (consisting of the Lords who did engage in the Cause of the Parliament
against the forces raised in the name of the late King, and so continued until 1648) had and have to be a part of the Parliament of
England." Some opposition was raised from the republican ranks, but
was overborne. On March 17, as a member reported to Sir Ralph
Verney, at "About 6 o'clock we passed the Bill of Dissolution with

---

*Tracts*, II, p. 773; Sir George Warner, ed., *The Nicholas Papers* (= Camden
Society, 3d Series, vol. 31) (Aberdeen, 1920), IV, p. 200; Thomas Carte, ed.,
*Duke of Ormond's Papers*, II, p. 311; Ludlow's *Memoirs*, II, p. 246.
[14] *Clarendon S. P.*, III, pp. 304-305; *Nicholas Papers*, IV, p. 200; M. M.
Verney, *Memoirs of the Verney Family*, Vols. III-IV (London, 1894, 1899), III,
p. 472.

a perfect salvo to the rights and privileges of the Lord's House." A
new parliament was to meet April 25.[15]

Parliament's was not the only salvo fired in the peers' behalf.
Prynne had issued a "Short, legal, medicinal, useful, safe, easie Prescription" in 1659 to recover the nation from "Dangerous, distrac-
tive, Destructive Confusion, and worse than Bedlam Madnesse". His
solution was not limited to the peers of 1648, but rather, "For all the
antient Nobilitie of the Kingdom ... to assemble themselves by Common consent at Westminster ...", and there proceed according to the
provisions of the triennial act to reconstitute the government of the
kingdom. This tract was followed by "Loyalty Banished: or England
in Mourning", which recounted his attempt to sit with the Rump.
From this point of departure, he went on to prove that parliament
was determined upon Charles I's death. This he argued from the
authority of doctrine laid down in the law books, because all writs
of summons abate at the king's death, because a parliament can be
called only by a king regnant (disregarding the triennial act now),
and because parliament is a corporation of king, lords, and commons,
"and if one of the three is extinct, the body corporate no longer exists".
His mourning concluded, in 1660 Prynne addressed some "Conscientious, Serious Theological and legal Quaeres" to the "twice-
dissipated, self-created Anti-Parliamentary Westminster Juncto". In
this pamphlet he trampled upon his particular enemies, those responsible for abolishing the lords and those he considered traitors to
the lords, "Mr. Cecil, the self-degraded Earl of Salsbury, Robert Cecil,
his son, ... and Mr. Herbert, the self-degraded Earl of Pembrook".
Eighty-eight other particular foes of Prynne were catalogued by name
and shortcoming. These three pamphlets concluded Prynne's efforts.
Evaluation of their effect varied. David Masson described Prynne as
a "rhinoseros in blinkers". Davies disagreed, and believed he "delivered many shrewd blows at the restored Long Parliament, and
rallied public opinion to the cause of ... the old constitution". Perhaps the judgment of the man most concerned should be most regarded. Charles II wrote to Prynne: "I have not only received par-

[15]  *Mercurius Politicus,* March 8-15, 1660 (#611), p. (1171), March 15-22, 1660
(#612), p. (1178); "A Perfect Diurnal of Every Dayes Proceedings in Parliament", March 13-16, 1660, B.M., E. 1016 (1); H. B. Wheatley, ed.,
*The Diary of Samuel Pepys* (London, 1896), I, p. 83; *Acts and Ordinances,* II,
p. 1472; G. Davies, *Restoration of Charles II,* p. 305; M. M. Verney, *Memoirs
of the Verney Family,* III, p. 473; *H. Mss. C., 7th Report,* Appendix, Part II,
Mss. of Sir Henry Verney, p. 463.

ticular information of your great services and indefatigable endeavours to awaken my people of England from that deplorable condition they have run themselves into, but have had the perusal of some of your labours myself; And I must believe that the efficacy of your pen has been so prevalent in the discovery of such designs, that it has and will facilitate my restoration." [16]

The events leading to that restoration were now beginning to move swiftly. The men who had been prominent shortly before now were subjected to scurrilous printed attacks. Henry Neville, who had spoken so strongly against the other house, was accused now of preferring the attentions of Lady DeLaWarr to his wife. The earl of Pembroke was accused of a similar transgression. The term of commonwealthsman was applied with derision to the earl of Carnarvon. Such low proceedings mirrored the change in England. By the end of February, 1660, it seemed certain that the old constitution, king and lords, would be restored. Only the question remained if there would be conditions upon the restoration. [17]

Charles trusted Monck to secure him an unconditional crown. Hyde wrote John Grenville, "Now ... the King resolves to conceal nothing of moment from the General, upon whose affection he relies entirely. ..." His trust was well placed. At every critical stage — the return of the secluded members, the dissolution of the restored Long Parliament, or the admission of the peers — Monck's intervention was decisive in favor of the crown. The general was chiefly responsible for Charles II's restoration without restriction or conditions. He, who had governed Scotland for Cromwell, Montagu, who had offered Oliver the crown, and Fairfax, who had served with him in his greatest victories, became the three men most responsible for the Stuart return. [18]

---

[16] *Somers' Tracts*, 1st Collection, IV, pp. 423-425; W. Prynne, "A short, legal, medicinal, useful, safe, easie Prescription. ..." (London, 1659), B.M., E. 722(1), pp. 2-3; J. Lingard, *History of England*, VIII, 574 n.; W. Prynne, "Loyalty Banished: or England in Mourning" (London, 1659), B.M., E. 986 (20), pp. 6-7; "Conscientious, Serious, Theological and Legal Quaeres. ..." (London, 1660), B.M., E. 722(3), pp. 4, 17, 21, 47-48; G. Davies, *Restoration of Charles II*, p. 96 n.; M. Coate, *Mordaunt Letter Book*, p. 126. David Masson, *The Life of John Milton. ...*, 7 vols. (New York, 1946), V, p. 449n.
[17] "Your Servant Gentlemen, or What think you of a Query, or two More" (London, 1660), B.M., E. 1016(9); C. H. Firth, *House of Lords*, p. 269.
[18] B.M., *Lansdowne Ms.* 1054 fo. 71; Keith Feiling, *A History of the Tory Party* (Oxford, 1924), p. 92; J. Campbell, *Lives of the Lord Chancellors*, III, pp. 163-164.

The efforts of these three were supported by other members of the council of state. Montagu had not accepted appointment to this body until Charles had approved his sitting. There he and Monck joined with Arthur Annesley, its president, to check those members anxious to impose terms on the king. Pierrepont, St. John, Holles, and Waller — all in close contact with the earls of Bedford and Manchester — led the fight in the council for the provisions of the Treaty of the Isle of Wight. Cooper and Sir Richard Onslow joined Monck's group in successfully blocking the movement for conditions there.[19]

Charles himself now began to play a direct role in the politics of restoration. From Brussels he sent a commission to Arthur Annesley to join with the trusted royalists Mordaunt and Grenville and two others as commissioners to treat with any but regicides to secure support for the restoration. He then issued a proclamation on March 20, to all peers of the realm. He exhorted them to take the lead in bringing the people of England to their former obedience. While he indicated to them his desire that they play a prominent role in the present affairs, the lords' response was mixed. Northumberland pessimistically wrote Manchester:

The peace and settlement of this nation ... is of most universal concernment, and in order to it, the restoring of the peers unto their rights will be found a necessary consequence — so as, the first being provided for, the other will follow of course; but, as businesses have been managed, I doubt neither are yet in a way of being well-secured. For the Lords to go about at present asserting their rights (considering to what some of their own number have lately consented), would, I think, be ill-timed, especially seeing that no part of the nation but ourselves has as yet expressed any desire that we should return to the exercise of our duties in Parliament; and all in power and authority have, either openly or impliedly, declared against it. What great matters the next meeting will bring forth, I am not able to judge; but those that believe it likely to do us right, or satisfy the nation's expectations, must have a stronger faith than your Lordship's affectionate and faithful servant,

Northumberland.

Say also wrote to Manchester, but in a different vein. On March 19, he explained that he had not yet come up to London because of his activities in the elections then being held for parliament. He expected to wait upon Manchester and the other lords about ten days before

[19] L. F. Brown, *The First Earl of Shaftesbury* (New York, 1933), pp. 92-93; Bodley, *Clarendon Ms.* 71 fo. 22; Clarendon's *Rebellion*, pp. 891, 893; "Perfect Diurnal", Feb. 23, 1660, B.M., E. 1016(1).

the opening of parliament, to consult on the means to be taken for the re-assertion of their rights and the good of the nation.[20]

It was not accidental that Northumberland and Say were corresponding with Manchester at this time. He was directing one last effort to effect a Presbyterian settlement of the kingdom. This party had difficulty making any headway during the Interregnum because Pride's purge and the abolition of the house of lords had deprived its leaders of a base of authority. Now these leaders had regained some influence. The exiled court was informed in early March that Manchester had written to all the lords of 1648, directing them to plan to sit when parliament met on April 25. He also urged them to join him in London before the opening to plan the securing of their old place in the constitution. In early April Pepys recorded that a number of peers and prominent Presbyterians were rather obviously in conference at the earl of Manchester's.[21]

Samborne wrote to Hyde that the earl of Bedford and Lord Wharton had joined with Manchester to effect limitations to the restoration. Mordaunt added to this that they planned to permit to sit neither the royalist lords, who had served with Charles I and his son, nor the young peers, who had come of age since the civil wars. Only seventeen peers would be admitted — seven earls, a viscount, and nine barons. Monck had agreed to this proposal, Mordaunt said, and this noble Rump "will have a negative voice on the Commons, and render ineffectual all those good intentions they come frought with". Another of Hyde's correspondents saw an even worse picture: "Besides, there is so insolent a spirit amongst some of the Nobility, that I really fear 'twill turn to Aristocracy. . . ." Northumberland was pictured as emerging as an equal to the king, "nay perhaps his superior". Bordeaux reported that the Presbyterian lords had gained Monck to their position and that he professed he could not restrain the army if those peers who had not been on the side of parliament were admitted to sit. Bordeaux placed the number to be admitted at fifteen. Barwick reduced this number to fourteen in his report to

---

[20] *Baker's Chronicle*, p. 658; *Bibliotheca Lindesiana. A Bibliography of Royal Proclamations of the Tudor and Stuart Sovereigns. . . .*, ed. R. R. Steele, 2 vols. (1910), I, p. 382; Duke of Manchester, *Court and Society from Elizabeth to Anne*, 2 vols. (London, 1864), I, p. 395; *H. Mss. C., 8th Report*, Appendix, Part II, Mss. of the Duke of Manchester, p. 65.
[21] D. Ogg, *Reign of Charles II*, I, pp. 214-215; *H. Mss. C., Mss. of the Marquis of Bath*, II, p. 144; *Pepys' Diary*, I, p. 106.

Hyde, and added that he saw no way to circumvent their plan.[22]

It was essential to Manchester and his followers to exclude all other categories of peers because of the program they wished to achieve. When Ormond was in England to sound them, Say had approached him on behalf of the Presbyterian interest. Say asked if the royalist lords would join in a restoration on the basis of the Treaty of the Isle of Wight. Ormond rejected this out of hand. The lords of 1648 knew that if they wanted this program, they alone could achieve it. The house of commons about to meet was expected to be very tender toward the king. The lords attempted to raise the spectre of an unrestrained king given rein to vengeance, but without notable success. They talked of the importance of establishing the monarchy upon the true basis of liberty and property. This to them meant the terms of the Treaty of Newport, or more particularly the Treaty of the Isle of Wight. In its main provisions this would give parliament control over its own meetings and adjournments, as well as the control of all military forces and militia for a period of years, with safeguards after that. All acts against the crown would be consigned to oblivion and all peerages granted after May 20, 1642, would be void. Other provisions would give parliament a major direction of finance and the court of wards would be abolished and a fixed annual revenue substituted. A Presbyterian church government would be set up. The general result desired by the lords of 1648 would be a limited monarchy and a powerful aristocracy, the twin institutions so favored by the Whigs, the intellectual inheritors of these men. Fittingly, the first of the great Whigs, Anthony Ashley Cooper, later earl of Shaftesbury, was now in communication with Manchester. Mordaunt reported him in this "cabal", which the royalist asserted to be dividing already the offices of state among themselves. Besides this concern for offices, the old lords desired the whole of the land settlement be confirmed as it existed. From Suffolk House these aristocrats seemed to be carrying their program toward success. On one point only they yielded.

[22] *Clarendon S. P.*, III, pp. 680, 705, 729; F. P. G. Guizot, *History of Richard Cromwell*, II, p. 412; Peers alive in 1660 who sat in 1648 were: earls of Denbigh, Lincoln, Manchester, Northumberland, Nottingham, Rutland, Salisbury, Stamford, and Suffolk; Viscount Say; and barons Bruce, Dacre, DeLaWarr, Grey of Warke, Howard of Escrick, Hunsdon, Maynard, Montagu, North, and Wharton. According to Mordaunt, all of these but two earls and one baron were to sit. Bordeaux eliminated two more, and Barwick, yet one more. Say is obviously Mordaunt's viscount. Earls certain to sit were Denbigh, Manchester, Northumberland, Salisbury, and Stamford. Among the barons all but Montagu and North would probably sit in a Rump. This would total a hard core of 14.

Contrary to the Treaty of the Isle of Wight, they were prepared to accept the restoration of episcopacy. This was the cause for which, strictly speaking, Charles I had laid down his life and its return was never really in doubt in 1660. Bishop Morley, on his reconnoitering mission into England, found this tacitly accepted by the Presbyterian leaders. Morley held out the hope that the institution of episcopacy could be integrated with some modified form of general Presbyterian church government.[23]

To circumvent the success of this junto, the royalists saw their best hope in the rest of the nobility. Hyde wrote to Mr. Hatton, "I know not what to think of Monk; but if the Lords do not concur together in doing some act towards the recovery of their right, or making the violence that is upon them, so notorious and visible, that the people may think themselves concerned to demand it upon their behalf, as a fundamental constitution of the Kingdom, they will lose all respect." These lords did appear to be proceeding timidly. Major Wood reported to Hyde five days before parliament opened that the lords could not decide whether to sit as a house of parliament in their own house, or privately elsewhere. Pepys wrote that the lords' sitting was uncertain, and feared "whether they will sit or no, it will bring a great many inconveniences".[24]

The inconvenience was to be to the Presbyterian lords. Too lightly they assumed it was for them to formulate conditions. They might possibly have succeeded in vetoing the return of the cavalier peers. They could not, however, reasonably exclude the younger generation of peers who had grown up since the civil wars. It was Mordaunt who seized upon this weakness. He wrote Hyde, "I have made it my business with the Earls of Oxford and Strafford to put them to asserting their privileges, who have equal right, without exceptions, with the other [peers]. . . . I hope at least so far to defeat the old Lords, as that they shall not sit, unless they admit the others, but for the King's Lords, we are not like to prevail with the General." [25]

---

[23] G. Davies, *Restoration of Charles II*, pp. 295-296; Thomas Carte, *Life of James Duke of Ormonde*, 6 vols. (Oxford, 1851), III, p. 663; T. Carte, ed., *Duke of Ormonde's Papers*, II, pp. 328-329; *Clarendon S. P.*, III, pp. 527-528; D. Ogg, *Reign of Charles II*, I, p. 11; W. D. Christie, *Life of Anthony Ashley Cooper, First Earl of Shaftesbury*, 2 vols. (London, 1871), I, p. 220; K. Feiling, *History of the Tory Party*, pp. 91, 126; L. von Ranke, *History of England*, III, p. 294; C. H. Firth, *House of Lords*, pp. 269-270.

[24] *Clarendon S. P.*, III, p. 701; *C.C.S.P.*, IV, p. 671; *Pepys' Diary*, I, p. 108.

[25] D. Ogg, *Reign of Charles II*, I, p. 28; *Clarendon S. P.*, III, p. 729.

Monck again became the key to the nature of the restoration. He could dictate who would and who would not sit. He was attacked from both sides. Clarendon reported him as fully engaged to the Presbyterian peers. Ludlow accused him of promising those peers that they only would sit, and then betraying his word. Mordaunt did report to Charles II a "close correspondence between some of the presbiterian lords and Monck...". But he added hopefully that the royalist lords, the marquess of Hertford and the earl of Lindsey, were seeking to approach Monck. Bordeaux reported only that Monck was in a state of irritation at the multitude of pressures the various groups of peers were bringing upon him.[26]

Monck appeared stalled, uncertain of how to proceed among the contending lords. Indeed, the critical issue at stake gave Monck good reason to hesitate. The consequence of his decision would be to determine the character of the upper house and its outlook on the subject of a conditional restoration. While Monck did not favor hard conditions for the king, he had by no means committed himself to a completely unconditional return of monarchy, as his advice to Charles indicated. In the end, as Clarendon observed, the younger Cavalier peers would abandon moderation and temporizing and force the issue upon Monck. The Cavaliers, for their part, were behaving with moderation and restraint at Charles's command. The royalists in London, led by the marquess of Dorchester and the earls of Northampton, Devonshire, and Norwich, issued a declaration that "We do sincerely profess, That we do reflect upon our past sufferings from the hands of God, and therefore do not cherish any violent Thoughts or Inclinations...". This statement was followed by others, signed by prominent royalist peers like lords Vaughan, Belasyse, Loughborough, Lexington, and Lucas. As evidence of their good will they declared "That we intend by our quiet and peaceable Behaviour, to testify our submission to the present Power ... in expectation of the future Parliament."[27]

On April 25, 1660, the Convention Parliament, called really at the summons of George Monck, assembled at Westminster. It contained a house of lords. The eleven years in the wilderness at last were

[26]  Clarendon's *Rebellion*, p. 894; Ludlow's *Memoirs*, II, pp. 260-261; M. Coate, ed., *Mordaunt Letter Book*, pp. 95-96; F. P. G. Guizot, *History of Richard Cromwell*, II, p. 412.

[27]  Clarendon's *Rebellion*, p. 897; B.M., *Egerton Ms.* 2618 fos. 75-76, *Lansdowne Ms.* 1054 fo. 72; J. Oldmixon, *History of England*, p. 464; *Baker's Chronicle*, pp. 722-723.

at an end and the lords entered into Sinai. The elect on that Wednesday numbered only ten. There was the melancholy and uncertain Percy, earl of Northumberland. The old fox, Say, had emerged from his den. The retiring but skillful Wharton was there. Lincoln, Suffolk, and Denbigh completed the earls' bench. Hunsdon, Grey, and Maynard sat for the barons. Their speaker was the earl of Manchester, the most prominent Presbyterian nobleman in the country. All ten had sat in 1648, all ten had opposed Charles I, but all ten had also stood against his execution. They gathered confidently to await the arrival of Sir John Grenville, bearing the Declaration of Breda and letters from their sovereign to his lords and gentlemen of parliament. Yet these ten represented only a fraction of their order. The day they sat there were 145 peers of England potentially entitled to sit in parliament, and a good number of these were now in London. It appeared momentarily that the remnant sitting would be the house of lords. But the strong tide of royalism could not be contained, or the impulsive young peers turned aside. The expansion of the house was to be a gradual process, with qualifications, until all classes of peers sat. The peers of 1648 were the first, but the young peers would have to be accommodated. Then there were the old royalists, who had stood by the house of Stuart from the start, and the creations since 1642, the peers ennobled for their service to the royal cause. Also to be considered were the recusants, the Roman Catholic peers, and lastly the peers of the royal blood and their fellow exiles. The rumor spread that the Presbyterian peers soon would have company.[28]

These lords, for their part, proceeded harmoniously with the house of commons, while, as Pepys reported, the young lords forbore to sit. The sitting peers sought to strengthen their hand by appointing Northumberland, Say, Wharton, and Hunsdon as a committee "to consider of such Lords as shall have Letters written to them, to desire their Attendence on this House". The committee nominated six names, all peers who sat in 1648. These were the earls of Nottingham and Rutland, and barons North, DeLaWarr, Montagu, and

[28] A. S. Turberville, "Lords under Charles II", XLIV, pp. 400-401; C. H. Firth, *House of Lords*, pp. 282, 285, 291. Firth's figures are based upon the *L.J.* A "Catalogue of the Peers of England", printed 1661, in *Somers' Tracts*, VII, p. 413, lists 147 peers, including Albemarle and Sandwich. The list in the *Old Parliamentary History*, XXII, p. 332, is dated May, 1660, but should read 1661. *L.J.*, XI, p. 3; Clarendon's *Rebellion*, p. 904; G. Davies, *Restoration of Charles II*, pp. 258-259; *H. Mss. C.*, 5th Report, Appendix, Part I, Duke of Sutherland Mss., p. 146.

Bruce. The earl of Leicester also wrote to Manchester, promising to add his vote to their party if his health permitted him to attend the house of lords. The peers then took up treating with Charles, as they long had planned. These plans at once started to crumble. Denbigh, quick to judge the intensity of the royalist gale now rising, went over to the king without reservation. Manchester and Northumberland told alderman Bunce the day before parliament opened that they would have propositions for the king, albeit easy ones. Three days later these propositions had become petitions, which indeed were never sent.[29]

In a letter to Hyde, Lady Willoughby had predicted this fate for the proposals as soon as the young lords should enter. On April 26, the earl of Strafford had communicated with Monck.

My Lord,
    I understood we had been all clearly absolved of any engagement & free to go into the house though however I confess it had been first to have understood it directly your Lordship & must desire your pardon for my heat in my other letter. I shall not offer to go to the house till I know certainly from your Lordship I am free in respect of what was promised & I doubt not but your Lordship will find the same from us all besides that could meet together, namely my Ld. of Oxford, m. L. of Bridgewater, & m. L. of Bolingbroke. My Lord I shall wait upon your Lordship after dinner . . ..

The next morning the young lords entered the house. Two of their number, the Earl Rivers and Baron Petre, had anticipated this by sitting in the afternoon of the 25th and on the 26th respectively. This action had raised tempers, Henry Coventry reported to Hyde, but the Presbyterian peers had no course but to give way graciously. Monck told the old peers that now they were in, he had no power to turn any lord out. For Monck, the admission of the young lords represented the final step to an immediate and unconditional restoration.[30]

The admission of the young peers pointed to the admission of all the peers. The case of the Presbyterians had broken down. They could actually claim no right to constitute exclusively a house of lords. They had not been summoned in the usual manner by writ. They could not now sit as a part of the Long Parliament, which was at last defunct.

---

[29] *C.S.P.V.*, 1659-1661, p. 141; *Pepys' Diary*, I, p. 110; *L.J.*, XI, pp. 3-4; *H. Mss. C., 8th Report*, Appendix, Part II, Mss. of the Duke of Manchester, p. 65; *C.C.S.P.*, IV, pp. 674, 683, 686.

[30] *C.C.S.P.*, IV, p. 685; D. Ogg, *Reign of Charles II*, I, p. 31; T. Carte, *Duke of Ormonde's Papers*, II, p. 328; Roger Coke, *Detection of Court and State in England*, 2 vols. (London, 1694), II, p. 102; K. Feiling, *History of the Tory Party*, pp. 93-94; B.M., *Egerton Ms.* 2618 fo. 70.

If they founded their case upon their birthright, as *consiliarii nati*, other peers were in possession of the same privilege. The old royalists and the new creations abstained from exercising that birthright for the time only to avoid cavil. The cavalier camp was in jubilation at their victory; other classes of peers could well wait; the young peers would secure them their majority. Hyde quickly had reports of the rapid and numerous entries of trusted peers. Barwick wrote that Say and Northumberland had converted to zealots for the king upon first sight of their new comrades. The earl of Berkshire, directing royalist admissions to the house, asked Charles for directions for filling it up.[31]

Bordeaux threw some question upon Monck's role in the young peers' sitting. He reported to Mazarin that on the 26th Monck had asked Strafford still to forbear sitting. The earl of Northampton, writing to Charles II, implied that it was the old peers who told the young ones to forbear because Monck would not tolerate their presence, but once they entered, they discovered he did not desire their exclusion. Bordeaux later reported that Monck approved the sitting of the young peers on the 27th. In fact the Presbyterians in the lords had already been joined by four other peers by the evening of Monck's meeting with Strafford. Two of these four, the earls of Dorset and Middlesex, had not taken any active role in royalist affairs after succeeding to their peerages, but neither had they been "peers of 1648". Taken together, these four sitting peers left Monck at a distinct disadvantage in his meeting with Strafford; either he had to let Strafford's group of young royalist peers in, or he had to turn out the four peers already sitting, and the possible consequences of this action he evidently was not prepared to risk.[32]

The actual entry of the young peers was orderly enough. The Journal reports only that "Signification being given to the House, 'That divers Lords were in the Lobby, ready to attend the Service of this House having never sat in Parliament since the death of their Ancestors'; ... The House gave the Gentleman Usher Authority to call them in, to sit in their Places in the House." No indication of debate occurs. Led by the earls of Oxford, Derby, and Strafford, they took their places. As the fathers of the last two had been executed for their services to the Stuart cause, the significance of their

[31] J. Lingard, *History of England*, VIII, pp. 615-616; *C.C.S.P.*, IV, pp. 679-680, 684, 687.
[32] F. P. G. Guizot, *History of Richard Cromwell*, II, p. 414; *C.C.S.P.*, IV, p. 679; *L.J.*, XI, p. 4.

admission could not be mistaken. Five others of their class came in with them; Viscount Conway, and lords Cromwell, Gerard, Teynham, and Capel. These alone did not overbear the Presbyterians, but before the house adjourned on the 27th, twelve more peers had come in. Four of these — the earls of Bedford, Nottingham, and Rutland, and Lord Howard of Escrick — were old parliament men. They were outweighed by the arrival of the earls of Bridgwater, Warwick, Bolingbroke, and Winchilsea, Viscount Hereford, and barons Berkeley and Craven. The earl of Scarsdale was also admitted, but only by the title of Baron Deincourt. The earldom, bestowed upon him after 1642, was not recognized, indicating the issue of all such titles was still unsettled.[33]

For a few days, Pepys was able to report the house growing gradually as Presbyterian and young peers came in. On the 27th summons were sent to the earls of Leicester and Clare, and Lord Paget, all now of royalist inclination. Lord Brooke, a young peer, was the next to sit, on April 30. A larger number came in on May 1. The earls of Salisbury and Stamford, and Baron Bruce swelled the Puritan ranks. The duke of Buckingham headed a young contingent of the earl of Carnarvon, and lords Morley and Chandos. Sir Richard Leveson explained the restraint of the old royalists, even when Monck promised not to restrict them, to the wish of the king. Charles asked them not to complicate matters until disputes over the election of unqualified members in the commons were settled, and that house firmly in hand. However, in the lords Mordaunt reported that the Presbyterians were finding the young lords most unrestrained. Fearing the introduction of wild measures, they approached the great royalist peers, Hertford and Southampton, to check the young peers' highness, if need be by coming in themselves. This did not at once happen, though many prominent young royalists like the earl of Berkshire were in the house, he allegedly to avoid his creditors. An important addition to the house was the entry on May 8 of James Compton, earl of Northampton, an able man who was to carry much of the work of the house for the next twenty-one years.[34]

At the end of April Monck had indicated that the old royalists who

<hr>

[33] *L.J.*, XI, pp. 4-5; C. H. Firth, *House of Lords*, pp. 282-283; A. S. Turberville, "Lords under Charles II", XLIV, p. 401.

[34] *Pepys' Diary*, I, p. 112; *L.J.*, XI, pp. 5-6; C. H. Firth, *House of Lords*, p. 284; *H. Mss. C.*, *5th Report*, Appendix, Part I, Duke of Sutherland Mss., p. 149; T. Carte, *Duke of Ormonde's Papers*, II, p. 330; P. H. Hardacre, *Royalists*, p. 143.

had borne arms for the Stuart cause were free to take their seats as peers of parliament. On May 14 the house of lords issued summons to the marquess of Hertford, the earl of Southampton, and five other prominent royalists to come in. This number included the earls of Lindsey, Peterborough, and Portland. On the 16th Lindsey took his seat with two other royalists, barons Lovelace and Paget, while Peterborough followed on the 17th. Hertford and Portland sat on the 18th, with the earl of Leicester. On the 21st the entry of the earls of Southampton and Devonshire completed the return of most of the prominent old royalists not in exile.[35]

However, as Bordeaux reported, one prominent group of royalists who remained in England were still uninvited to sit. On May 4 the house of lords had started the wholesale issuing of summons, but with a proviso: "Ordered, That Suspension be made of issuing out of Letters for attending this House, to those Lords that are Recusants, until the further Pleasure of this House be known." Bordeaux correctly observed of this, "they have excepted the Catholic peers from this invitation, without however refusing them admission". When the restriction was proposed there were already two recusants, lords Teynham and Petre, sitting in the house. The other Catholics honored the restriction for eleven days, then, on the 15th, Viscount Stafford came in. The earl of Shrewsbury sat on the 19th. He was followed by the marquess of Winchester and barons Abergavenny, Arundell, and Stourton two days later. This entry effectively terminated any further consideration of a religious exclusion.[36]

There remained a possible legal exclusion of the peers created since May 20, 1642. The title of these lords had been denied many times over in the legislation of the Interregnum. These lords approached Monck on May 13 and the general attempted to dissuade them from sitting. He concluded with the qualification that if the lords now in the house thought it their due, and were willing to admit them, he would oppose no man's right. The lords in the house did not yet think it their due. On May 4 they had ordered "that no Lords created since 1642 shall sit". So affairs rested until Charles II entered London on May 29. Two days later the earl of Berkshire rose to acquaint the house "That he was commanded by His Majesty, to signify His

[35] *L.J.*, XI, pp. 12, 27, 33; F. P. G. Guizot, *History of Richard Cromwell*, II, p. 417; C. H. Firth, *House of Lords*, p. 286; A. S. Turberville, "Lords under Charles II", p. 401.
[36] F. P. G. Guizot, *History of Richard Cromwell*, II, p. 424; *L.J.*, XI, pp. 13, 28.

Desire to the House, that those Lords who have been created by Patent of His late Majesty at Oxford do sit in this House of Peers". The house instructed the earl to return to Charles "that Matters of Honour do belong to His Majesty; and this House does acquiesce in His Majesty's Pleasure". The house further ordered the restriction of May 4 vacated. The king's action also terminated a move in the commons to send up a bill legally barring these lords.[37]

The civil war creations (or promotions) of Charles I entered the house in large numbers on June 1. The most prominent of the new arrivals were the marquesses of Newcastle and Dorchester and the earls of Chesterfield, Lichfield, and Norwich. Entering with them were lords Belasyse, Byron, Clifford, Hatton, Lucas, and Vaughan, and four others. The same day Edward Hyde took his place on the woolsack. Charles's wish also assured that his own creations could sit. He had made only eight creations or promotions during his exile, and these were slow to come in. Among the first were Lord Berkeley of Stratton, Hyde's old foe, on June 5, and Viscount Mordaunt two days later. This influx was not particularly well-received by the old royalists any more than by the Presbyterians. Peers eligible to sit now outnumbered those eligible in 1642. Many of the new creations were looked upon as distinctly of "mean quality and less fortune". Actually their wealth was little less than that of the old peers. The assessments of the committee for the advance of money on 85 old peers averaged £ 3,433; on 15 new peers, £ 2,700. The average worth estimated by the committee for compounding for 34 old peers was £ 27,231. Seven new peers had an average wealth of £ 26,680. These new peers were the last controversial group to enter the house of lords, and their sitting almost completed the return of the temporal peers to Westminster.[38]

Lord Wharton, in a list he compiled of the different classes of peers re-entering parliament in 1660, set apart the lords who had gone into exile with the king as a special group. These men represented both the highest conception of the royalist cause as well as the leading royalist statesmen. On the last day of May its most honored represen-

---

[37] B.M., *Egerton Ms.* 2618 fo. 29; C. H. Firth, *House of Lords*, pp. 286-290; *Clarendon S. P.*, III, p. 748; P. H. Hardacre, *Royalists*, p. 144; *L.J.*, pp. 13, 50; A. S. Turberville, "Lords under Charles II", p. 401; F. P. G. Guizot, *History of Richard Cromwell*, II, p. 438.

[38] *L.J.*, XI, p. 50; Clarendon's *Life*, II, p. 14; *G.E.C.*, V, pp. 785-786; P. H. Hardacre, *Royalists*, pp. 143-144, 144 n.; *H. Mss. C.*, *5th Report*, Appendix, Part I, Duke of Sutherland Mss., p. 153.

tatives were welcomed into the house with great ceremony. These were the two princes — James, duke of York and Albany, and the young Henry of Oatlands, duke of Gloucester. They were joined the following day by Henry Jermain, earl of St. Albans and a leader of the French partisans. Barons Crofts and Langdale came in during June. Hyde, not yet elevated to the peerage, was sitting as lord chancellor of England. Ormond, by his English title of earl of Brecknock, concluded the representation of this group when he sat in July. The reconstruction of the house of lords had taken about four months.[39]

This reconstruction was of temporal peers only. As the abolition of the house of lords was considered an illegal act of the army and Rump, no legal bar was recognized against the return of the lords temporal in 1660. The case of the lords spiritual was different. They had been excluded by due process of law. An act of parliament, passed by both houses, had been passed into statute law by Charles I on February 14, 1642. Thus a statute was needed to restore the bishops. As the temper of the commons in the Convention Parliament was still anti-episcopal, it was decided to wait on this statute until a new royalist parliament could be assembled. The nine bishops still living would have to wait better than a year until the death of Charles I was fully vindicated, and their place as peers with it.[40]

Charles II had written to William Morice, "... yet there is as little question, that there are some persons both within and without both Houses, who desire to keep up the memory of the old jealosies & animosities, & to prevent such an entire union as can only make us all happy; Next to the blessing of God, nothing can so absolutely disappoint those designs, as my presence with you, which those men will endeavour to destruct & defer all they can, & I am sure you will as much endeavour to hasten...." The opening up of the house of lords to its full temporal membership had contributed to hastening the king's return, but the memory of old animosities remained. A swift rebuilding of the old order was necessary. This period opened a new time of testing for the house of lords. It could draw neither inspiration nor solace from the last eleven years. The house had been humbled, its members humiliated, and their privileges disregarded. If the chamber were to enjoy its former prestige it had much leeway

[39]  Bodley, *Carte Ms.* 81 fo. 63; B. M., *Add. Ms.* 32,455 fo. 43; *Baker's Chronicle*, p. 734.
[40]  A. S. Turberville, "Lords under Charles II", p. 401; C. H. Firth, *House of Lords*, p. 291; L. von Ranke, *History of England*, III, p. 315.

to recover. The last years had also dealt a final blow to personal monarchy of the style of the Tudors and the early Stuarts. A parliament without the support of public opinion had likewise been rejected. Thus the whole position both of monarchy and legislature was altered. The attempt to establish a clearly defined relationship within the trinity of crown and both houses, the crown in parliament, was to occupy the next three decades. The rise of the lords after 1690 was laid on the foundations of the restoration period.[41]

The lords took a lead in restoring the formal conventions of the constitution. They promptly moved that, "according to the ancient and fundamental laws of the kingdom, the government is, and ought to be, by king, lords, and commons". They then voted that means should be devised to secure the king's return to his people. A series of orders from the lords set the tone of affairs in the early part of May. On the third they ordered that the statues of the late king should be put up in the same places from where they had been pulled down. The same was ordered for the arms of the Stuart family. Charles II was ordered prayed for by all ministers. Statues of Monck were to be erected in appropriate places. Ermine robes, crown, and sceptre for the king were ordered by parliament on May 15. On the 25th the lords dispatched a letter welcoming the king on his safe arrival in England, and four days later the house adjourned to wait upon their dear and dread sovereign at Whitehall.[42]

The king's word had proceeded him into England. On May 1, after consulting with Monck, Sir John Grenville presented himself at the bar of the house of lords and delivered two letters to the earl of Manchester. The first was a letter to the house of lords specifically. In it Charles spoke not of the past behavior of the lords but of their present state. "We cannot have a better Reason to promise Ourself and End of Our common Sufferings and Calamities, and that Our own just Power and Authority will with God's Blessing be restored to Us, than that We hear you are again acknowledged to have that Authority and Jusrisdiction which hath always belonged to you, by your Birth and the fundamental Laws of the Land. ..." The second document was the famous Declaration of Breda. It held out the pro-

---

[41]    B.M., *Egerton Ms.* 2618 fo. 75; A. S. Turberville, "Lords under Charles II", p. 400; W. S. Holdsworth, *History of English Law*, VI, p. 161; D. Ogg, *Reign of Charles II*, II, p. 450.
[42]    G. Davies, *Early Stuarts*, p. 259; D. Ogg, *Reign of Charles II*, I, p. 32; *C.J.*, VIII, p. 7; *L.J.*, XI, pp. 11-12, 29, 41, 46.

mise of a peaceful resumption of a moderate monarchy, with a tenderness for men's consciences. Of particular interest to the peers was its land provision. "And because ... many Grants and Purchases of Estates have been made... We are likewise willing, that all such Differences, and all Things relating to such Grants, Sales, and Purchases, shall be determined in Parliament, which can best provide for the just Satisfaction of all men who are concerned." This provision promised to be of immense benefit to the nobility.[43]

To benefit in the restoration settlement, the upper house needed first to make good its relations with the commons. On the second day of parliament the lords sent to the commons the request for a conference concerning the setting of a day of fast and thanksgiving. Only two voices questioned the proceeding in the commons. Luke Robinson rose to ask the Speaker who made the other chamber a house of lords. He wished to know the feeling of the commons concerning the other chamber sitting at Westminster. The commons gave almost total support to it. The earl of Manchester managed the conference with the commons on the lords' vote that the government is of king, lords, and commons. Again the commons quickly concurred with the lords in their vote. The commons also ratified the earl of Manchester to be a commissioner of the Great Seal, a futile Presbyterian move to side-track Hyde's ascent to the woolsack. On May 8 the two houses joined in proclaiming the king. On the 11th they jointly issued a declaration that all commissioners in military, judicial, and revenue offices from April 25 forward "shall and are hereby authorized and required to proceed forthwith in the execution of their Commissions ... in the King's Majesty's Name and Style". Together the houses showered largess on the royal family: £ 25,000 for the duke of York and £ 17,000 for his younger brother. Henrietta Maria was to receive £ 20,000; to the Queen of Bohemia and the Princess Royal each went £ 10,000. The commons recorded no objections to lordly participation in these financial proceedings. The two houses showed promise of working in harmony.[44]

In this burst of harmony the two houses had dispatched their joint commission, to be composed of six lords and twelve commoners, to

---

[43]   Baker's Chronicle, p. 723; L.J., XI, p. 7.
[44]   F. P. G., Guizot, History of Richard Cromwell, II, p. 414; H. Mss. C., 5th Report, Appendix, Part I, Duke of Sutherland Mss., pp. 146, 208; C.C.S.P., IV, p. 678; L.J., XI, pp. 5, 8, 10, 16, 19, 25; Pepys' Diary, I, p. 115; B.M., Add. Ms. 35,906 fo. 15.

The Hague to welcome in the king. The lords were a mixed lot, headed by the dependable earls of Oxford and Middlesex, and Viscount Hereford, along with lords Brooke and Berkeley. The earl of Warwick, troubled with gout, did not bother to go. Since the entry of the young lords had ended the possibility of conditions, the commissioners had no importance. However, the unsettled conditions in England were sufficient to make the royalists anxious to secure the realm with all possible speed. In England the complexion of the militia changed sharply. The earls of Oxford, Middlesex, and Suffolk led the midlands levies. Lords Maynard and Berkeley, aided by Sir John Carew in Cornwall, led in the west country. Sir Horatio Townshend was charged with Norfolk. These were only temporary measures before enough time had passed properly to appoint lords lieutenant for the shires. A more important step was the appointment of Monck as captain-general of all the land forces in England, Scotland, and Ireland. This legalized the *status quo*. John Maitland served as secretary of the council in Scotland. As earl and later duke of Lauderdale he held his native land firmly to Stuart policy. Ireland also was held quiet by Charles Coote and Roger Boyle, Lord Broghill, both old servants of the Commonwealth. Monck was briefly appointed to the Irish lord lieutenancy with Lord Robartes as his deputy. Neither appeared in Dublin, and Irish affairs were shortly transferred to the diligent Ormond.[45]

The three kingdoms were quiet. A policy of moderation seemed indicated. The Declaration of Breda held out this hope. In the council the earl of Southampton saved the public records of the Interregnum from destruction. Many groups had contributed to the politics of the restoration; now several pass from an active or influential role in public affairs. Power had come at last to the exiles and had returned to the lords as well. The humble royalist hardly tasted it, and his desire for revenge went unsatiated. The cavalier leaders could afford to be moderate, however much the impecunious royalist rank and file grumbled of indemnity for the king's enemies and oblivion for his friends. Through the past years of trial the exiles and the peers had never lost their grip on the royalist party. The restoration settlement, then, would be a settlement on their terms. This settlement is best

---

[45] *Baker's Chronicle*, p. 729; John Evelyn, "A Character of England. . . ." in *Somers' Tracts*, VIII, p. 415; *Mercurius Politicus*, March 29-April 5, 1660 (#614), p. (1113), April 4-12, 1660 (#615), pp. (1243)-(1244); *L.J.*, XI, p. 3; D. Ogg, *Reign of Charles II*, I, pp. 169, 172, 175.

understood in regard to the position and policy of these royalist leaders. Almost to a man they sat in the house of lords. It is natural, then, to take up the study of the restoration settlement in the house of lords, and by a survey of the position of the peerage in the England of 1660.[46]

[46] J. Oldmixon, *History of England*, p. 473; D. Underdown, *Royalist Conspiracy*, p. 388.

V

## THE ENGLISH PEERAGE IN 1660

The French traveller, Sorbière, in reflecting upon his journey through
England, believed that country's recent troubles could be traced to
the king unwisely having weakened the nobility. His observation was
not unique. Of all classes of English society, the peerage drew naturally the most attention. The minister could only expound divine
purpose revealed to men in the order of the universe and in human
society. The peer was the living embodiment of that purpose; for
as only God can make an heir, the existence of a landed aristocracy
was obviously "a proof of intelligent design in the shaping of the
universe". This view was held by Anglican and Presbyterian alike. The
peerage was part of the natural order of things. Yet a peer who left
England in 1641 and returned in 1660 would perceive at once that
his place in the natural order was not so immediately and completely
accepted as it once had been. There was not the same support in
public opinion. There was less respect and more criticism. The peer
of 1660 was not likely more proud or overbearing than his ancestors
of Elizabeth's time. But more men challenged his behavior. The
spread of democratic ideas in the two decades past sapped the
moral basis of the claims of the nobility. Ultimately the standing of the
individual peer had come to rest less on the social advantages of his
caste, and more upon his personal character and his record of public
service. Hyde had wisely indicated this transformation to the peers.
"Your Lordships will easily recover that Estimation and Reverence
that is due to your high Condition, by the Exercise and Practice of
that Virtue from whence your Honours first sprang; the Example of
your Justice and Piety will inflame the Hearts of the People towards
you." The opportunity of the peers was great. They were less restricted in the scope of their activities than any nobility in Western
Europe.[1]

---

[1]  Samuel Sorbière, *A Voyage to England, Containing many things relating to*

In the divine order of society, the peerage stood closest to the king. By the laws of England they were his hereditary counsellors. Hyde had told them that from their practice the people "will make a Judgement of the King Himself. They know very well, that you are not only admitted to His Presence, but to His Conversations, and even in a Degree to His Friendship; for you are His Great Council." Yet the earliest reports of royal association with the peerage did not fulfill Hyde's hopes of counsellor statesmanship. The news sheets in June of 1660 noted that his majesty found great pleasure in the entertainments of Wallingford House, now the residence of the duke of Buckingham. The name of Buckingham was not honored in many English homes. The king was reported hunting with the earl of Middlesex. The house of Cranfield was no more popular than Villiers with most Englishmen. The king was entertained by the earl of Bristol. The earl was the most outspoken recusant peer, and the most obnoxious to the public. In hard fact, there were few noble names honored in England in 1660. Therein lay the first challenge to the nobility.[2]

The peerage did bring certain advantages to meet the challenge that faced them in 1660. In age, they possessed a reasonable balance of youth and maturity, promising vitality tempered by experience. The age of 149 of the 157 peers living in 1661 can be determined. Nine of these were minors. There were only twelve peers in their twenties, but there were thirty-six in their thirties, the largest single group. Thirty-one peers in their forties constituted the next largest block. In all, seventy-nine peers eligible to sit in the house were under fifty. These were balanced by sixty-one peers over fifty. Twenty-eight were in their fifties and another twenty-three in their sixties. A remarkable ten had passed their seventieth birthday, one of whom, the earl of Dover, was eighty. The peerage was also added to by Charles at a fairly rapid rate, although numerous extinctions kept the total number of peers fairly constant. The four creations of 1660 were all substantial gains for the noble order: Monck as duke of Albermarle, Montagu as earl of Sandwich, Ormond, and Hyde. In 1661 the king

---

the State of Learning, Religion, and other Curiosities of that Kingdom (London, 1709), pp. 58-59; D. Ogg, Reign of Charles II, I, pp. 136, 224; C. H. Firth, House of Lords, pp. 292-293; A. S. Turberville, "Lords under Charles II", p. 77; L.J., XI, p. 238.

[2] L.J., XI, p. 238; "An Exact Accompt, communicating the chief transactions of the three kingdoms . . .," June 15-22, 1660, June 29-July 6, 1660, B.M., E. 186(7), p. (13); Mercurius Publicus, August 30-September 9, 1660, B.M., E. 186(34).

advanced Hyde to earl of Clarendon; Baron Capel became earl of Essex and Baron Brudenell earl of Cardigan. At the same time Charles Howard became earl of Carlisle, Arthur Annesley, earl of Anglesey and John Grenville, earl of Bath. Six new barons completed the coronation honors, most notable being Anthony Ashley Cooper as Lord Ashley. Among Charles's creations of later years would be such prominent figures as the marquess of Halifax and the earl of Danby.[3]

Annesley's title was made possible by the death of the old earl of Anglesey, and other notable losses occurred in the noble ranks. Lord Colepeper, long servant to the Stuarts, died on July 12, 1660. Lord Finch, another old royalist of notable service followed him on November 20. The year 1660 also claimed Esmé, duke of Lennox and Richmond, and William, duke of Somerset and marquess of Hertford. The most prominent loss was Henry of Oatlands. He was first reported ill of the smallpox on September 11, and the doctors reported his condition good. Then, sometime before 11 P.M. on the 13th, he suddenly died. The responsibility for his sudden turn for the worse was blamed on the doctors in attendance. Pepys said he died "by the great negligence of the doctors". When Charles II dispatched some of them to assist at the earl of Oxford's sick-bed, who also suffered from smallpox, one of his gentlemen announced he would run through the first who dared enter the sick room. No doctor entered. The earl recovered.[4]

Numerous deaths and numerous creations steadily changed the complexion of the peerage. In Charles's reign fifty-four peers succeeded to titles, and there were frequent creations or promotions. Yet in 1685 the net increase in temporal peers was only three, so brief was life in the seventeenth century. In the first years of the reign there was a slight increase, for the restoration rewards included the grant of sixteen patents between June of 1660 and May of 1661. While Charles was generous to those instrumental in his return from his travels, he evidently was anxious not to inflate the peerage. Clarendon wrote that by 1664 the king had resolved "to create no more noblemen, the number whereof [is] already too much exceeded...". Charles was relatively faithful, for him, to this resolution. There were

[3]   B.M., *Add. Ms.* 35,828 fos. 259-260; A. S. Turberville, "Lords under Charles II", p. 403.

[4]   *H. Mss. C., 5th Report*, Appendix, Part I, Duke of Sutherland Mss., p. 151; *Mercurius Publicus*, July 12-19, 1660, B.M., E. 186(20); White Kennet, *A Register and Chronicle Ecclesiastical and Civil* (London, 1728), p. 315; *Baker's Chronicle*, p. 752; *Pepys' Diary*, I, p. 222; B.M., *Add. Ms.* 32,324 fo. 60.

only ten creations altogether from 1662 to 1670. Five of these occurred in 1664, and one was the passing under the great seal of the
patent of Baron Frescheville, whose warrant dated from 1645. The
patent had been long delayed by questions concerning the conditions
under which Charles I had issued the warrant. Charles II finally
resolved to honor all possible grants of his father.[5]

Another creation of 1664 was Henry Bennet as earl of Arlington.
With Buckingham, Bennet represented a less than desirable element
in the peerage, young men who dabbled in politics while earning the
appelation of restoration rakes. Bennet was at least a foreign expert
of some ability but Buckingham was not so redeemed. The latter was
more noted for his quarrels with other peers, closely missing possible
death at the hand of Sandwich. Sandwich had challenged Buckingham to a duel for cheating at cards. As the outcome between the
dilettante Villiers, albeit trained by the marquess of Newcastle, and
the professional soldier Montagu could not be in doubt, the earl of St.
Albans intervened and Charles patched up the quarrel. Although the
rakes attracted considerable attention, they did not characterize the
restoration peerage. To this body heredity granted the same diversity
to be found in any miscellaneous body of men. The earl of Southampton
was prominent for his virtues of honor and diligence. He and his close
friends Clarendon and Ormond united in their objections to the king's
mistresses on grounds of morality and decorum. Southampton, as
treasurer, objected as well to their expense, and Clarendon feared
their influence on Charles's policy. If the propriety of these three
was founded upon the faith of the Anglican communion, their
Presbyterian colleagues were as well represented. Manchester, Say,
and Northumberland all led respected private lives.[6]

In the Presbyterian ranks of the peerage Charles found new servants of the monarchy. Baron Robartes, among the "most formidable"
of their leaders, became so devoted a Stuart agent that he was rewarded with the earldom of Radnor in 1679. Manchester was entrusted with the post of lord chamberlain of the household and Ashley
became chancellor of the exchequer. The latter gained the earldom
of Shaftesbury for his services before he broke with Charles and

[5] A. S. Turberville, "Lords under Charles II", pp. 402-403; Sir George Clark,
*The Later Stuarts* (Oxford, 1955), p. 10; Clarendon's *Life*, II, p. 233.
[6] A. S. Turberville, "Lords under Charles II", p. 404; D. Ogg, *Reign of
Charles II*, I, pp. 138, 152; *Pepys' Diary*, I, p. 318; Clarendon's *Life*, II, p. 22;
G. N. Clark, *Later Stuarts*, p. 8; J. Oldmixon, *History of England*, p. 470.

became his most formidable opponent in parliament. Ashley was a man of wit and considerable intelligence. In this respect the lords were generally acknowledged the superiors of the commons. If many of the nobility were poorly educated, and possessed of narrow prejudices, they were still generally better than the squirearchy. The lords were well redeemed from mediocrity by the presence of men like Buckingham, Bristol, Ashley, and later Halifax. The great personalities of the political world, dominated by Clarendon, were either in the house of lords or soon promoted there. The foremost historian of the period was a peer. The most famed soldier sat in the upper house. The earl of Anglesey built one of the first great libraries of an English noble, and many of his class were to imitate him. The earl of Devonshire deserves consideration for his patronage of Thomas Hobbes. Against such virtues, the lords had sufficient vices. Few sought the traditional military service of their order in the Dutch wars, despite the example of York, Rupert, Albemarle, Buckingham, and Sandwich, the last dying in service. Clarendon wrote (not quite fairly) of the notorious rake, Rochester, that he "saw danger at a distance with great courage, and looked upon it less resolutely when it was nearer, ...". More degrading was the conduct of the two sons of the earl of Dorset, who robbed and murdered a wayfarer. They were convicted of manslaughter at the Middlesex sessions in Easter term of 1662, but pardoned by the king. By any standard the character of the peerage varied greatly. If the Sackville family produced criminals, the North family had jurists. If most peers were Anglicans, there was a strong Presbyterian cadre, and seventeen openly professed the old religion. Foreigners were represented by Rupert as duke of Cumberland and Charles Polliander of Kirkhoven, Baron Wotton. The cosmopolitan character of the nobility was strengthened by numerous foreign wives. Yet this diverse group could seem homogeneous enough. In gathering the rewards of the restoration they were of one mind.[7]

"Every one was ready to celebrate and display his own particular Merits; but never more plausibly, than when they related to the glorious Work of the Restoration", wrote Clarendon. In this respect

---

[7] A. S. Turberville, "Lords under Charles II", p. 404; D. Ogg, *Reign of Charles II*, I, pp. 152, 272-275, II, p. 467; A. S. Turberville, *House of Lords*, p. 233; S. Sorbière, *Voyage to England*, p. 13; Clarendon's *Rebellion*, p. 826; *C.S.P.V.*, 1661-1664, p. 115; P. H. Hardacre, *Royalists*, pp. 53, 53 n.; Bodley, *Rawlinson Ms. B 13*, p. 8.

two groups in particular were rewarded. Both those who had shown long and undeviating loyalty to the Stuart cause and those whose change of heart was crucial to the royal return gained recognition, as the bestowal of peerages illustrated. Honor was granted as well by the Garter. This insignia of the oldest knightly order was personally bestowed on Monck, on May 26, by the king, and the same day the Garter was borne to Montagu, still in the Downs. The marquess of Hertford and earl of Southampton, elected to the order long before, finally received the formal tokens of their long loyalty. Clarendon declined the Garter, asking that his place go to the young earl of Lindsey, whose father had worn the Garter when he fell in battle for Charles I. The young earls of Oxford and Strafford were similarly honored. The earl of Manchester was the only prominent Presbyterian admitted to the conclave that met at Westminster on April 16, 1661. Only one of the twenty-six stalls of the order was empty, that reserved for the Prince of Wales. Three peers, Northumberland, Salisbury, and Berkshire had met before, in 1625. The others, including Ormond, Newcastle, and Bristol, sat for the first time. No commoner wore the blue riband.[8]

If honor went predominantly to the peers, so too went responsibility. Giavarina reported that Monck, Hyde, Ormond, and Manchester appeared to be the most influential figures about the new court. All four were summoned to the privy council. Although this body had little of the power of former times, it still served as the central agency where the direction of the government originated, and was indeed Charles's personal council in the early years of his reign. He picked its members with a careful eye. When William Morice was recommended to serve as one of its secretaries, Charles wrote Mordaunt, "I have never heard of Morice before, and you shall do well in all such cases, to give me as large information as you can...." The king was also firm in excluding those in disfavor, as Giavarina reported at one point was the case with Buckingham. Charles attended the meetings of his council regularly, usually twice a week, at the opening of his reign. His wit was present at the council table as his notes to Clarendon reveal. Once Clarendon pointed out affairs would be long as the marquess of Dorchester and earl of Anglesey both desired to speak and "since I presume they will differ both

[8]   L. Echard, *History of England*, III, p. 6; *Baker's Chronicle*, pp. 733, 758; Clarendon's *Rebellion*, p. 910; Clarendon's *Life*, II, p. 82; *C.S.P.D.*, 1660-1661, p. 3; Bodley, *Rawlinson Ms.* B 115 fos. 34, 39-40, 42, 45-47, 52-53, 55, 59.

from their learning last published in this place". The king's sharp reply was, "If those two learned persons could be sent to supper, we might dispatch it now, but by my Ld. Dorchester's face I fear his speech will be long which will be better for a collation than a supper." [9]

When Charles's privy council first met on May 31, 1660, it showed a varied composition of cavalier, Presbyterian, and old servant of the Commonwealth or Protectorate. The first group was naturally led by Hyde, with Ormond, Southampton and secretary Nicholas. Hertford, Lindsey, and Dorchester were also in this category. Northumberland, Anglesey, Say, and Robartes led the Presbyterian contingent. Monck, Montagu, and Charles Howard sat for the third class. The later addition of Norwich and St. Albans swelled the cavalier ranks without adding to their unity. Ashley had also come in by September of 1660. Lauderdale was a member, but usually absent in Scotland. Naturally the duke of York sat. Of the twenty-nine members of the council only five did not also sit in the house of lords. Lauderdale had no English title; the two secretaries, Nicholas and Morice, were commoners. Sir Charles Berkeley and Sir George Carteret were the other two members. The twenty-four peers represented in particular the hereditary duty of their order to serve as the counsellors of the king, since the house of lords had grown too large easily to fulfill this function. [10]

In the eyes of Hyde, the privy council also suffered from its size, and from the diversity of opinions represented by its various members. The Venetian resident wrote to the Doge and Senate that the privy council occupied itself with such affairs as issuing proclamations against "vagabonds and other rogues", but no discussions of consequence had taken place. The Venetian correspondents shrewdly noted with their observations on the privy council that Hyde appeared the sole director of affairs, and that matters "derive their substance from the opinion of the Lord Chancellor". Hyde, true to his interpretation of the constitution, believed that the king in privy council should be the guiding power of the government. However, the

[9] C.S.P.V., 1659-1661, pp. 159, 170-171; Sir Arthur Bryant, ed., The Letters, Speeches and Declarations of King Charles II (London, 1935), p. 82; Clarendon S. P., III, p. 709; W. D. Macray, ed., Notes which passed at Meetings of the Privy Council (London, 1896), p. 50.
[10] D. Ogg, Reign of Charles II, I, p. 189; Clarendon's Life, p. 992; K. Feiling, History of the Tory Party, p. 103; E. I. Carlyle, "Clarendon and the Privy Council", E.H.R., XXVII (London, 1912), pp. 257-258.

administrator in him advised a smaller body to expedite the complex functions of governing, and the politician in him nodded agreement. He developed a number of committees about the privy council, to carry out specific executive functions or to serve as links to the traditional government offices. To these committees he drew experts and able men, often regardless of party. In the royal commission "for the managing and improving of trade", Hyde sat with as diverse a group as Southampton, Albemarle, Robartes, and Ashley. One central committee was more restricted. The committee on foreign affairs Hyde used as a cabinet, in many ways by-passing the privy council. The hard core of the committee's membership was only seven. The king, Clarendon, Albemarle, Ormond, and Southampton were the debating members. The two secretaries Nicholas and Morice attended, but primarily to dispatch business. From this body emanated the operation of government throughout the realm.[11]

The peers predominated not only at the policy forming level of government, but also in the main offices of state. Hyde had been made chancellor in 1658, but he had hardly entered into the powers of the office before he was raised to the peerage. The lord stewardship went to Ormond and was largely honorary, appropriately so because the noble Butler was fully engaged in his duties as lord lieutenant in Ireland. Hyde's two deputies — Jeffrey Palmer, the attorney-general, and Heneage Finch, the solicitor-general — were both commoners; as were the two principal secretaries of state, Nicholas and Morice. The lord high treasurer was Thomas Wriothesley, earl of Southampton. This old and loyal royalist was preferred over Manchester, who desired the post. For a few months in 1660 Southampton served as chancellor of the exchequer. This office was passed on to his nephew by marriage, Lord Ashley. Manchester had to be content with the post of lord chamberlain, of little responsibility. Albemarle had the heavy duty of captain-general of all the forces, which had been specifically granted to him for life. Viscount Say was briefly lord privy seal but as he retired more from active politics Lord Robartes was entrusted with that seal. The ornamental posts of lord high constable and earl marshal were granted to Northumberland and Suffolk respectively. The effect of the division of offices was control of the places of power by the old royalists. Of the Presbyterians only Robartes held much influence by

[11]  C.S.P.V., 1659-1661, p. 161, 1661-1664, p. 87; G. N. Clark, *Later Stuarts*, p. 13; B.M., *Add. Ms.* 34,729 fo. 112; J. Campbell, *Lives of the Lord Chancellors*, III, pp. 168-169; Clarendon's *Life*, II, p. 49.

his office. Albemarle was a separate case. The ascendancy of Clarendon, established in the structure of cabinet council and privy council, was further extended by the settlement of the principal offices of the realm and government.[12]

The offices of the central government and of the state increased the power of particular peers rather than of the house of lords. For the peerage in the reign of Charles II it was true, as it usually was, that their parliamentary authority was rivaled by their power outside parliament. The major prop to this authority was the office of lord lieutenant. The lieutenant combined executive with military functions. He served as the royal vice-regent in the shire, commanded the local militia, and was usually custodian of the county archives. As head of the county commission of the peace, he formed the link between the council on one side and the many local officials on the other. This office went almost invariably to a great landholding noble, who gained both influence and experience. The significance of this post was increased at the restoration by the revival of the old militia organization, which had fallen into decay when eclipsed by the professional army of the Commonwealth. The militia now formed an armed counter-weight to the army, which was being rapidly disbanded. As the lords lieutenant had extensive control of appointments, it was important to the crown who appointed them that they were both well affected toward the central government and of sufficient influence in their respective shires to carry out the policy of the government.[13]

Charles and Clarendon proceeded at once on a program of careful manipulation of lieutenancies, designed more to confine the court's enemies to the less important shires than to block them out altogether. The circumstances of the restoration left Clarendon this policy of opportunism by necessity. He did well. At one time he and his two most trusted associates, Ormond and Southampton, held among them six shires — Hampshire, Kent, Norfolk, Oxford, Somerset, and Wiltshire — returning 117 members to parliament. Despite such accomplishments, there were some shires where the court never

[12] K. Feiling, *History of the Tory Party*, p. 103; M. Coate, ed., *Mordaunt Letter Book*, p. 178; D. Underdown, *Royalist Conspiracy*, p. 316; D. Ogg, *Reign of Charles II*, I, pp. 151-152; *C.S.P.D.*, 1660-1661, p. 253; Clarendon's *Life*, p. 1006; P. H. Hardacre, *Royalists*, p. 147.
[13] A. S. Turberville, "Lords under Charles II", p. 76; D. Ogg, *Reign of Charles II*, II, pp. 486-487; James Robeson Tanner, *English Constitutional Conflicts of the Seventeenth Century* (Cambridge, 1928), p. 223.

gained influence. In the privy council Clarendon pushed his chances
and in June of 1660 gained Shropshire and Buckinghamshire for the
well affected Baron Newport and earl of Bridgwater respectively.
But Bucks and Salop were not the serious problem Middlesex was.
The earls of Dorset and Berkshire shared the lieutenancy here, but
Berkshire was seventy-two and notably ineffectual. Clarendon judged
the Middlesex militia to be in the worst state of any in the realm and
pressed Charles in the council for Berkshire's removal. This took place
and the militia improved, but by the appointment of Albermarle,
not entirely to Clarendon's satisfaction. In other cases Clarendon
was more successful. The earl of Cleveland went to Bedford and the
earl of Devonshire was named lieutenant of Derby. Clarendon
desired Viscount Hereford for Herefordshire, but Charles vetoed the
choice on grounds that the viscount was both unpopular and ineffectual.[14]

The lord lieutenancy traditionally acknowledged the paramount
interests of the greatest of the landed families. Thus Lord Herbert
of Raglan, cadet of the house of Somerset, held the lieutenancies of
Gloucester and Hereford. The earl of Northumberland held both the
shire of his title and Sussex. In the North, Cumberland and Westmorland were the provinces of the earl of Carlisle. Viscount Fauconberg
was lieutenant of both Durham and the North Riding of Yorkshire. In
the West, Cornwall, rich in parliamentary seats, was the preserve of
the earl of Bath. Albemarle held the choice lieutenancy of Devonshire. The most traditional lieutenancy was that of the earl of Derby
for Cheshire and Lancashire. Traditional, too, was the circumstance
that the haughty Stanley would be a problem to the court. He could
not easily be denied the post, but the court could and did send him
detailed instructions. These largely concerned the security of the realm,
ranging from the apprehension of vagabonds to the careful sur-
veillance of all men of known republican sympathies. The assessment
of peers for the militia fees was also included in the council's instructions to Derby. The commission ended on the hopeful note that
the lord lieutenant would speedily inform the crown of anything
that might concern the peace of the realm. The commission was not
very well regarded, for Clarendon was soon urging Charles to dis-

---

[14] Andrew Browning, "Parties and Party Organization in Reign of Charles II",
*T.R.H.S.*, 4th Series, XXX (London, 1948), pp. 32-33; W. D. Macray, ed., *Privy
Council Notes*, pp. 1, 20; *C.S.P.D.*, 1660-1661, pp. 41, 145.

patch sharp notes to Derby to settle the militia and regularize the executive proceedings in the two shires.[15]

Closely tied to the office of lord lieutenant was that of *custos rotulorum*, the chief justice of the peace and master of the county sessions records. Peers often held this post concurrently with a lord lieutenancy, but commoners sometimes discharged the duties of the office. On May 22, 1660, parliament ordered that all peers displaced as *custos rotulorum* in the time of Oliver Cromwell were to be restored. This brought back such men as Manchester, Suffolk, and Wharton. The royalist peers had to wait some months before gaining similar appointments.[16]

The main political benefit of the shire offices was electoral influence. Turberville put the case well in saying:

> A lord who scarcely ever appeared at Westminster, in virtue of his membership of the Upper House, was able to exert the widest authority as a territorial magnate. This territorial power reacted upon the influence of the House of Lords viewed as a corporation. The House was in the main an assembly of great landowners, of men bound together by the ties of common interest, and because of their authority in their respective districts able to wield a great authority in Parliament. Tangible proof of this was given in the extensive nature of aristocratic control over elections and the composition of the House of Commons.

The peers had returned to their electoral influence before they returned to the house of lords. There were several instances of their efforts in the elections to the Convention Parliament. Sir Ralph Verney attempted to gain the support of the marquess of Hertford in his campaign for election to that parliament. He was unable to gain the marquess's patronage and failed to win election. One of the most determined electoral battles occured in Essex, and ended in the discomfiture of a peer. Two cavaliers, Sir Edward Turner and Sir John Bramston, stood for the shire against the Presbyterians, Sir Harbottle Grimstone and Mr. Raymond. The earl of Warwick took up the Presbyterian cause. Bramston described the alignment in the shire as all the nobles save Warwick, most of the gentry and the greater part of the yeomanry for the two royalists; Warwick, and all the old justices of the peace, committee men, and sequestrators for the Presbyterians. According to Bramston, Warwick "mistooke his strength, supposeinge,

---

[15]  B.M., *Egerton Ms.* 2543 fos. 91-93; W. D. Macray, ed., *Privy Council Notes*, p. 75.
[16]  B.M., *Hargrave Ms.* 178 fo. 94; *L.J.*, XI, p. 38; Kennet's *Register*, p. 156.

UNIVERSITY OF VICTORIA
LIBRARY
Victoria, B C.

because soe manie of the nobilitie and gentrie were against him, that the numbers on our side were swelled by the servants and attendants of those noblemen and gentlemen more than by freeholders havinge voices...". Thus the earl rejected an offer to share the two seats between the two parties, declaring for "both or none". The royalists carried both seats. Warwick was not deterred. During the elections to the Cavalier Parliament the king sent Manchester to tell Warwick not to oppose the two royalist knights. "He appeared not, but sent all he could against me." Both Turner and Bramston were again returned. But most lords had better luck than Warwick, and so did the ladies, too. Marlborough, in Wiltshire, was in the pocket of Lady Herbert and the duchess of Somerset in the 1661 election. Clarendon, for his part, recommended only the name of Heneage Finch to the vice-chancellor of Oxford University and was "surprised" at the generosity of the university in returning Finch and Clarendon's younger son, Laurence. So formidable did the electoral power of John Grenville, earl of Bath become — secure as he was as steward of the duchy of Cornwall, lord lieutenant of that county, lord warden of the Stannaries, and groom of the Stole — that he was known as the "Prince Elector". His influence spread into Devon as well. Thus seventy members of parliament had to consider in varying degrees his influence.[17]

Control of the militia was only one of the functions of the security of the realm entrusted to the peerage. Certain garrisons were maintained after the restoration and the command of some of these was entrusted to peers. The earl of Portland was commissioned governor of the Isle of Wight of such significant memory. Portland, Weymouth, and Sandfoot Castle were entrusted to Lord Sandys. Lord Belasyse became governor and captain of the garrison of Kingston-upon-Hull. The peers received some stipend for this service; in the case of Lord Belasyse it was 10s. a day for his own care and 8d. a day for each of twenty soldiers.[18] Peers were employed for service

---

[17] A. S. Turberville, House of Lords, p. 232; M. M. Verney, Memoirs of the Verney Family, III, pp. 475, 477; Clarendon S. P., III, p. 731; Richard, Lord Braybrooke, ed., The Autobiography of Sir John Bramston (London, 1845), pp. 114-115, 119-120; B.M., Add. Ms. 32,324 fo. 76; Kennet's Register, p. 393; D. Underdown, Royalist Conspiracy, p. 334; D. Ogg, Reign of Charles II, II, p. 474.
[18] Parliamentary Intelligencer, July 30-August 6, 1660, B.M., E. 186(25); An Exact Accompt, June 29-July 6, 1660, B.M., E. 186(13); Calendar of Treasury Books, 1660-1667, ed., W. A. Shaw (1904), 1661-1667, p. 211; C.S.P.D., 1660-1661, p. 429.

outside as well as within the realm. In July of 1660 Lord Crofts was dispatched to Paris, the most important ambassadorial post. Within a year he was replaced there by the earl of St. Albans, confidant of Henrietta Maria. The earls of Bristol and Sandwich received roving commissions from the crown, for example in the search for a wife for Charles. The impoverished earl of Winchilsea persuaded the king to recall the old ambassador at Constantinople and allow him to negotiate for the post. As he would represent both England and the Levant Company, he sought an opportunity to build a fortune. The earl was willing to represent Venetian interests as well, Giavarina reported to the Doge and Senate, for a sufficient bribe. The earl appeared "full of idle talk, informed about many things, but not very steady, rather inclined to be light and volatile...", and the Venetian resident wasted no money on him. The Levant Company was more generous and in exchange for five years' service promised the earl his expenses to and from the Porte with a suite not exceeding thirty persons, and an additional £ 600 for expenses. In addition the company would pay the charges for all official presents and a salary of 10,000 dollars in Spanish pieces of eight. After a difficult journey the earl took up his post and thereby made his fortune. The importance of the ambassadors was not great, for Clarendon kept all the strings of foreign affairs in his own hands. The instructions to the ambassadors were limited to minor affairs, and these usually were issued from Clarendon rather than through the two secretaries. Important matters Clarendon conducted directly with the foreign authorities concerned.[19]

Perhaps the most unpleasant duty that befell any of the peerage involved the responsibility for Irish affairs. Somehow, this lovely, fertile island brought forth at once the most unfortunate characteristics in any Englishman so unlucky as to be in any way connected with its affairs. The dark curse was working in 1660. Pepys correctly anticipated this in recording that "there was like to be many factions at Court between Marquis Ormond, General Monck, and the Lord Robartes, about the business of Ireland; as there is already between the two Houses about the Act of Indemnity". Ormond was the English statesman most experienced in Irish affairs, and he held vast

[19] *Mercurius Publicus*, August 9-16, 1660, B.M., E. 186(28), Paris, August 7, 1660; D. Ogg, *Reign of Charles II*, I, pp. 151-152; *C.S.P.V.*, 1659-1661, pp. 168-169; *C.S.P.D.*, 1660-1661, pp. 270, 582; J. Campbell, *Lives of the Lord Chancellors*, III, p. 169.

tracts of land there. Albemarle, too, had great holdings, and Clarendon recorded that he was determined to limit Ormond's power there. The general started with the initial advantage of the lord lieutenancy. However, Ireland was distasteful to him and English affairs required his attention, so the dispatching of a deputy to Dublin was debated. In the privy council Charles proposed Lord Berkeley, whom Clarendon opposed. In the end Berkeley was not appointed, and Lord Robartes was named deputy. Pepys wrote that Robartes did not like "to be deputy to any man but the King himself". Clarendon held much the same opinion. Albemarle and Robartes soon quarrelled, neither went to Ireland, and finally the king sent the trusted Ormond.[20]

A more pleasant duty that fell to the peers was the assumption of the chancellorships of the two universities. On May 8, 1660, Richard Cromwell resigned the chancellorship of Oxford. The house of lords, on the 26th, voted the restoration of the marquess of Hertford to the office, and the convocation of the university approved this on June 6. About the same time Oliver St. John was discharged from the chancellorship of Cambridge and the house of lords restored the earl of Manchester to the post. Hertford was shortly succeeded to the chancellorship of Oxford by the earl of Clarendon, to the mutual benefit of the university and the memory of the earl. Clarendon well illustrated the range of offices and services the peerage fulfilled at the executive level of government. He was both lord high chancellor of England and chancellor of Oxford. To a significant degree the ability of the peerage to fulfill these duties depended upon their strength as a social class, and the economic base which supported their position.[21] The economic base of the peerage had been but precariously preserved during the years without the house of lords. If the house hoped again to play a prominent role in the government of the realm, then its members collectively had to strengthen their economic position, particularly in the land; this was a message they could not fail to read in the events recently past. The improvement of their economic status, then, became the first order of business for the restoration peerage.

---

[20] *Pepys' Diary,* I, pp. 210-211; Clarendon's *Life,* pp. 1031, 1050, 1058; W. D. Macray, ed., *Privy Council Notes,* p. 6; A. Bryant, ed., *Letters of King Charles II,* p. 99.

[21] Kennet's *Register,* p. 141; *L.J.,* XI, p. 42.

# VI

## THE LORDS AND THE LAND SETTLEMENT

The restoration did not at once return to the nobility the political powers they had held, although it afforded them the opportunity to regain that power insofar as they were able. Political power, like social position, was in good measure dependent upon economic strength, still measured in no small degree by the breadth of a man's acres. As the acreage available in 1660 was limited, and the number of claimants many, not all could be satisfied. The first years of the restoration, then, saw a determined effort waged in the land settlement by all politically active persons. In this struggle it quickly emerged that the peers were prepared to close ranks and to make hereditary dignity their first test of merit. This attitude did not escape comment. To his social inferiors the nobleman presented an unpleasant appearance. Evelyn observed of the nobility "that they kept at such a surly distance with the gentlemen, even of family, that methought I never beheld a ruder conversation". Sorbière found the nobility "for the most part intolerably proud and haughty in England. It looks as if a Lord took himself to be of other species than a Gentleman, so imperiously he carries himself." Sir Ralph Verney felt the peers were "tedious persons to waite on". However, most waited, for the peerage could bestow benefits and secure advancement for the ambitious. The peers were noted for their extravagance and increasingly for their costly country homes, coming in this period to absorb much of their income. Magalotti referred to the fine noble homes he visited in his account of his journey through England. Sorbière saw another aspect of this display. "The English nobility cannot regulate their Incomes and Expence as they ought to do, because they must Let their Lands to Farmers and Receivers at a low Rate, if they would keep up the Respect and Obeysance due unto them; and if they do not keep good Houses they will be soon dispised." [1]

[1] A. S. Turberville, *House of Lords*, pp. 227-228; *Somers' Tracts*, VII, p. 184;

The economic supports of noble grandeur were still rather frail in 1660. The sales Sorbière noted were providing only temporary relief. Lord Townshend's account books for 1661 give a picture of the complexity of mortgages and debts many peers were enmeshed in. Townshend listed twenty-seven separate debts in excess of £ 100. Seven of them were in the form of mortgages, upon which £ 7,300 was due in 1661. Loans on bonds due totalled nine items of £ 3,900. His total debts reached £ 15,050, of which he was able to pay £ 4,100 that year. Many aristocratic families were equally encumbered. The marquess of Newcastle sold lands valued at £ 56,000 to pay debts. The parliamentary levies upon the lands and incomes of the peers in the last fifteen-odd years now appeared in a mass of mortgages, and when those could not be met, yet further loans inadequately supported them until the shaky income of the noble could no longer support the paper edifice erected upon it; next came alienations and sales. The revenue of offices, a major source of income, was cut off by the civil wars and often not regained. The financial necessity of offices tended to increase the noble's reliance upon the favor of the court and weakened his position as an independent agent in English politics. A yet greater blow to the noble landowner grew from the "sensational" monetary depreciation which Richard Tawney found to characterize the whole of the middle years of the seventeenth century. Against this sort of inflation landed wealth was particularly vulnerable, becoming, in Tawney's words, "an obsolete anachronism". Clarendon recorded that rents underwent a sharp decline and that "all this mischief" fell most heavily upon the nobility and other great landholders. Income was rendered uncertain from the land and fees from offices were unpaid or paid partly and late more often than not, for the crown was chronically short of money too. So prominent a courtier as the earl of Lindsey could not extract his salary from the government, even when his relative, Danby, held the white staff. In some cases the extravagance of particular peers completed the ruin incipient in the conditions of the period. Clarendon, admittedly a biased observer, related that the earl of Bristol paid £ 10,000 to purchase Wimbledon from the queen mother and spent that amount again on the buildings and gardens there. The debts of the duke of

S. Sorbière, *Voyage to England*, pp. 30, 50, 66; M. M. Verney, *Memoirs of the Verney Family*, IV, p. 8; *C.S.P.D.*, 1660-1661, p. 45; Lorenzo Magalotti, *Travels of Cosmo the Third, Grand Duke of Tuscany, through England* (London, 1821), pp. 141-142.

Richmond for the years 1661 and 1662 were calculated at £ 57,300. His financial agent was properly wild with concern at this immense figure; meanwhile the duke was planning to erect a new house in London. In 1664 the agent was busy selling the ducal lands for income. The whole style of living was a serious drain upon noble revenues. The earl of Westmorland calculated the expense of £ 173/13/4 in fees at his creation in 1629. The cost was much greater now. John Oldmixon, a partisan source, spoke not without some truth in saying that the cavalier lived better under sequestration and the dominance of modesty and sobriety than when fully restored to his estate but possessed by luxury and extravagance. Against this must be put the duchess of Newcastle's eloquent defence:

But perhaps some will say, that if My Lord had enjoyed his estate, he would have spent it, at least so much as to maintain himself according to his degree and quality.

I answer; that it is very improbable My Lord should have spent all his estate, if he had enjoyed it, he being a man of great wisdom and prudence, knowing well how to spend, and how to manage; for though he lived nobly before the time of the wars, yet not beyond the compass of his estates, nay, so far he would have been from spending his estate, that no doubt he would have increast it to a vast value, as he did before the wars . . . notwithstanding his hospitality and noble housekeeping. . . .[2]

Despite such formidable economic strains the peers were hardly reduced to poverty. In 1688, when it was more expensive to live, Gregory King estimated the family income of several classes of the English population. A common laborer earned £ 15 a year, a skilled artisan £ 40. A farmer he estimated to gain £ 44 and a tradesman £ 45. A gentleman's income was set at £ 280 and a baronet's at £ 880. In 1663 the militia census for Cheshire revealed the income of Lord Delamere at £ 1212 from his lands in that county alone. The earl of Carlisle's lands in Cumberland yielded him £ 1,000. The duke of Norfolk, not a great landholder in that county, still realized £ 500 from his estates there, and the earl of Northumberland £ 600. Baron Wharton's lands in Westmorland had a revenue of £ 800. Chamberlayne, in 1669, estimated a peer's average income at £ 10,000 a

[2]   B.M., *Add. Mss.* 11,324 fo. 1; 21,947 fos. 7, 12; 28,076 fo. 102b; 34,217 fos. 2-5; 41,656 fos. 140-141; J. Thirsk, "The Sales of Royalist Land During the Interregnum", p. 205; Bodley, *Rawlinson Ms.* A 119, p. 2; *C.S.P.D.*, 1660-1661, p. 72; R. H. Tawney, "Harrington's Interpretation of His Age", p. 217; Clarendon's *Life*, pp. 1099, 1108; J. Oldmixon, *History of England*, p. 491; Margaret, duchess of Newcastle, *Life of the First Duke of Newcastle*, pp. 101-103.

year, as compared to £800 for an average knight. In 1660, when Edward Noel, son and heir of Viscount Campden, married Elizabeth Wriothesley, daughter of Southampton, they had at least 16,490 acres settled on them in Middlesex, Kent, Rutland, and Gloucestershire. This did not constitute poverty. Nor did the expenditures of the bishop of Winchester, who spent on his houses and castle £ 20,281/1/1 in the years 1662-1684. The expense in 1662 alone was £ 1,438/15/8. His benefactions and charities added £ 28,951/16/2 to his debit ledgers in twenty-two years. While his charities properly exceeded his personal expenses, the bishop had hardly taken up an anchorite's existence. Clarendon himself, despite ministerial discretion, lived in a succession of palatial homes: Dorset House, once residence of the bishops of Salisbury, Worcester House in the Strand, and finally the unfortunate edifice of his own construction, opprobriously known as "Dunkirk House". When Clarendon went into his second exile in 1667 his list of major debts was £ 41,436/13/9, only £ 400 of which was for the infamous house. On the other hand, in the same year the rents of the duke of Newcastle were estimated at £ 22,393. From this maze of wealth and poverty the peers themselves saw one goal clearly. The case of Lord Byron was the case of many of them. His predecessor's lands had gone in the Commonwealth's first act of sale and he succeeded to a total wealth of £ 1,200. To him and most of his colleagues, redress for the deprivations of the past two decades was an economic first principle.[3]

The land policy of the restoration settlement started with the Declaration of Breda, whose main virtue was that it offended no one because it settled nothing. The responsibility of a settlement was simply left to parliament. The house of lords took the declaration at its word and before any policy of government and both houses was decided upon, issued a series of proclamations. These proclamations, in themselves a bold exercise of authority, indicated what the policy of the house of lords would be in the months to come. Their earliest

---

[3] B.M., *Add. Ms.* 36,922 fo. 22; *Hargrave Ms.* 47 fos. 138-140; *Stowe Ms.* 541 fos. 138-140. Hargrave has misdated *Ms.* 47 as 1673, evidently on the evidence of "13th yr of our Reign. Ch. II". Of course the 13th year as Charles dated his reign was 1661, and further internal evidence as well as Cokayne makes Hargrave's date impossible. *H. Mss. C., 12th Report,* Appendix, Part VII, Mss. of S. H. LeFleming, p. 30; J. Campbell, *Lives of Lord Chancellors,* III, p. 223; T. H. Lister, *Life of Clarendon,* III, pp. 535-539; D. Underdown, *Royalist Conspiracy,* p. 324; Margaret, duchess of Newcastle, *Life of the First Duke of Newcastle,* pp. 98-100.

order, that a stop be made to wastes on all lands once the king's, was expected. Pepys had made the obvious enough observation that the royal and church lands would never be confirmed in their new hands by any parliament. Another proclamation of the lords seemed to promise a moderate approach to the land issue by declaring that no person in possession should be disturbed until parliament had settled the disposal of the land in question. However, the lords did not apply this general policy to their own members. Wherever possible the lords entered upon their lands. The upper house ordered on May 23, 1660, that the duke of Buckingham, the earl of Derby, Lord Craven, "and all other Lords that are in the like Condition" were to be put in possession of any of their lands which had been held by regicides and were now forfeit. This was followed by an order that the duke of Buckingham, the marquess of Winchester, Lord Powis, and others were to have possession of all their lands sold without their consent. All estates of peers seized or sequestrated for recusancy, other than upon conviction by due course of law, were ordered discharged to their original owners. From the start the house of lords treated the noble victims of the Commonwealth acts of sale as a special group and like crown and church assured them the return of their lands forcibly sold.[4]

The lords now had to carry through their program as part of the general land settlement. That settlement was going none too well. The difficulties were formidable. The distribution of crown and church lands had started as far back as 1643 and 1646 respectively. Reams of transaction papers covered over the original dispositions in many cases. It was attempted to wipe all this out, without particular regard for any person involved. In addition to transactions between individuals and the state there were many others between private persons. Any party to any of such transactions could question the validity of the transfer. Impatient royalists did not wait on the law, but forcibly expelled new owners from their lands. Loyal grumbling increased as no general action against purchasers was taken. Even royalists whose lands were confiscated without legal process were put at a disadvantage. Their lands were not returned outright, but rather it was left to each of them as individuals to proceed at common law within five years to regain their lands. An effort in the house of

---

[4] J. Thirsk, "Restoration Land Settlement", p. 316; B.M., *Add. Ms.* 32,455 fo. 21; *Pepys' Diary*, I, p. 141; *L.J.* XI, pp. 38, 46, 67, 95-96, 103; D. Ogg, *Reign of Charles II*, I, pp. 161-162.

commons to open the whole land issue to legislative inquiry and remedy was defeated by the government. The result greatly favored the lord over the commoner. Without an automatic return of lands by general statute, only the courts or private acts could afford the royalist remedy. And the highest court of law and the clearing house of private acts for redress at law was the house of lords. If anyone were to be cared for, it would be that house's own members.[5]

The general result was a restoration of lands for crown, church, and royalist magnates. The rank and file, forced to sell their lands to pay delinquency fines, were left to suffer. Few of this last class were in a position to fight long proceedings at law, and indeed, if they sold their lands "freely", which was construed to be any condition short of direct government duress, they had no case in law. This policy had a serious effect upon the nation. It completed the alienation of many of the lesser gentry from the court which had been developing from the time of Elizabeth. Central control of the localities weakened; to maintain public order was difficult and to collect taxes was harder. Charles II therefore relied upon the house of lords to carry through his policy when the house of commons balked at its moderation. Charles himself did not help matters by his vacillations and many yieldings to importuning courtiers. He had originally intended that all the Irish lands of the regicides would be reserved for the duke of York. However, he was persuaded to make many grants out of these lands. When Clarendon attempted to hold him to his word, the king passed grants under the great seal of Ireland, thus circumventing the irate lord chancellor.[6]

Whatever the demerits of the Irish settlement, it was a clear cut arrangement. The defective nature of the English land legislation resulted in a heavy docket of private bills to clog the legislative channels for two full years. The new owners of most flimsy pretext did not as a rule give up their land until moved by civil actions or orders resulting from special petitions to the house of lords. Loss of titles in the civil wars, as well as faked and contradictory conveyances, added to a burden that could be lightened only by legislation. In a

---

[5] T. H. Lister, *Life of Clarendon*, III, pp. 33-35; P. H. Hardacre, *Royalists*, pp. 153, 156-157; *Old Parliamentary History*, XXII, p. 412; J. Thirsk, "Restoration Land Settlement", pp. 317-318.

[6] K. Feiling, *History of the Tory Party*, p. 101; G. N. Clark, *Later Stuarts*, p. 5; J. B. Kenyon, "The Reign of Charles II", *Cambridge Historical Review*, XIII (Cambridge, 1957), p. 84; Clarendon's *Life*, pp. 1066-1067; T. H. Lister, *Life of Clarendon*, II, p. 103.

situation that cried for justice, it quickly became apparent that for securing a favorable judgment the privilege of a peer was more valuable than any other qualification. Although not yet restored to the upper house, the lords spiritual levied their own justice with a strong Old Testament flavor. They ruthlessly seized their lands and tenancies, building even more ill will. The temporal lords were content to proceed by orders and legislation. They could well be content. Within two years the lords had not only regained many acres parted with in the last two decades, but on occasion managed to regain that land under terms that cancelled legitimate debts and mortgages of long standing. In addition, new lands and other sources of wealth were assiduously solicited and obtained. Any attempt to obstruct the peers' policy resulted in the offender being taken into custody. The lords were in deadly earnest about securing their position on the land and wasted no sentiment on commoners. Of fifty royalists owning lands in the southeastern counties who had suffered from confiscation or sales, only three, all peers, obtained what they sought by private acts.[7]

One of the first peers to seek redress by private act was Lord Craven and his case was the most litigious of any peer who suffered under the republicans. In his initial petition to the house of lords he desired a stop to the wasting of his old lands until he could proceed further, and this was granted on May 10, 1660. Early in June he submitted to the committee on petitions his claim for redress. His estate had been totally confiscated by the usurping government and he "has been already damnified above £ 200,000, besides the total loss of all his real estates". As his lands had been dispersed by the act of sale of 1652, and regaining them would require a multiplicity of suits, Craven asked to be granted repossession by act, and to regain all arrears of rents and profits. A counter-petition was filed against Craven's by Lady Grey, wife of Lord Grey of Groby, the noted republican. She asked consideration for the exchange of her jointure for lands of Lord Craven which her late husband had gained. On June 6, after two days of deliberation, the committee on petitions reported its findings to the whole house. The committee found that the real and personal estate of Lord Craven was voted confiscated without hearing, summons or charge; there was neither proof of

[7] D. Ogg, *Reign of Charles II*, I, pp. 162-163; Clarendon's *Life*, pp. 1047, 1083; D. Underdown, *Royalist Conspiracy*, p. 335; J. Thirsk, "Restoration Land Settlement", pp. 318, 320-321, 321 n.

pretended offense nor trial by peers. The house of lords then ordered that all the proceedings against Lord Craven be declared null and void and they voted Craven restored to all his personal and real goods, "in whose hands so ever the same is", together with arrears of rents and profits. On June 23, the lords were informed that their order was being defied. They promptly re-affirmed it, and warned that anyone disobeying the order would answer to the house. The lords were as good as their word, incarcerating one Edward Baker, who begged the pardon of the house and was shortly released. The house also summoned two other persons for reprimands for balking at Lord Craven's entry into his lands. In July Craven was given the governorship of Shrewsbury Castle as an additional benefit. His proceedings attracted notice, particularly by some old army men, who feared that parliament might take similar action with estates sold to them. Parliament, however, was too wise to do this. Voices were also raised in the house of commons accusing Craven of much double-dealing under his guise of injured innocence.[8]

The case of the duke of Buckingham was typical of most peers who sought to re-enter their lands. He first obtained a stay from the house of lords against the felling of timber or other abuses to his estates. All rents were also stayed in the tenants' hands, until the question of possession was settled. Two days later the house of commons ratified the order unanimously, as had the lords originally. The lords then proceeded to examine the evidence presented, and concluded that the proceedings against him were illegal, having been done without concurrence of the house of lords and for acts committed when a minor. The duke then entered a formal petition with the committee for petitions, which reported after a day's consideration in Buckingham's favor. This judgment was then confirmed by a second order restoring all the lands the duke had held into his possession. As with Lord Craven's case, no act was passed.[9]

All re-entries were not as simple as Buckingham's. Ormond needed an act of restoration. A bill that would return to the marquess of Or-

---

[8] *Acts and Ordinances,* II, pp. 591-598; K. Feiling, *History of the Tory Party,* p. 97; *L.J.,* XI, pp. 23, 52, 55, 74-75, 78; *H. Mss. C., 7th Report,* Appendix, House of Lords Mss., p. 93; P. H. Hardacre, *Royalists,* pp. 153-154; H.L.R.O., *Orders Books of the Committee for Petitions,* I, p. 16; *Mercurius Politicus,* July 6-12, 1660, B.M., E. 186(18); T. Carte, ed., *Ormonde Papers,* II, pp. 341-342.
[9] *L.J.,* XI, pp. 11-12, 17, 24, 59, 61, 63; *C.J.,* VIII, p. 14; *Parliamentary Intelligencer,* April 30-May 7, 1660, B.M., E. 183(12); B.M., *Add. Ms.* 32,455 fo. 53.

mond all lands in his possession on October 23, 1641, and any day thereafter passed its first two readings in the house of commons on July 18, 1660. It was engrossed on the 20th, received its third reading on the 23rd, passed, and was sent up to the lords the same day. The lords were as expeditious as the commons. Its first reading was completed the same day the bill was sent up. The second and third readings passed the lords on the 24th. On July 28 the bill received royal assent. Clarendon recorded that Ormond was easily restored to his lands because of his great position and merit and the fact that his lands had been reserved by Cromwell, thus there was no sizable body of new owners to contend with. The marquess of Winchester also needed an act of parliament, but for a different reason. His restoration to his lands had proceeded in much the same manner as the duke of Buckingham's. An additional order was necessary in the case of two intransigent new owners and a bill was started in the house of lords but not proceeded with. However, in February of 1662, the marquess found it wise to secure the records of his estate. Most of his deeds and evidence had been burnt and lost at the storming of his castle of Basing during the civil wars. The bill passed its third reading in the lords on February 25, and became law on May 19, 1662.[10]

The marquess of Newcastle and Baron Colepeper benefitted from private acts in their behalf. Orders were sufficient for the entry of the marquess of Worcester and earls of Northumberland, Suffolk, and Lichfield. Barons Gerard of Brandon, Chandos, Maynard, and Poulett also gained orders from the lords facilitating the repossession of their estates. Of the Roman Catholic peers, who suffered from recusancy as well as delinquency fines, Baron Arundell needed an act of restoration. The recusants had been frequent victims of confiscation; Winchester, Worcester, and Powis, as well as Arundell, had suffered this fate. In the end it made the restoration of their estates a fairly simple affair, as the basis of restoration was made the illegality of the acts of sale. The other recusants had their recusancy proceedings terminated. This was usually accomplished on grounds of their never having been convicted as recusants, and that their privileges as peers had been violated. Viscount Montagu pleaded this, as did Lord Petre. Baron Vaux had his estates discharged from sequestration on similar

<hr />

[10]  *C.J.*, VIII, pp. 92, 95, 99; *L.J.*, XI, pp. 13, 15, 73-74, 102-104, 109-110, 162, 385, 388, 391, 393; *S.R.*, V, pp. 206, 434; Clarendon's *Life*, p. 1051; *H. Mss. C., 7th Report*, Appendix, House of Lords Mss., pp. 160-161.

grounds. In all, twenty peers were aided by acts or orders of the house of lords in regaining their lands.[11]

The process of economic recovery was uneven. Even while twenty peers were regaining their lands, the position of others had become severe enough to require sales. Baron Abergavenney applied for an act to enable him to sell some of his lands. The chaos of the last twenty years had rendered his estate, never great, even poorer. His dual aim was to pay his many debts and to be able to provide some settled sum for his brother and sisters. The act passed through both houses quickly and became a law on July 30, 1661. A much longer affair concerned the lands of Ferdinando, late earl of Huntingdon. The earl had died in debt while engaged in selling his lands. In November of 1660 a bill to confirm these sales was brought into the house of lords but never proceeded with. A second bill was introduced into the Cavalier Parliament and was sent to a special committee appointed for the bill. The concern of the lords was for the interest of the young earl, a boy of eleven years. The second bill provided for additional sales to clear the youth's estate of all encumbrances. In February of 1662 the committee reported to the lords that they believed the act for sales would be in the best interest of the young earl, and that his mother consented to the proceedings. Reassured on this point, the lords passed the bill and Charles approved it on May 19, 1662. The whole matter had taken over a year and a half and throughout the proceedings the lords had shown themselves careful to protect the interests of a minor member of their order. The wish to provide portions for his younger brother and sisters was Lord Widdrington's basis for petition to be able to sell lands. Mary, Lady Widdrington challenged this petition as violating a life interest she had in the lands with tail to her sons. Widdrington appeared to have triumphed over his stepmother when the house of lords passed the necessary bill. However, Lady Widdrington had the last word, for the bill never became law. Baron Willoughby had to ask the crown for the grant of the remainder it possessed in the priory of Hevening, manor of Knaith, and the old monastery of Tupholme. This he secured; he was then able to alienate the lands to pay the debts he had contracted during "the late troubles".[12]

---

[11] *L.J.*, XI, pp. 20, 36-37, 59-60, 67-74, 87-89, 116-125, 134-149, 160-164, 177-184, 386, 396, 453; *C.J.*, VIII, pp. 141, 212, 218; *C.S.P.D.*, 1660-1661, pp. 61, 430; *H. Mss. C.*, *7th Report*, Appendix, House of Lords Mss., pp. 124-126 130, 160, 162; *S.R.*, V, pp. 252-253, 302, 434.

[12] *L.J.*, XI, pp. 275-276, 350, 359, 384, 387, 393, 412, 418; *H. Mss. C.*, *7th*

Of all the royalists in the house of lords, the earl of Cleveland fared worst at the restoration. His misfortune was of his own making. Before the civil wars his extravagance and mismanagement had placed him deep in debt. When the treason trustees came to sell his lands under the Commonwealth, they sold them to the earl's creditors. Their claims on him were sufficiently strong that he never regained Hackney manor or Bishop's Hall, Stepney. Purchasers at second hand in his estate in Toddington, Bedfordshire, gained leases of 99 years with the earl's acquiescence. This still did not relieve the earl of the clamor of his creditors. Thus an act was presented to vest all the lands and manors of the earl in trustees to be sold to satisfy the earl's debts and those of his son, Lord Wentworth. The bill passed the lords but narrowly avoided rejection in a light house of commons on December 24, 1660. A second act was passed in the Cavalier Parliament confirming the terms of the first act. The earl of Winchilsea also resorted to an act to place the priory of Watton and other lands in Yorkshire in the hands of trustees for sale. A bill to enable the earl of Banbury to fell the woods on his lands for payment of debts passed two readings in the house of lords but was not further proceeded with, the house addressing itself to the validity of Banbury's title and the legitimacy of his birth. All told, seven peers found themselves in such precarious finances that their only recourse was to alienate their land. The land legislation of the restoration was not entirely to the benefit of the nobility.[13]

The general land settlement afforded occasion to some peers to improve their land holdings. The earl of Dorset was one of these. His uncle, the late earl, had conveyed three manors in Kent to Henry Smythe of London, who had vested the lands in trustees with their annual income of £ 130 assigned to the benefit of the poor of the parishes of St. Saviour's, Southwark; St. Olave's, St. George's, and St. Mary Magdalen's, Bermondsey and some other parishes. The earl wished to regain these choice manors and the excellent messuage of Knole. He proposed to levy a perpetual charge of £ 130 on his manors of Bexhill and Cowding in Sussex in exchange for the possession of the three manors. The advantage to the earl in this arrangement was

---

*Report*, Appendix, House of Lords Mss., pp. 137, 144, 152, 160; S.R., V. pp. 320, 434; C.S.P.D., 1660-1661, pp. 502, 578.
[13] J. Thirsk, "Restoration Land Settlement", pp. 323, 327; L.J., XI, pp. 125-140, 150, 307-309, 396, 412, 419-420, 423;*H. Mss. C., 7th Report*, Appendix, House of Lords Mss., pp. 125, 127; C.J., VIII, pp. 141, 226; S.R., V, pp. 252, 303, 320.

sufficiently obvious to the house of commons for them to reject the bill in the Convention Parliament. The earl tried again when the Cavalier Parliament met, this time with success. The earl's income was further supplemented by a royal grant of forestry rights and income in Ashdown Forest, near his property in Sussex.[14]

While the position of the lords gave them substantial advantages over commoners in the land settlement, and these advantages were occasionally exploited by members like the earl of Dorset, in general the front of legality was preserved in the lords. This policy was re-enforced by the desire of the leading members of the government to settle the nation as quickly and quietly as possible. They did not wish overbearing nobles to trample upon property rights any more than Cromwell had desired the property rights of the nobles trampled on. This program now clashed directly with one of the most over-bearing of the noble houses, that of Stanley, in the persons of Charles, seventeenth earl of Derby, and his mother, the countess dowager of Derby. Vast tracts of Lancashire, Cheshire, northern Wales, and the Isle of Man composed the greater part of the Stanley domains. From this base the family had relentlessly pursued a royalist course, which cost the sixteenth earl his life. The burden in fines and confiscations was also great, and to avoid the weight of these, as well as pay for their debts incurred in supporting the crown, the Stanleys resorted to a multiplicity of conveyances of varying degrees of legality. But most important, these transfers were entered into freely, and were thus considered binding at the restoration. The Stanleys' own cleverness told against them. This was not evident when the earl of Derby gained on May 10, 1660, the order that when any act concerning land sales came up from the commons, he should have a provision considered, protecting his interest in all his and his father's lands, regardless of conveyances. Here the general land case rested while the earl and countess dowager launched legal assaults on each other's title to the Isle of Man. The lords had ordered the Isle restored to the earl on May 23, but on June 6 the petition of the countess dowager had sent the whole matter into the committee for petitions. From that body the earl of Pembroke reported that the lords committees "chose rather to try how an Agreement might be made between the two Stanleys, rather than to have the Business

[14] *H. Mss. C., 7th Report*, Appendix, House of Lords Mss., pp. 134, 142; *L.J.*, XI, pp. 194, 197, 254, 256-258, 268-269; *S.R.*, V, p. 319; *B.M., Egerton Ms.* 2979 fos. 119-120.

proceed in a legal Way". The committee succeeded in making an agreement which both parties and the house of lords approved. Charles approved the restoration of the government of Man to the earl a month later. His family feuds concluded, the earl was more free to turn his attentions to his lands' purchasers.[15]

The earl obtained the usual order to prevent wasting and to stop rents on lands whose possession he was to acquire. However, the order for possession was carefully hedged. It stated that the earl was to "be put into Possession of those Lands of his that are now in Sequestration and are not passed away to any other by himself". The earl was hardly content with this, and succeeded in having a bill brought in for recovery of the manors of Hope, Mold, and Hawarden. This bill was read twice on June 13, 1660, and sent to committee. The committee found that Serjeant Glyn had bought Hawarden, paying £ 1,700 to the late earl and his wife, and £ 9,000 to Sir John Trevor and others, who were the original purchasers of the three estates, all sequestrated. Trevor and the others would not convey Hawarden to Glyn until the earl acknowledged their right to Hope and Mold. This done, the three manors were alienated for a total sum of £ 10,700, of which the earl and his wife claimed to have received only £ 1,700. The actual value of the estates was placed at £ 30,000, for which purchasers had paid £ 12,000. The committee argued "that it appears ... that the Fraud, which was in the Beginning contrived for depriving the Earl and his Tenants of their Pre-exemption ... seconded with the Force and Necessity which the Earl was kept under, do destroy the Freedom of all the consequent Acts". The committee ordered the earl of Derby restored to the manors, upon payment to Trevor and the others of their purchase price of £ 12,000. Serjeant Glyn was to receive £ 1,700 and interest from the new earl and the countess dowager, and £ 9,000 and interest from Trevor and his companions. However, the earl's version of the case soon appeared to vary considerably from that of Trevor and the other purchasers. Evidence showed that the earl had made an agreement with the purchasers that they should buy his sequestrated estates from the government and hold them in trust for the Stanley family on specific terms that called for the earl to repay the purchase price within a certain time. The earl had freely made this agreement and then failed to meet its terms. At this point the whole business went into commit-

---

[15] *L.J.*, XI, pp. 22, 39, 54, 57; *Mercurius Publicus*, July 5-12, 1660, B.M., E. 186(18); see also *Parliamentary Intelligencer*, July 7, 1660.

tee hearings for a month. In August of 1660 a bill was presented entitled: "An Act for the Preserving of the Earl of Derby's Right of Action and Entry unto the Manors, Lands, and Hereditaments, heretofore sold by William [sic] Earl of Derby." This bill passed a second reading on August 23. Then the whole affair took another strange turn. The bill was never mentioned after August 23, and two days later a new bill appeared in its place, entitled, "An Act Restoring Charles, Earl of Derby to the Possession of the Manors, Lands, Tenements, and Hereditaments, belonging to James late Earl of Derby, his Father." This vastly different bill passed its third reading in the lords on August 29 and was sent down to the commons the following day. There William Prynne was waiting for it. Prynne may have been a champion of the lords, but only as a function of his championing of the law. The bill, Prynne justly observed, violated the act recently passed for the confirmation of legal proceedings, for it would invalidate legal acts of sale. The commons set the bill aside without an order for a second reading.[16]

The earl, believing that the extraordinary efforts and sufferings of his house on the behalf of the Stuart cause entitled it to special consideration, took further action. His belief was shared by many in both houses, and accordingly there was support for the introduction of yet a third bill. On May 25, 1661, the third bill, identical in title to the second, had its first reading in the house of lords. Upon its second reading, June 5, Sir John Trevor petitioned against it. The bill was then sent to a special committee charged to see if it violated the acts of indemnity and confirmation of judicial proceedings rather than back to the committee for petitions. Of this committee of twenty-six members, ten were later to go on record against the earl's case. The committee found that the bill's title, indicating the apparently innocent intention of restoring the earl to his estates, was a false front. It emerged that Derby had asked his tenants to buy their farms from the treason trustees and had granted them a release in return for money equivalent to three years' purchase. Derby's bill, to get around this, contained a clause invalidating any conveyances the earl had made during the Interregnum. As this and another provision, concerning rent payments made before 1660, were breaches of the act confirming judicial proceedings, strong opposition was

[16] *L.J.*, XI, pp. 59-62, 91-94, 96, 132, 137-138, 147, 149; *H. Mss. C.*, *7th Report*, Appendix, House of Lords Mss., pp. 127, 143; P. H. Hardacre, *Royalists*, p. 98; *Old Parliamentary History*, XXIII, pp. 49-50.

raised. The bill disappeared into the committee on June 7, 1661, and did not reappear.[17]

Three bills had now been lost; yet a fourth appeared. On December 10, 1661, this bill, to restore to the earl the manors of Mold and Moldsdale, Hope and Hopesdale, county Flint, had a first reading in the lords. Surely by now even brave men fled before the sight of the irrepressible argent stag of Derby. Again the bill went to a special committee. This committee of twenty-one members was more favorably inclined toward the earl; only four of them later registered opposition to the bill. The committee did amend this bill and reported it back to the house, where it passed its third reading on February 6, 1662. This passage produced the sharpest outburst yet. There were ninety-three peers in the house on the sixth, seventy-five lords temporal and eighteen spiritual. Twenty-five of the temporal lords recorded their protest against the bill's passage, an unusually large number.

In fact the recorded protest of even one member was uncommon in these years. The names of the protesters were significant. Clarendon led the list, followed by his friend Ormond. The leading Presbyterians were represented by Manchester, Robartes, Bedford, and Northumberland. Five of these six held posts in the government. The earls of Bridgwater and Portland, two of the three most active peers in the daily conduct of business in the lords, protested. The protesting signatories held that the sales the earl sought to overturn were voluntary, and therefore legal and binding. They further held that the bill was a breach of the terms of both the act for confirmation of judicial proceedings and the act of indemnity. The bill successfully passed the house of commons this time and was presented to the king on May 19, 1662. To the presentation of the bill he replied, *Le Roy s'avisera*. Thus the royal veto stopped the fourth and last bill. The purchasers were confirmed in their holdings and Charles promised the earl a grant of lands and money, which he duly made. The affair was not soon forgotten by the proud Marcher family. In 1732, when Hanoverians reigned in England, the earl of Derby erected on his lands an edifice bearing the inscription, "James, Earl of Derby, was beheaded at Bolton, 15 October, 1652, for strenuously adhering to Charles II, who refused a bill passed unanimously by both Houses

[17] *L.J.*, XI, pp. 256, 271, 273-275; J. Thirsk, "Restoration Land Settlement", p. 324.

of Parliament for restoring to the family the estate lost by his loyalty to that King." [18]

The Derby lands case concluded a major part of the economic settlement of the restoration for the lords. The next stage was one of special grants in restitution for losses loyally sustained between 1642 and 1660. Lord Willoughby had loaned parliament £ 3,155/15/10 during the late troubles and was paid only £ 1,000. He now presented his claim for the remainder, which the house of commons approved. The lords concurred in this, although Lord Mohun entered his dissent. The money had hardly been put to loyal purposes. Lord Willoughby was still paid his £ 2,155/15/10. The duke of Buckingham made good his claim to seven horses in Oliver Cromwell's stable; Charles ordered these returned to the duke. The marquess of Winchester tried for much more, but did no better than the earl of Derby. He had three bills brought in to reimburse him for moneys given to parliament by Robert Wallop out of the marquess's estate, which Wallop temporarily possessed. The first bill provided that the marquess be paid £ 19,000 damages. This bill passed three readings in the lords but did not pass the commons. The second bill provided for £ 10,000 damages, but was rejected by the lords upon its first reading on May 15, 1661. The third bill again asked for £ 10,000. It passed two readings in the lords, but foundered upon the report of the legal officers that it was contrary to the act of indemnity in attempting to extract this sum out of the estates of Robert Wallop. The earl of Bristol met the same result when he attempted to obtain £ 6,500 from the estates of Carew Raleigh in a cause like that of the marquess of Winchester. Bristol's bill passed three readings in the lords but failed to pass the commons. The earl did not renew the matter. Lord Lexington had no better fortune. He wished to raise £ 2,680 and damages out of the estate of John Hutchinson. Hutchinson petitioned against the bill, which passed the lords. Again the commons refused to pass such a measure and threw out Lexington's bill on the second reading. Because the Convention commons obviously would not tolerate private bills for financial restitution, and the act of indemnity made them illegal in the Cavalier Parliament, some other means of satisfying the economic claims of the loyal (and

[18]   *H. Mss. C., 7th Report*, Appendix, House of Lords Mss., pp. 152, 155; *L.J.*, XI, pp. 348, 362-363, 372, 378-379; J. E. T. Rogers, *A Complete Collection of the Protests of the Lords*, 3 vols. (Oxford, 1875), I, pp. 22-24; J. Thirsk, "Restoration Land Settlement", p. 324; Andrew Amos, *The English Constitution in the Reign of King Charles the Second* (London, 1857), p. 219.

not so loyal) had to be found. The method resolved upon was royal grants of lands, offices, and revenues.[19]

Charles granted the earl of Derby the office and revenues of chamberlain of the county palatine of Chester for his life and that of his son. Other royalists received similar offices with attached revenues. For a rental of £ 46/13/4 a year the marquess of Ormond gained a 31 year lease of the forest and castle of Exmoor, timber rights excepted. To the earl of St. Albans and Baptist May went the office of registrar in the court of chancery with its traditionally lucrative revenues. Viscount Mordaunt was particularly well treated. The priory of Reigate with its house and lands in Surrey was granted to him and his heirs at a nominal rent. The king also named him Constable of Windsor castle in reversion and keeper of its forests and parks for his life. He received the manors of Currey Mallet and Shepton Mallet in Somerset to be held by him and his wife jointly for 31 years. He further received with two others a shilling on each chaldron of coal shipped from the Tyne for 31 years beginning December 25, 1660. Lord Herbert of Raglan was rewarded with the office of Constable of the castle of St. Breville's in the forest of Dean for his life. To Lord Vaughan went the offices of constable of Radnor Castle with the stewardship of its accompanying manors and the stewardship of Brecknock. Both grants were for life with an annual fee of about £ 20. The earl of Portland gained as a royal favor the manor and parks of Berkhampstead for 31 years at an annual rental of £53/14/9, although the land was rated at £543 a year. The earl of Dorset was granted the office of master of Ashdown Forest with perquisites of courts, underwoods, and coppices for the trivial rental of £ 5. The earl of Monmouth received the park of Rudfen for 21 years at a rent of £ 200, upon payment of an £ 800 fine. As the park was surveyed at a value of better than £ 394, this promised the earl a fair profit. Lord Belasyse gained a lease of 10,000 acres of fen lands at a rent of £ 1,500 a year, or about half the rents of the improved portions.[20]

Several choice grants went to the duke of Albemarle. For the token of 4d. a day he received the possession of Middlesex Park, North

[19]  C.J., VIII, pp. 91, 272; L.J., XI, pp. 91, 115, 117, 125, 133, 137, 149, 167, 254, 307; B.M., *Harleian Ms.* 7158 fo. 96; *Egerton Ms.* 2618 fo. 93; *H. Mss. C.*, *7th Report*, Appendix, House of Lords Mss., pp. 117, 124-126, 142, 147-148.
[20]  Bodley, *Rawlinson Ms.* A 119, pp. 2, 11, 13, 18, 30, 40-41, 51, 57; *C.S.P.D.*, 1660-1661, pp. 69, 138-139, 142, 213, 266, 327, 487, 496, 523-524, 577; *Cal. Tr. Bks.*, 1660-1667, pp. 54, 62, 106, 109, 179.

Park, Bushy Park, and South Park of Hampton Court, all valuable properties. He was named bailiff of Teddington, also in Middlesex, and Byfleet and Ashstead in Surrey. In addition, he gained sufficient royal lands to assure him of £ 7,000 annual revenue. This included the great estate of Theobalds in Hertford, as well as other lands in Middlesex, Nottinghamshire, Hampshire, Sussex, Yorkshire, and Lincolnshire. The earl of Manchester had to be content with two small grants in Huntingdon. The earl of Suffolk fared better; he received the receipts from the sealing of writs from the courts of king's bench and common pleas. For this 25 year grant the earl had to pay £ 1,654/14/-, but it was considered a good bargain. Lord Loughborough received the farm of customs on the import and export of sheep and horses between Ireland and England for 21 years. His rental was £ 400 a year for the first seven years, then £ 500. Again this was a good bargain as the normal customs was estimated between £ 1,000 and £ 1,100 annually.[21]

In his grants Charles usually followed two policies; he granted lands and offices, seldom cash, and usually attached some fees to bring him a revenue. He granted for a period of years or lives, but seldom alienated the lands or offices irrevocably. But on occasion he departed from these rules. The young earl of Rochester was granted a pension of £ 500 a year, in memory of his father's services to the crown. Clarendon received the handsome grant of £ 20,000. He also gathered in many parcels of land. The rent on his holdings in Wychwood Forest in Oxfordshire was reduced from £ 140 to £ 40 a year. He also accepted the manor of Withcote in Leicestershire and 40 acres of Lyfield Forest in Rutland. The magnificent tract of Cornbury Park in Oxfordshire was granted him in August of 1661 and all of the offices for Wychwood Forest. In 1662 the manors of Langley, Leefields, and Ramsden, all in Oxfordshire, were added to his already princely holdings in that county. Clarendon's revenues were further enriched by the grant of a half-year's rent due from the soldiers settled in the Irish counties of East and West Meath, Wexford, and Kilkenny. Tracts in Westminster and Lambeth followed this. Later grants made him steward and ranger of the royal manor of Woodstock and ranger of the New Forest, and he gained additional manors while chancellor. Clarendon added to his grants by purchases at reasonable prices set by people anxious for his favor. Only Albemarle

[21] Bodley, *Rawlinson Ms.* A 119, pp. 26-27, 33, 91, 100; *C.S.P.D.*, 1660-1661, pp. 174, 430, 523, 577; *Cal. Tr. Bks.*, 1660-1667, pp. 53, 127, 221.

could approach him in the benefits bestowed by royal bounty. Others who performed great service at the restoration did well too. John Grenville, as earl of Bath, drew a salary of £ 2,000 as groom of the Stole and first gentleman usher of the bedchamber. Charles also honored his father's promise to the earl of Leicester that he should be no loser for his services as that monarch's ambassador to France. The earl accordingly received £ 3,033/6/8 due him from that service.[22]

A traditional if small source of income was restored to the peers in 1660. An ordinance of 1652 had terminated the payment to the peers above the rank of baron their creation money, sums paid annually to a peer in proportion to his title. These charges were usually placed against the regular revenue and had consequently not been paid for a decade when they were formally abolished. Some few had been assigned against particular estates or corporations, and were also officially terminated. Eight days after the lords returned to parliament, the earl of Lincoln moved for a creation money impost. The house judged the following day that creation money might be claimed, not by looking backward, but by consideration as a right by patent to be enjoyed in the future like all other rights conferred by a patent of nobility. On May 12, the lords directed the committee for privileges to investigate the subject with a backward look to those responsible for denying the peers their payments as well as a forward look to securing again the income. The house finally resolved that creation money was an undoubted right of all peers which no alienation or similar process could invalidate. The house further moved to have their arrears paid. The arrears were never paid. The Treasury paid the creation money regularly from 1660 on. Barons were not provided with regular grants. Viscounts received 20 marks, or £13/6/8; while earls were paid £ 20. Marquesses were paid 40 marks, or £ 26/13/4; dukes received £ 40. A peer was paid accordingly for every English title he held above the rank of baron. Thus the earl of Bridgwater received 20 marks for his title of Viscount Brackley and £ 20 for his earldom. The duke of Buckingham collected handsomely from the profusion of titles that had been showered upon his father. Creation money was usually paid twice a year. The first warrant for payment was issued to the earl of Denbigh on January 5, 1661, and was followed

[22]   Bodley, *Rawlinson Ms.* A 119, p. 92; *C.S.P.D.*, 1660-1661, pp. 298, 523, 558; 1661-1662, pp. 65-66, 78, 131; T. H. Lister, *Life of Clarendon*, II, p. 82; III, pp. 522-528; *Cal. Tr. Bks.*, 1660-1667, pp. 82, 315; J. Campbell, *Lives of the Lord Chancellors*, III, p. 117; Clarendon's *Life*, p. 1069.

rapidly by a succession of warrants until the upper ranks of the lords were enjoying their perquisites of old.[23]

The restoration of creation money nearly completed the economic benefits accruing to the house of lords after Charles II gained his throne. The house did attempt to examine a number of deeds and conveyances which its members claimed had been forced from them. These concerned the surrender of noble rights over tithes, rectories, and rent charges assigned for religious support. The claimants stated that the papers were in the hands of the clerk of the commons now, but the commons would not acknowledge that he had them. The lords did not secure the papers. Equally unsuccessful was a bill to enable Richard Boyle, Lord Clifford, to proceed at law against those involved in seizing his goods contrary to the articles of York under which he had surrendered them. This was contrary to the purposes of the government as represented in the act of indemnity, and was rejected at its third reading in the lords. Viscount Campden, on the other hand, succeeded in securing the grant of a mansion and lands in Kensington, Middlesex by an act in 1662. A series of orders commanded the return to various peers of papers and deeds seized or called in by various Commonwealth committees or officials.[24]

The lords fared well at the restoration. All those who had lost lands by confiscation regained them promptly, sometimes less encumbered than they had been before the civil wars. Where legislation was required, either to make good a questionable title, or facilitate the sale of lands by those peers who found such action necessary, the house of lords promptly provided a bill. Only in a few cases, notably that of the earl of Derby, were the claims of loyal service imperfectly balanced against the goals of an ordered and peaceful settlement. However, the loyalty that suffered in such a balance was sufficiently recompensed in the grants of lands and offices which Charles bestowed. The lords were no more successful than lesser cavaliers when they attempted to proceed in an arbitrary and illegal manner, but they had a full and favorable hearing when their case was just. The peerage at the least maintained their own in the economic aspects of the restora-

---

[23]   *Acts and Ordinances*, II, p. 585; *L.J.*, XI, p. 26; H.L.R.O., *Minute Books of the Committee for Privileges*, I, pp. 4, 24; Edward Chamberlayne, *Angliae Notitia* (London, 1679), p. 272; *Cal. Tr. Bks.*, 1660-1667, pp. 182, 189-190, 192, 195, 197, 207-208.
[24]   *L.J.*, IX, pp. 81-89, 109, 123, 133, 151, 163, 403, 408, 410; *C.S.P.D.*, 1660-1661, p. 391; *H. Mss. C.*, *7th Report*, Appendix, House of Lords Mss., pp. 125, 162.

tion settlement. In comparison to lesser cavalier groups their gains were substantial. The stake in the land they had fought so tenaciously to preserve was secured to them. By 1662 the position of the peerage was firmly established on the two foundations of the house of lords and landed estates.

In the course of restoration rewards the monarchy honored the ancient claims of two noble families. The house of Howard was the first of these. On August 30, 1660, the house of lords heard the first reading of a bill to restore Thomas, earl of Arundel, Surrey, and Norfolk to the dignity and title of duke of Norfolk. The progress of the bill was slow. The earl of Arundel was insane, and if he was Protestant, the rest of the family were very much Roman Catholics. Both these facts gave pause to the desire to buttress the prestige of the lords by reviving some of the great titles of their order. A committee of forty-one peers, very large for 1660, eventually considered the bill. They duly reported, as the Rump had done a year before, that the earl was "a perfect lunatic". The committee finally approved the bill and reported it fit to pass on November 19. The same day the lords appointed a committee of seven — including Hyde, Ormond, the earls of Bristol and Peterborough, and Baron Robartes — to wait on the king to know his pleasure in the matter. The chancellor reported to the house on the 22nd that the king had no objection to the proceeding. The bill passed its third reading the same day. It then faced a shorter but stormier session in the commons. The heaviest debate came on December 3, the day the bill was given its third reading. Serjeant Maynard and William Prynne led the attack on the bill; they argued that Mr. Henry Howard, the earl's brother and perhaps the leading papist in England, promoted it for his own advantage. This was probably true enough; he succeeded to the dignity in 1677. Sir Richard Onslow, Sir Robert Paston, and Sir George Downing led in arguing the case for the bill. None of these were Catholic; Onslow often led government bills in the house, Downing was decidedly disinclined to favor papists, and the Paston and Howard families had often clashed over Norfolk affairs. This variety of support carried the measure by 187 to 116, after six hours of debate. Charles approved the bill and a bill of the following year confirming the restoration.[25]

[25]    L.J., XI, pp. 149, 155-156, 183-185, 187, 189, 198; C.S.P.V., 1659-1661, pp. 220, 226; Old Parliamentary History, XXIII, pp. 32, 35-37; C.J., VIII, p. 196; New Parliamentary History, IV, pp. 154-155; E. S. de Beer, ed., The Diary of John Evelyn, 6 vols. (Oxford, 1955), III, p. 326; S.R., V, pp. 302, 349.

The house of Seymour was the second family to regain a dukedom. Here proceedings were complicated by two claims. The marquess of Worcester, a Roman Catholic, and head of the house of Somerset, claimed the duchy of Somerset by virtue of a patent issued him by Charles I. The marquess of Hertford, an Anglican, and head of the house of Seymour, claimed the right to the dignity by restoration. The house of lords referred the contending cases to a committee of the most prominent members of the house on August 10, 1660. The committee reported that the marquess of Worcester admitted that he held the patent from king Charles I only on certain conditions of service he had been unable to fulfill during the civil wars. On September 3, the house was informed that the marquess of Worcester had surrendered his patent to the king. At this point the committee received a bill repealing an act of Edward VI's reign which closely limited the lands that a person bearing the title of duke of Somerset might hold. This emerged from committee in a new bill. This bill provided for the restoration of the marquess of Hertford to the dukedom of Somerset. It quickly passed both houses and was approved by the king on September 13, 1660. In his speech Charles spoke of the trusty old servant of the crown who had conducted the body of his royal father to its burying place.

I cannot but take Notice of One particular Bill I have passed, which may seem of an extraordinary Nature, that concerning the Duke of Somersett; but you all know it is for an extraordinary Person, who hath merited as much of the King My Father and Myself as a Subject can do; and I am none of those who think that Subjects by performing their Duties in an extraordinary Manner do not oblige their Princes to reward them in an extraordinary Manner. There can be no danger from such a Precedent; and I hope no Man will envy him because I have done what a good Master should do to such a Servant.

The old servant did not long live as duke of Somerset. Since the restoration he had seldom been well enough to leave his lodgings. On October 24, 1660, hardly a month after Charles's speech, Somerset was dead. As his son, Lord Beauchamp, was already dead, the heir and new duke was the eight year old grandson of old Hertford. Hertford had arranged before he died that his daughter-in-law should have the guardianship of her son as long as she remained a widow. She had, however, remarried and the old duke had obtained a promise from Charles II that the wardship of the child might be vested insofar as possible in the duchess dowager. For this purpose the duke had placed substantial property in trusteeship. The young duke's mother, now Lady Herbert, petitioned the lords for custody and the duchess filed a counter petition. The lords quickly dropped all proceedings when the king indicated he would honor the old duke's wishes and watch the young duke's interest himself. The lords did initiate a bill to pay the debts of the old duke but it never emerged from committee after its second reading. The original act of restoration was confirmed by an act in 1661. The role of Charles II in the two ducal restorations made clear that to the peerage the king was the fount of all honor. The monarch raised them, and as memories of Norfolk provided, the monarch could set them down. The relationship of king and peers was described by Charles in terms of master and servants. The peerage enjoyed, however, another and different relationship with king, that between crown and house of lords.[26]

---

[26] *L.J.*, XI, pp. 133, 138, 151-153, 156-159, 173, 219, 353-354, 358, 418; *C.S.P.V.*, 1659-1661, pp. 190, 199; *H. Mss. C.*, *5th Report*, Appendix, Part I, Duke of Sutherland Mss., p. 155; *7th Report*, Appendix, House of Lords Mss., p. 164; *S.R.*, V. pp. 253, 349; Clarendon's *Rebellion*, p. 698; *C.S.P.D.*, 1660-1661, p. 380.

# VII

## THE LORDS AND THE LAW

Colonel Rymer recorded in his diary on November 11, 1661, his experience at the opening of a session of parliament: "The Black Rod came down and commanded us up to the King where we found him sitting on the throne with his crown on, and his robes and all the Peers and Bishops with their robes also, so as in my judgment I never saw so majestic a sight in all my life...." The king ordinarily communicated directly with the commons only when their Speaker presented his traditional demands at the opening of parliament and the money bills at the close of a session. Usually the lords served as the agents of formal communications. In September of 1660, when it was unclear if the king wished parliament to adjourn, or merely to recess for a short time, the commons requested a conference with the lords that the latter might ask the king his meaning. The lords duly commissioned the lord chancellor to carry the request to the king on their behalf and when he reported, they conveyed the king's reply to the commons. Accordingly, when the commons wished an adjournment delayed that they might complete some bills, they sent the message through the lords. When Charles decided to adjourn the Convention Parliament, he so informed the upper house, who requested a conference with the commons to inform them of their sovereign's wishes. Petitions might be joint proposals of both houses, but were directed to the king through the lords, as in the case of a parliamentary protest on excessive Dutch tariffs. The peers themselves had to address requests to the king to leave their duties in parliament. More than in a simply parliamentary sense, the law for a peer began with the king, and as *consiliarii nati*, the peers had special obligations to him. Thus many peers obtained particular pardons from the king, erasing all wrongs to the crown, at the time of the restoration. Such peers as might be expected laid hold of this offer: the earl of Northumberland and the earl of Denbigh. But they were not alone. Although the earl of Clare and Viscount Fauconberg had done much to secure themselves with the king, they still exercised the ancient practice of securing pardons. Even the duke of Buckingham found it politic to do so. The royal pardon also was a last escape for a peer from the law. The earl of Chesterfield had to seek his Sovereign's mercy for slaying a man; Charles granted the pardon. The Stuarts were generous with their pardons to highly placed persons to the degree that it became a public abuse. The consequent effect upon an already too lawless society was unfortunate. As peers easily gained such pardons, some were all the more free in their behavior, which again had unfortunate effect upon the reputation of the peerage generally.[1]

The royal pardon was only one of the legal benefits of the peer. In seeking such mercy he differed from the commoner only in the degree of favor or disfavor he might incur. But the individual peer enjoyed, outside the particular privileges attached to him by virtue of his being a peer of parliament, many rights in law which no commoner had. Some of these privileges were still important; others were relics of an earlier time. In this latter category was the benefit of clergy without being able to read. By the seventeenth century this provision no longer had much meaning, although it was faithfully cited in any compilation of peers' rights. The peer still retained useful benefits in civil processes. A plaintiff wishing to proceed in any suit or action against a peer of the realm could not avail himself of a day of grace by favor of the court. When the case came to trial, at least one knight must sit on the jury, or the case was dismissed, or rather the "Array may be quasht by challenge". Further, if the civil proceeding should go against the noble, no award might be given against the body of a peer. He could not be incarcerated in a debtor's prison, or held in custody for a settlement. Sir Robert Sawyer was to rule later in the seven Bishops' case that the privilege extended to misdemeanors. This provision respecting the body of a peer was maintained with great care by the lords, and its principle extended into criminal jurisdiction. They successfully maintained a peer could not be imprisoned by attachment out of chancery. They attempted to maintain such privileges for peers in a bill to preserve the king's person in 1661. The house of commons would not yield on this privilege in cases of treason and the lords had to retreat. Peers were, however, exempt from jury duty in civil cases, and also free

---

[1] B.M., *Egerton Ms.* 2043 fo. 17; *L.J.*, XI, pp. 150-153, 157, 164, 189, 224, 236, 240; *C.S.P.D.*, 1660-1661, pp. 34, 41, 44, 214, 479.

from being impaneled for inquests, even if the matter lay between two peers. If a peer should ever be impaneled, a special writ existed for his discharge. When any peer was called to testify, under any circumstances, he was never bound to good behavior, or put to swear not to break the peace. In all cases peers promised such behavior only upon their honor, which Chamberlayne recorded "was ever accounted so Sacred, as upon no termes to be violated".[2]

Not only was the peer privileged in legal proceedings, but his privileged position was secured from popular criticism. Chamberlayne put it thus:

The Laws of England are so tender of the Honour, Credit, Reputation, and Persons of Noblemen, that there is a Statute on purpose, to hinder all offence by false Reports, whereby any scandal to their Persons may arise, or debate and discord between them and the Commons; and because it is to defend, not only Lay-Lords, but Bishops and all Great Officers of the Realm, it is called *Scandalum Magnatum.*

The scope of this protection was great and not lightly transgressed, for it could reach to minute matters. The *Parliamentary Intelligencer* reported one case.

Here we cannot but advertise you, how that foolish lying spirit, that for many years hath filled this great city with contradictions and forgeries, did this week begin to peep forth again, particularly a paultry paper, called (forsooth) a petition of one Rich lately a servant to Mr. Cleypoole, which pretended that some servant belonging to Charles Lord Gerrard, has unduly seized upon his horse; but wether the horse was his, or Mr. Cleypoole's, or Mr. Cleypoole's father-in-law's, is now so manifest that Rich himself, for his ridiculous lying paper, must give appearance for so impudent a scandal against a Peer of the Realm.

This legal concept had emerged when every lord was considered a great officer of state, because he was required to support the king by his advice. In the reign of Richard II the concept was given statutory force. Although few peers were still great officers of state, the obvious advantages of such a statute were zealously maintained. However, the temper of England after the Puritan Revolution did not adjust gently or peaceably to the re-enforcement of the statute. In 1660 the earl of Suffolk learned this for all the lords. In December one Alexander Peper was brought before the bar of the house of lords for speaking scandalous words against the earl. These were

[2]  B.M., *Egerton Ms.* 2043 fos. 10-11; *Lansdowne Ms.* 506 fos. 1-2; E. Chamberlayne, *Angliae Notitia*, pp. 257-259; *L.J.*, XI, pp. 269-271, 276.

alleged to be "That the Earl of Suffolke was a Fool and a Knave; and he did hear that the Lords would choose him of their House of Parliament; but he did hope they had more Wit than to choose such a Fool". Peper was further alleged to have described the earl as "a base stinking Fellow". Now arraigned before all the might and majesty of the lords in parliament assembled, Peper was called upon to explain himself. His reply was "he did not speak those Words, but he might say, the Earl of Suffolke showed himself so". He was promptly committed to custody. The lords decided that since Peper's words were spoken before the passage of the act of indemnity they were pardoned by the general terms of the act and Peper was discharged free from any criminal proceedings. However, the house also judged that the earl of Suffolk's right to proceed in a civil cause was not barred by the act, and Peper was left to face proceedings for indemnity.[3]

While the peer made full use of the privilege of *scandalum magnatum*, other rights were less often exercised. In the seventeenth century there was not too much need to appeal to the old privilege that a peer of the realm might not be put to the rack, or otherwise tortured, to discover the truth, though accused of high treason. Still of considerable consequence was the right of trial by peers, one of the most cherished of the lords' privileges. When indicted of a criminal offense, the noble placed himself on his peerage and claimed the right of trial by his peers acting as a jury. This jury was headed by the chancellor when parliament was in session or by an elected lord steward if parliament were not sitting. The jury of peers found their verdict, of course, on their honor, and not under oath. The noble jurors were particularly privileged. They were judges both of law and fact, a right for which common jurors still had to wait. All this was not entirely to the lord's benefit. If he might choose trial by peers in most criminal offenses, he must stand trial before his peers if indicted of a felony or treason. Nor could he challenge his noble jurors for they were all peers, who could not "be guilty of Falsehood, Favor, or Malice". Further, if parliament were not in session, not all peers need be summoned to the court of the high steward. This potentially permitted a coterie of one's enemies to be assembled to judge an indicted peer. Lord Cornbury wrote Ormond in 1667 that his father, Clarendon, feared that parliament would be prorogued in order that

---

[3] E. Chamberlayne, *Angliae Notitia*, pp. 259-260; *Parliamentary Intelligencer*, B.M., E. 186(29); D. Ogg, *Reign of Charles II*, II, p. 465; *L.J.*, XI, pp. 198-199, 202-203, 211-212.

this might be done in his case. In fact, 1667 marked the beginning of a long struggle of the lords to get the commons to accept a bill requiring all peers to be summoned to the court of the high steward. Not until 1696 was such an act secured, and that after a culminating six years' struggle with the lower house. The Convocation of 1661 clarified the position of bishops in these proceedings. There it was declared safe and lawful for bishops to be present at trials for blood in the lords, though not to vote. In these cases as in all other legal proceedings, peers called as witnesses gave evidence upon their honor, and not upon oath.[4]

There were a few minor privileges peers held not directly connected to their role as peers of parliament. The noble might kill one or two deer in the king's forests when travelling by royal summons. He could not be summoned for service in the *posse comitatus*. His home was secured from search for arms except by special warrant from the king by an act of 1661. The chaplains of peers might be pluralists. Each duke might have six chaplains, marquesses and earls five, viscounts four, and barons three. A peer might retain in his employ six resident aliens.[5]

All these privileges, and the great ones associated with nobility by virtue of being peers of parliament, rested upon the individual's legal status as a peer. A formidable body of peerage law upheld this status. This law had largely passed under the control of the house of lords. Only as recently as 1625 the house had won a battle with the crown. When the earl of Bristol did not receive a summons to the parliament of that year, the lords refused to sit. After this incident the principle that every eligible peer was to be summoned to parliament was maintained. In the last half of the seventeenth century the house secured control of peerage legislation. The lords initiated all bills concerning peers and allowed the house of commons either to accept or reject the measures, but not to amend them. The house, in 1660, exerted the right to examine all patents of nobility. Upon information "That several Grants have been surreptitiously gotten, since the year 1642, which have been prejudicial to the King, and the Peers of

---

[4]  E. Chamberlayne, *Angliae Notitia*, pp. 257, 260; D. Ogg, *Reign of Charles II*, I, p. 137; W. S. Holdsworth, *History of English Law*, I, p. 191, VI, pp. 232-234; B.M., *Hargrave Ms.* 216 fo. 32; A. Amos, *English Constitution in the Reign of Charles the Second*, pp. 259-260; White Kennet, *A Complete History of England*, 3 vols. (London, 1719), III, p. 252.
[5]  B.M., *Lansdowne Ms.* 506 fos. 1-2; E. Chamberlayne, *Angliae Notitia*, pp. 259-260; D. Ogg, *Reign of Charles II*, I, pp. 136-137.

this House", the lords ordered that the matter "be referred to the Committee for Privileges, who are to consider, and examine the same [grants], and to report the same to this House, what remedy they think fit". The house yielded to Charles's will on the matter of patents granted during the Interregnum. They did insist that no new peer be admitted to sit in the house, in 1660, unless his patent was read during the proceedings. This rule was followed for the introductions of Albemarle, Sandwich, Brecknock, and Hyde as a baron. In 1661, faced with the admission of eleven new titles in one day, the house waived the reading of the patents. The lords required that patents be presented to the house, and were satisfied with the reading of the writs of summons. The lords also deviated from custom, though not from law, in the sitting of the duke of Gloucester. The prince sat and participated in the house at the age of twenty, one year short of the age traditionally observed. The minimum age did not become a fixed rule until May 22, 1685.[6]

The subject of the patents issued between 1642 and 1660 refused to stay dead. Many royalists had strong feelings that some of the honored were of little desert. Many of the older peers hardly desired the expansion of their order. Despite the royal opinion, two attempts to judge upon those patents developed, involving lords, commons, and chancery. The commons moved first, discussing a bill to abolish all titles conferred by Charles I after his retreat to Oxford. This proceeding was quickly lost. The lords brought in a bill "for preventing Inconveniences which may arise by Patents and Grants, made, or pretended to be made, during the late troubles". This bill spent much time in committee, and finally provided that all patents obtained from the crown between June 1, 1642, and May 22, 1660, be brought into the court of chancery to be viewed and examined. If a patent were not brought in, it was to be declared void. The bill was further modified by excepting several peers by name from the operation of the act. The lords passed this version but after two readings the commons sent it to committee and did not recall it. The result of these proceedings was some discontent; the king maintained his right.[7]

[6] J. R. Tanner, *English Constitutional Conflicts of the Seventeenth Century*, p. 217; W. S. Holdsworth, *History of English Law*, I, pp. 365-392, VI, pp. 249-250; *L.J.*, XI, p. 27, XIV, p. 10; B.M., *Add. Ms.* 15,574 fo. 416; *Harleian Ms.* 7158 fo. 271; *Hargrave Mss.* 131 fo. 60, 167 fos. 5-6; L. O. Pike, *Constitutional History*, p. 275.

[7] *Clarendon S. P.*, III, p. 740; *H. Mss. C.*, *5th Report*, Appendix, Part I, Duke

The eighteen years without regular government and eleven years' absence of a house of lords created more controversies than that of the patents of that period alone. In 1660 the house of lords had five cases concerning peerage law to consider, as opposed to only six during the remainder of Charles's reign. Two petitions claiming the dormant barony of Fitzwalter were presented by Mr. Cheeke and Mr. Mildmay. The king asked the house of lords to consider the rival claims in August. During the following month the lords examined the petitions, but recognized neither. While the king had been willing to leave the determination of the Fitzwalter barony to the lords, he took the lead in the case of the barony of Windsor. On June 16, 1660, he "created" Thomas Hickman Baron Windsor. The creation was important in establishing the king's right to declare, when a barony descends on female co-heirs, which line the dignity shall run through. The late Baron Windsor had two sisters and no heirs when he died. The elder of the sisters married Dixie Hickman, and had a son, Thomas. The signet office docket book for 1660 duly recorded that "it belongeth to his Majesty to declare which of the said co-heirs shall enjoy the dignity of their ancestry". In this case the king judged the barony to pass through Elizabeth, the elder sister, to her son, Thomas. As the doctrine of abeyance was not yet established, the recall was treated as a creation. Clearly the principle was emerging; the house of lords did not seat the new lord at the bottom of the barons' bench, but gave him the precedence of the original patent for the barony.[8]

The king called upon the lords for judgment again in the case of the earl of Banbury. Nicholas Knollys had taken his seat in the house of lords, and as there was considerable doubt regarding the legitimacy of his birth, he petitioned the king that his title be secured. Charles sent the petition to the house of lords with a royal request that he not have a writ of summons. In making this request Charles acknowledged the victory of the peers over his father in the Bristol affair of 1625. The lords were happy to receive the king's request, as some of them had already moved that the earl should not sit in the house. However, the lords encountered some difficulty with the law. While Knollys' legitimacy was most doubtful, his aged "father" had died

---

of Sutherland Mss., pp. 150, 153, 156; *7th Report*, Appendix, House of Lords Mss., p. 131; D. Ogg, *Reign of Charles II*, I, p. 166; *L.J.*, XI, pp. 156, 158.

[8]  B.M., *Hargrave Ms.* 178 fo. 226; *L.J.*, XI, pp. 67, 135, 157; L. O. Pike, *Constitutional History*, pp. 133-135, 138.

before his birth and he had never been declared illegitimate. Further, he was probably the son of Baron Vaux by the countess of Banbury. The earl of Northampton, reporting from the committee for privileges, concluded that Nicholas Knollys was in the eyes of the law the son of William, late earl of Banbury. Thus the lords were advised to inform the king that he should issue a writ to Banbury. This decision did not sit well with the house, and a bill was brought in declaring Nicholas, called earl of Banbury, to be illegitimate. The lords did not proceed with the bill but neither did Knollys, or Vaux, resume sitting in the face of the lords' hostility. The lords learned a lesson from this case, and in 1662 proceeded with a bill to illegitimatize a child named Ignatius, born of Lady Anne Roos. Lady Anne was wife of Lord Roos, heir apparent of the earl of Rutland, but had long been living apart from her husband. The bill did not pass, but an act illegitimatizing all the children of Lady Anne passed in 1668, two years after an act of divorce between the lord and Lady Anne.[9]

The lords also settled a principle of peerage law in the case of lords Berkeley and DeLaWarr. Lord Berkeley petitioned the house for precedency over Lord DeLaWarr on the grounds of his ancestors having held a barony by tenure before Lord DeLaWarr's ancestors had, but a Lord Berkeley had not been summoned to parliament until after a Lord DeLaWarr. In other words, in peerage law did barony by tenure take precedence over barony by patent? The lords first received petitions on the matter on July 24, 1660, and considered the case until 1669. The records revealed that there had been Lords Berkeley in England since 1120, but no summons to parliament until 1463, while a Lord DeLaWarr had been summoned as early as 1299. The final decision of the house of lords was to declare barony by tenure obsolete and recognize only baronies by patent. Lord Berkeley had to be content with the fourth seat on the barons' bench. The lords further refined their definition of a barony by patent in the Frescheville peerage case of 1667. They then held that a writ of summons alone did not create a parliamentary barony; they required proof that the summons was obeyed.[10]

Peerage law became entangled with criminal law in the case of

[9]  L.J., XI, pp. 90, 272, 305, 315; B.M., Add. Ms., 38,141 fo. 207; H. Mss. C., 7th Report, Appendix, House of Lords Mss., pp. 165-166.
[10]  L.J., XI, pp. 104, 197, 257, 261-262, 268, 274; B.M., Add. Ms. 38,141 fos. 166-167; W. S. Holdsworth, History of English Law, I, 178 n., D. Ogg, Reign of Charles II, II, p. 461.

Viscount Purbeck. On June 15, 1660, the earl of Monmouth accused him of saying, "Rather that the late King should want one to cut off His Head, He would do it himself." Upon this information the house ordered the gentleman usher to take Purbeck into custody and bring him before the house to answer informations of high treason as well as other "high Misdemeanors". On June 16, Purbeck came before the house to hear the informations against him. In addition to the statement of the earl of Monmouth, a further allegation declared that Purbeck had praised Bradshaw for his action against the "tyrant", Charles I. Purbeck was said to have stated in Richard Cromwell's presence his hatred of Charles I and his cause. Various atheistical speeches were also attributed to him. Purbeck for his part readily admitted that he hated Charles Stuart, and hence his own name of Villiers, which he had changed to Danvers. He continued that he was not a peer, and had applied for an order from the attorney-general to clear him of any possible title. He maintained that his honor was but a shadow, without substance, his estate was too small to maintain an honor, and the noble family of his birth had never recognized him, or left him any estate. Purbeck further pointed out that he was presently a member of the house of commons, and asked the lords to first decide if they could try him or not, before he answered the accusations against him. The lords considered this and told him that he was faced with informations, not charges; they desired his response to them. Purbeck declined to answer on the ground that he had a seat in the house of commons, and the lords re-committed him to custody. The lords proceeded to summon legal advice. While this was still in progress, Purbeck on July 14 petitioned for release from custody because of ill health. This sufficiently hastened the law experts to bring in their report to the lords on the 16th. The attorney-general added a new charge on that date, that Purbeck stated he would "rather wash his Hands in the King's Blood, than in the Blood of any Dog in England". Charges the lords had in sufficiency; less certain was their right to prosecute the charges.[11]

A slightly more humble Purbeck, or as he preferred, Robert Danvers, then addressed a formal petition to the lords. He stated that no man had a more high and honorable esteem of the lords than he, but he lacked a writ to sit among them. Of course no peer had a writ of summons to the Convention Parliament. He further pleaded poverty

[11]   B.M., *Add. Ms.* 27,590 fos. 38-41, 43-45; *L.J.*, XI, pp. 64-66, 75-76, 93-94.

as disqualifying him. Concurrent with their list of charges presented
on July 16, the lawyers reported upon Purbeck's contention that he
was not a peer. They concluded that Purbeck could legally surrender
his peerage to the king with the royal consent alone needed. They
cited the cases of the earl of Norfolk in Edward I's reign, the earl
of Pembroke in the reign of Edward IV, Viscount Lisle's surrender
to Henry VIII, and most recent, Baron Stafford in the time of Charles
I. The affair was allowed to end here without a clear decision by the
lords. The act of indemnity rendered nugatory the charges, or "informations", against Purbeck, and he was initially bailed on £ 10,000
security on July 27, and then released from any custody on a bond
of the same amount in September. It is not clear how the poverty
stricken Purbeck was able to raise £ 10,000. He had alleged in his
petition to have not £ 1,000 left against debts of £ 5,000. The poll
of the house of lords on November 25, 1661, did not contain Purbeck's name. The lords ordered the committee for privileges to consider again the question of Purbeck's peerage. He himself made good
his rejection of the title. When, in 1678, his son claimed the title,
the lords unanimously judged that no fine levied to the king could
bar a title of honor or the right of any one claiming such title as
heir to the person against whom the fine had been levied. The problem of how to dispose of an unwanted title was thus left to confront
the second Viscount Stansgate.[12]

The difficulties encountered in several of these cases moved the
house of lords to consider a heralds' bill, which would provide for
the recording of matches and descents of the nobility. It also included provisions for the regulation of noble arms. The bill passed
two readings and died in committee. Although the lords did not
possess an absolute domination of all proceedings regarding the legal
status of a peer, they had a considerable voice and exercised it. While
the king still retained unchallenged his complete freedom in the creation of peers, hence forward the community of peers in the house of
lords largely regulated matters concerning honors. The influence of
the house of lords extended beyond regulation, for it conferred upon
its members valuable privileges. Added to trial by peers and *scandalum magnatum* these rights made the possession of an honor the

---

[12]   B.M., *Add. Ms.* 32,455 fo. 89; *H. Mss. C., 7th Report*, Appendix, House of
Lords Mss., p. 110; *L.J.*, pp. 58, 93-94, 103, 107, 166-167, 337; *Old Parliamen-
tary History*, XXII, p. 382; L. O. Pike, *Constitutional History*, pp. 271-272;
W. S. Holdsworth, *History of English Law*, VI, pp. 244-245.

key to unusual status. The house of lords, as a legislative and judicial body, was vital to the importance of its members as landed magnates. Ultimately it was this alone which distinguished them from the most powerful of the gentry and gave more than honorary value to a peerage. The fate of the peerage during the absence of a house of lords was convincing proof that the house was vitally important to the English nobility. And its importance to the nobility was dependent upon its importance to the government of England.[13]

[13] *H. Mss. C., 7th Report*, Appendix, House of Lords Mss., p. 148; *L.J.*, XI, pp. 337-339, 358-359; W. S. Holdsworth, *History of English Law*, I, pp. 192-193.

# VIII

## THE HOUSE OF LORDS IN 1660

If the peers were, as individuals, subjects of the king, as members of the house of lords they often acted as if they wished to be at least his equals, if not superior to him, in political power. The Puritan Revolution had made clear that the prerogative could no longer claim full sovereignty in the state. If the king were kept without an army he could not in the long run hope to resist the will of parliament. In this sense ultimate sovereignty had passed to parliament. However, constitutional law did not yet reflect this conclusion, and during all of the reign of Charles II and that of his successor the controversy to decide who was to be the dominant partner in the state would continue. In forcing this decision the house of lords co-operated with the house of commons, and at times took the lead in subordinating the Stuarts to parliament. At the same time the houses conducted a running battle for powers and for privileges and the lords sometimes co-operated with the crown to check the lower house. The peers who took their seats in 1660 were very sensitive of their rights and aware of the power which the lower house had displayed, often at their expense, during the past two decades. So sensitive was the upper chamber that when messengers from the house of commons implied that the commoners might set the time of meeting of a free conference between the houses, the lords deemed it to be a breach of privilege. The source of the lords' sensitivity lay much deeper than such matters of privilege. They knew that the nation gave most attention to the deliberations of the house of commons. True, Englishmen were in favor of two houses, but the houses gradually seemed to acquire different functions. The lords might have judicial authority, but the commons had finance. The victory of the commons in financial matters was not yet complete, and would be challenged as late as 1741, or even 1909, but they held a decided advantage over the lords. In the rivalry between the houses, the lords had advantages of their own. On the issue of impeachments, lords and crown closed ranks against a frustated house of commons, which was able to claim only one victim by this method — an aged peer of little influence whose main crime was his Roman Catholicism. Charles himself had not calculated upon his return how valuable the lords were to prove in protecting his ministers. He as much as anyone was impressed by the lords' ability to give the commons a good battle in legal and financial disputes. The lords did hold some advantages which they could put to good use. They were largely spared the odium that attached in some degree to the house of commons for the excesses of the Interregnum. They could claim by the language of their writs of summons, *ad consentiendum et deliberandum de omnibus arduis regni negotiis*, as opposed to the commons' *quibusdam*, the right to a fuller role in and a broader right to consider all matters of state. Peers did not have to meet the religious requirements that the commons imposed on its members, and could claim to give a seat to those of their members who did not and would not accept the communion according to the rites of the Church of England. The membership of the lords contained many able and experienced men who were consistently superior to any counterparts in the commons throughout Charles's reign. The lords needed these advantages to maintain their place in the constitution through the unsettled years between the Puritan and Glorious Revolutions.[1]

The position of the upper house was substantially aided by the privileges of its members by virtue of being peers of parliament. As against the king, the lords' freedom of speech was subject only to the review of their own colleagues in the house. Charles II never repeated the mistake of his father in trying to breach the sanctuary of either house at Westminster, although he later would attend debates in the lords. As against the commons, the lords early moved to redress the wrongs they had suffered in the past. In June of 1660, they ordered the committee for privileges to consider "the great Violation that hath been committed upon the Peers of this Realm, by restraining their Persons, burning them in the Hand, refusing their Privileges

---

[1] J. R. Tanner, *English Constitutional Conflicts of the Seventeenth Century*, p. 218; W. S. Holdsworth, *History of English Law*, VI, pp. 208, 258; B.M., *Hargrave Ms.* 167 fo. 44; C. H. Firth, *House of Lords*, p. 296; J. P. Kenyon, "The Reign of Charles II", pp. 85, 85 n.; A. S. Turberville, "Lords under Charles II", XLIV, p. 406, XLV, p. 63; R. W. Perceval, "The Origins and Development of the House of Lords", p. 40; D. Ogg, *Reign of Charles II*, II, pp. 458, 465; *C.J.*, VIII, p. 289; F. P. G. Guizot, *History of Richard Cromwell*, II, p. 435.

when they have been claimed, or any other Breaches". They empowered the committee to summon offenders for examination. In this frame of mind, the lords cherished their privileges. These were of varying significance, just as their extra-parliamentary privileges were. They could and did pass bills and give judgments without the assent of the lords spiritual, but it concerned them more that no peer could be called to answer before the lower house only on an information or charge. However, the privilege perhaps most characteristic of their parliamentary status was the right of proxy.[2]

The right of proxy permitted a lord to cast his vote although he was absent from the house, by entrusting it as a proxy to another lord who did attend. It recognized the status of the peer whose voice was to be available to the king on all issues and at all times. There were certain regulations upon the use of proxies. While they had been recognized in some form as far back as the time of Edward I, or at least it was so argued, the use of proxies was not regulated until 1626. The abuses of the right of proxy by the first duke of Buckingham, who might have held as many as a third of all votes in the house on a given day, had led to this reform. The new rule allowed no peer to hold or vote more than two proxies. All proxies from spiritual lords must be made to spiritual lords, and from temporal lords to temporal lords. Any given proxy was good for the duration of one parliament only, and then only while the peer was actually absent. If he returned and left again, a new proxy was necessary, just as a new proxy was necessary at the opening of each new parliament. The clerk of the parliament kept records, or proxy books, which determined which proxies were in force. Their use was not too frequent. Only fourteen were made during the Convention Parliament. Only two peers, the duke of Albemarle and earl of Manchester, held two proxies. The proxy books for 1661 and 1662 no longer exist, but by 1663, the use of proxies had not risen greatly. In the session of that year twenty-seven proxies were made by twenty-six peers to twenty-one peers. Albemarle, Clarendon, Manchester, Ashley, and Lord Arundell held two.[3]

When parliament was in session peers had immunity from suits and

---

[2] D. Ogg, *Reign of Charles II*, II, p. 463; L. von Ranke, *History of England*, III, p. 325; *L.J.*, XI, p. 58; W. S. Holdsworth, *History of English Law*, VI, p. 244; B.M., *Add. Ms.* 22,181.

[3] E. Chamberlayne, *Angliae Notitia*, p. 257; B.M., *Hargrave Ms.* 168 fo. 14; House of Lords Record Office, *Proxy Books*, 1660, 1663.

ordinary civil proceedings at common law. Lord Mohun was faced with suits in the court of common pleas and with an action of eject- ment, that is an action charging the lord with a trespass upon the lease of a freeholder. The lords ruled that the cases could not proceed unless Lord Mohun waived his privilege of parliament. A peer could abuse this privilege as a means of avoiding just debts and other obli- gations. In 1661 the Earl Rivers had thirty-four declarations filed against him. There was a strong suspicion that the earl was evading substantial justice, but the lords duly ordered the actions against him halted. This privilege could also be extended to cover dependents of peers, as in the case of the earl of Strafford, who was able to stop proceedings against a tenant of his on grounds that the action would threaten his lordship's interest in the land. In other cases the lords declined to take a stand. Lord Petre had invoked privilege of parlia- ment in a suit against him by Lord Stourton. Stourton petitioned the lords either to hear the case themselves or to order Petre to waive his privileges, as the cause lay between peers. The lords did not act upon his petition. Lord Petre himself also petitioned the lords against the marquess of Worcester, arguing consideration of unique circum- stances in the case. His petition too went unanswered. In the case of Lady Dacre the lords did act. She requested the lords to stay a trial against her in common pleas. The lords judged that she had lost her right to privilege by having appeared in court to defend the action. In discussing the case, the legal aides asked if her marriage to a commoner had not terminated any claim at all to privilege. The lords judged that it had, and Lady Dacre lost on both grounds. Quite possibly the fact that the plaintiff was Sir Edward Nicholas prompted the attention the lords gave the case, but the house's decision had become the standard one.[4]

Peers not only had protection from suits but their goods and homes had a special security as well. The goods of peers could not be attached without legal proceedings, which of course were limited to time outside parliamentary sessions. The Westminster bailiffs had seized goods of the notorious debtor, the earl of Chesterfield, and he promptly complained to the house. He secured an order, though only after an eleven day wait, requiring the return of his goods. The house took no action against the bailiffs, perhaps suggesting that

---

[4] L.J., XI, pp. 187-188, 257, 269; H. Mss. C., 7th Report, Appendix, House of Lords Mss., p. 149; B.M., Add. Ms. 36,102 fos. 63-64, 80; C.S.P.D., 1661-1662, p. 32.

while they would preserve the privileges of their members, they would not condone the conduct of the earl. The lords also protected the houses of peers from search except under certain exact conditions. They required a warrant for the search under the sign manual, with the ratifying signatures of six members of the privy council, at least four of them peers. In 1662 the act for the ordering of the forces of the realm specifically barred the lords lieutenant, although peers, from searching the houses of any peers for illegally possessed arms. They had to request a particular and express order of the crown so to proceed.[5]

The most commonly exercised privilege was the immunity of peers and their servants from arrest in time of parliament. Upon this point the house was most punctilious; it constantly considered cases of this kind, usually concerning servants. In fact the whole scope of privilege, to both lords and commons, appeared to comprise a set of rights as vague and elastic as that high royalists claimed for the prerogative. Not until 1695 did courts gain authority to pronounce upon a privilege claimed by the house of lords, when Chief Justice Holt established the principle in Rex vs. Knollys. The only case of a peer being arrested in the early years of the restoration period came in May of 1660, when conditions were still unsettled and some over-zealous persons arrested the earl of Lincoln. The house of lords promptly summoned them to appear, but an action was not pursued. Cases involving servants were numerous. Those responsible for the arrests were either summoned to the lords to be reprimanded and to make their submission, or were detained in prison a while between those two steps. The gentleman usher served as private sheriff for the house of lords and had deputies appointed to help him handle the seizure of delinquents who transgressed the house's privileges. These unfortunates usually earned a short stay in the Fleet. The peers were usually reasonable about such offenders and requested their release after about a week's confinement. The house forbade in December of 1660 issuance of protections to servants who worked as menials on the estates of peers. The house also threatened punishment for the counterfeiting of protections. This privilege had no force in cases of treason, felony, or breach of the peace.[6]

[5]   B.M., *Add. Ms.* 36,922 fo. 7; *L.J.*, XI, pp. 56, 66; E. Chamberlayne, *Angliae Notitia*, p. 260.

[6]   A. S. Turberville, "Lords under Charles II", XLV, p. 74; W. S. Holdsworth, *History of English Law*, VI, pp. 257, 270-271; *L.J.*, XI, pp. 11, 25, 27, 29, 97, 107, 113, 214, 252, 261; *Steele*, I, p. 402.

Control of finance was largely the province of the commons, but the lords still retained the privilege of assessing themselves. Two weeks had not passed from the date of the lords' first sitting in 1660 when the house asked the committee for privileges to consider the subject. The committee reported on the restricted topic of militia assessments: "That their Lordships think it fit the Peers of this Kingdom do assess themselves with Horse and Arms for the Militia; and not to be rated and cessed by the Commissioners of the County." This decision flowed naturally from the traditional military service of the peerage to the crown. On May 9 the lords issued a proclamation affirming the statement by the committee. The lords did not confine their claim of assessment by themselves to the militia levies, but appointed in August John Clutterbuck to serve as collector of their money toward the disbanding of troops. Clutterbuck quickly gained semi-official prominence and continued to serve as collector of peers' moneys for poll bills. The lords revived the keeping of records by the old order of precedence among peers to facilitate the collecting and recording of peers' taxes. The most frequent of these was the poll tax.[7]

The poll tax was, roughly speaking, a tax upon the status of an individual, a sort of seventeenth century income tax with a graduated scale that rose to the £ 100 levied upon a duke or archbishop. Poll tax bills, like all money bills, were largely the business of the house of commons, which was especially tender of its rights wherever finance was involved. However, the lords were equally tender at the thought of being assessed by commoners. Thus the first poll bill in 1660 became a test to determine whose privileges would stand higher. In the test the lords achieved a clear victory. The bill came into the lords as a money bill from the commons, and merited quick passage. The lords, however, sent it to committee and boldly proceeded to make numerous amendments. They struck out a provision for taxing recusants double; they put in commissioners for collecting the tax in Cornwall. The lords also named commissioners for the Cinque Ports. Most important the lords provided for their own assessment. They then returned the bill to the commons. The house of commons rejected every amendment. In the first conference on the bill, on August 14, the lords held that "For the assessing of the Peers; were not the Proviso added, they might be assessed by Commoners; which

---

[7] B.M., *Harleian Ms.* 7158 fo. 2; *L.J.*, XI, pp. 15, 19, 21, 147, 231; *Steele*, I, pp. 385, 393.

their Lordships no way think fit, as not agreeable to their Right, and therefore have named Commissioners." When the conferees reported this, the commons agreed to the proviso in covering cases of peers assessed above the normal tax for their given ranks. The commons continued to insist that recusants pay double, and thus intended to place the Roman Catholic peers in the category of the proviso. In the second conference on August 15 the lords argued that the recusant provision trenched upon the privilege of peers. The lords also held out for the sole right of the house of lords to tax its members. The commons yielded on the recusant issue. The lords, with two victories won in the struggle over the bill, pressed for the third and most important. They offered a proviso that the effect of the act should not extend to peers, who would be assessed by lords appointed commissioners by the act. This was too much for the commons; they rejected the proviso by a vote of 86 to 70. At a conference the lords modified the proviso to leave the assessment to "such as are appointed by this act". The commons accepted this as not being a precedent and the bill became law. The lords had won the substance of the third point, since they had the right to appoint their own commissioners; the commons had only saved face. The commissioners, eleven in number, were all peers, headed by Clarendon, Southampton, Ormond and Manchester, the usual quadrumvirate. In the course of debate on the bill an old friend was heard from. Prynne, who had little good to say of the Cromwellian lords during their brief existence, now proposed that their titles might be recognized — to the extent of assessing them as peers. His proposal was dropped as being a penalty, and contrary to the act of indemnity.[8]

The principle the lords had established in the poll bill they attempted to apply to levies for support of the militia. They had pronounced their exemption from militia levies soon after their restoration. Later in 1660 they asked the committee for privileges to consider "how to provide to maintain the Privileges of Peers, in Point of the Militia, and paying of assessments...". The committee upheld the principle that no peer could be assessed toward the militia but by his own house. In late 1660 and 1661 the house of lords issued declarations to that effect. Not before March of 1662 did the house of

[8] D. Ogg, *Reign of Charles II*, II, p. 436; A. S. Turberville, "Lords under Charles II", XLV, p. 65; *L.J.*, XI, pp. 91-92, 97, 100-101, 127, 130, 153, 219, 232; *C.J.*, VIII, pp. 109-110, 121-122, 166-169; *Old Parliamentary History*, XXII, pp. 422-424, XXIII, pp. 45, 75-79.

commons challenge this concept, in the militia bill of that year. When the bill reached the lords, the upper chamber considered the challenge serious enough to examine the bill in committee of the whole house on four separate days. On April 17, the lords agreed to the proviso: "That the Peers of this Realm shall, according to the Proportion in this Act appointed, be assessed and charged with Horse and Arms, by Five or more of His Majesty's Privy Council, being Peers of this Realm, and not otherwise; any Thing in this Act to the contrary thereof notwithstanding." The commons objected to the proviso. They held that peers should be assessed as others in the bill, for the basis of the tax was land, not honors or position as in the poll tax. The lords were willing only to modify the proviso in terms of a committee of peers for collecting the lords' assessments, and added a device for collecting unpaid assessments of peers by the lords lieutenant. Again the commons objected; again the lords offered a modification — they would leave it to the king to name the commissioners to assess the peers. A third and a fourth conference between the houses followed on the peers' proviso. On May 17, about two months after the bill had started its course through parliament, the commons, though still objecting to the principle, gave way on the proviso, because the end of the session was near. Even so the final vote of the commons was a narrow 91 to 89. In its final form the proviso read that no peer should be charged with arms and horse but by themselves under a commission appointed by the king. Peers defaulting should not be imprisoned but distresses might be taken on their lands by the appropriate lords lieutenant. In the militia act as in the poll act, the house of lords had maintained its right of self-assessment against the commons' power of the purse.[9]

The lords for their part made strenuous efforts to collect the assessments due from their members, who were not accustomed to being pressed on bills. At first they used the lord chancellor's steward as collector, although they never confirmed his appointment. John Clutterbuck served as collector on the poll bills of 1660 and 1661. With the militia bill of 1662 pressure upon delinquent lords increased; from London the twelve lords commissioners appointed by the king made demands of them, and in the shires the lords lieutenant did the same. The lords not only fulfilled their statutory obligations but came to the aid of the crown with "free and voluntary presents".

[9]  E. Chamberlayne, *Angliae Notitia*, p. 260; *L.J.*, XI, pp. 193, 213, 233, 345, 413, 427-431, 454-466; *C.J.*, VIII, p. 433; *S.R.*, V, pp. 363-364.

These were sometimes given statutory form, as in 1661, but heavy expenses in paying off the fleet and garrisons led Charles to make sudden calls upon the nobility. Figures on the lords' generosity show that it varied. David Ogg credits them with £ 13,400 in the free and voluntary gift of 1661. A copy of Clutterbuck's acount for the poll bill in the *Lansdowne Manuscripts* gives a figure of £ 24,940 paid and £ 6,450 levied but still due. Certainly in free and voluntary gifts the peers approached their usual contributions in poll bills. The usual rates in these latter were £ 100 for dukes, £ 80 for marquesses, £ 60 for earls, £ 50 for viscounts, and £ 40 for barons. The levy upon a bishop was £ 60; a knight paid £ 20; and a gentleman of £100 annual income paid £5. Thus the average poll bill hardly touched the peer's pocketbook in proportion to its demands upon a gentleman. The voluntary gifts usually started at £ 100 and ran up to £ 400. Clutterbuck's account listed no return under £ 100, although Lord Powis paid £ 140 in two installments of £ 60 and £ 80. Dukes, marquesses, and officials of state usually paid £ 400. A few did not meet this standard. The marquess of Winchester paid only £ 200, and Ashley £ 300. On the other hand, lords Berkeley and Coventry both gave £ 400, as did the earls of Salisbury and Clare. Earls seemed to favor £ 200 and barons £ 100, although the individual wealth, generosity, and interest of various peers created frequent variations.[10]

The lords lost only one point regarding their claim of financial privileges in the early years of the restoration. A bill presented in 1662 provided for taxing the offices men held in order to raise £ 60,000 for loyal but indigent commissioned officers in the late conflict. The lords offered a proviso that "nothing in this Act contained shall be drawn into Precedent, as to the disposing of Monies formerly granted to the King or to the taxing of any Sort of man [*i.e.*, officeholders] distinct from the Body of People". The lords limited their concern to noble office-holders, as their declaration revealed when the commons rejected the proviso. The upper house then declared that they agreed to allow peers to be taxed by others than peers for their offices only because of the press of time and their concern for the indigent officers. They added that this was not to be taken as a precedent for taxing peers by others than peers. Despite this minor

---

[10]   B.M., *Add. Mss.* 34,217 fo. 73; 36,102; 36,922 fo. 14; *Lansdowne Ms.* 805 fos. 69-75; *L.J.*, XI, pp. 262, 264; D. Ogg, *Reign of Charles II*, II, p. 432; *C.S.P.V.*, 1661-1664, p. 85; "The Copy of an Order ... wherein every man is rated according to his Estate ...", in *Harleian Miscellany*, I, pp. 278-279; H.L.R.O., *Committee Appointment Books*, 1661-1664.

setback, the record of the house of lords in defending their privilege
of self-assessment was impressive in these years. The upper house
had shown determination to maintain its rights and success in its efforts toward that end.[11]

The lords enjoyed, in fact, a considerable measure of authority that
was only gradually regulated. A steady flow of orders from the lords
encroached upon executive and judicial functions usually vested in
crown or courts of law. Only as conditions became more settled did
the flow of orders subside, as a result of the firm opposition from the
commons. The largest category of these occasional orders gave peers
the right of general entry to search for goods of theirs lost or seized
during the late unpleasantness. In May of 1660, the lords gave the
earl of Northampton the right to search for valuable household possessions, and instructed the law officers "to break open, in the Day-
time", any door, trunk, chest, box, or other bar to access as should be
deemed necessary. In June they granted similar orders to the marquesses of Winchester and Worcester, earls of Derby, Dorset, and
Newport, Viscount Stafford, and Lord Arundell. Orders followed to
the earls of Bristol and Berkshire, and Lord Brudenell. Later orders
empowered a peer to seize his goods, "Wherever he shall find them".
Lord Craven and the countess dowager of Derby gained such powers.
When the proceedings of the peers on these orders were challenged,
the lords ordered the offender secured and called before the house
to answer for his temerity. Current complaints about the highness
of the lords' proceedings had foundation.[12]

While the house was usually deaf to protests rising outside its
walls, it provided for the hearing of protests from its members within
the chamber. The right of any peer to enter a recorded protest was as
ancient as the reign of Edward VI; the first signed protests appear in
the *Lords' Journal* in 1542. The protests were fairly numerous under
the two lesser Tudors, thirty-seven being recorded in Edward VI's
reign and twenty-two in Mary's. In Elizabeth's reign the protests fell
off precipitously, and only two were recorded after her first two
years. There was no recorded protest in James I's reign. Protests not
only increased in the reign of Charles I, but the innovation of protesting with reasons was added in 1640. The practice of fairly frequent
protests and the giving of reasons continued after the restoration. The

[11]   L.J., XI, pp. 436-439, 444-445, 466-467.
[12]   A. Amos, *The English Constitution in the Reign of Charles the Second*, p.
76; L.J., XI, pp. 76-79, 83, 88-89, 139-140, 142.

right of protest concludes the privileges peers possessed by virtue of their membership in the house of lords.[13]

The formal organization of the house of lords had been established in 1539 by the statute 31 Henry VIII, *cap.* 10. It provided that on the right side of the house from the throne should sit the archbishop of Canterbury, the archbishop of York, and the bishops of London, Durham, and Winchester. The other bishops were to sit in the order of their consecration. On the left side of the house, sitting above all dukes, except those who were the king's son, brother, uncle, nephew, or sons of his brothers or sisters, were the lord chancellor, lord treasurer, lord president of the council, and lord privy seal. The following officers sat first on the bench of the estate to which they belonged, regardless of antiquity: lord great chamberlain, constable, marshal, lord admiral, lord steward, and chamberlain of the house. If the chief secretary of the king were a peer or bishop, he sat above barons or bishops not holding offices. Peers not holding offices should sit according to their antiquity, in estates of duke, marquess, earl, viscount, and baron. If the lord chancellor, lord treasurer, lord president of council, lord privy seal, or chief secretary should not be peers, they were to sit on the upper part of the woolsack, in the center of the house of lords, either there to sit upon one form, or upon the uppermost woolsack, one above the other according to their rank of office. The twelve officers of the crown held precedence from the lord chancellor at the top, through the lord treasurer, lord president of the council, and lord privy seal to the lord great chamberlain, lord high constable, lord marshal, lord admiral, lord grand master, lord steward and the chamberlain of the house, with the king's chief secretary lowest. The order of the house was slightly modified after the act of Henry VIII. The lord chancellor, or lord keeper of the great seal, moved from the left side of the house to preside on the woolsack. The lord treasurer moved to the head of the earls' bench. At the restoration, the king directed that his brothers should sit immediately at the left hand of the chair of state, and Prince Rupert as duke of Cumberland was left to occupy the first place on the ducal bench. The lords otherwise adhered to the old order and dignity. They were still without robes in the Convention Parliament, but wore them at the opening of the Cavalier Parliament.[14]

[13]   J. E. T. Rogers, *A Complete Collection of the Protests of the Lords,* pp. v-vii, xiii.
[14]   B.M., *Add. Ms.* 28,792 fos. 6-7; *Hargrave Ms.* 167 fos. 5-6; *Stowe Ms.* 296

The Speaker of the house of lords was to be the lord chancellor or lord keeper. The Speaker occupied the woolsack, and did not possess the authority of the Speaker of the house of commons. Whether he be a peer or not, he was uncovered whenever he addressed the house in his capacity as Speaker. If he wished to speak substantively to a bill, he went down to his own place to speak and then returned to the woolsack. The Speaker might not without approval of the house adjourn the house or do any other thing but conduct the ordinary course of bills. And even in the routine of legislation, the house might overrule the Speaker. The lords in 1660 added to the role of the office of Speaker. When Clarendon took his place on the woolsack it was evident that the range of his duties would often take him out of the house, and a deputy would be needed. The lords resolved "That it is the Duty of the Lord Chancellor, or Lord Keeper of the Great Seal of England, ordinarily to attend the Lords House of Parliament; and that in case Lord Chancellor or Lord Keeper of the Great Seal be absent from the House of Peers, and that there be none authorized under the Great Seal from the King to supply that Place in the House of Peers, the lords may then choose their own Speaker during that Vacancy." The king, however, supplied the vacancy by appointing Sir Orlando Bridgman, lord chief baron of the exchequer, to preside when Clarendon was absent.[15]

Despite the provision of an alternate Speaker, the chancellor usually presided in the lords. Edward Hyde had received the custody of the great seal of England at Bruges in January of 1658. At that time the chancellorship entitled him to little more than a salary of £ 848 a year, unpaid. However, on June 1, 1660, Hyde, still a commoner, entered upon the regular discharge of his parliamentary duties, and took his place upon the woolsack. On November 11, 1660, he presented his patent as Baron Hyde of Hindon to the house, and was escorted to the last place on the barons' bench for a short while before returning to the woolsack. When parliament reassembled in 1661, he came in as earl of Clarendon. Clarendon was regularly in the house; he had one long absence due to ill health from the late summer of 1661 until December 19 of that year. Clarendon's handling of the house was distinguished, and as chancellor his formal addresses won

fo. 21; "A Perfect Catalogue of the Peers of the Realm of England . . ." (London, 1661), pp. 6-9; L.J., XI, p. 48; Pepys' Diary, I, p. 233.
[15]  B.M., Add. Ms. 36,102 fos. 9, 11; Hargrave Ms. 118 fo. 19; L.J., XI, pp. 55, 58-59.

acclaim for their eloquence. And for another reason, as Oldmixon justly observed, "the Lord Chancellor, according to Echard, made a handsome Speech; indeed it was handsomer than most of the rest of the Lord Chancellor's Speeches, because it was shorter." [16]

Beneath Clarendon, at the head of the earls' bench, sat the lord treasurer, Thomas Wriothesley, earl of Southampton. Unlike Clarendon, he played a steadily declining role in the house of lords, particularly after the death of a favorite daughter, which brought a heavy melancholy upon him. The next officer of note was the lord privy seal. William Fiennes, Viscount Say and Sele, briefly held this office in 1660. Say did not desire to retain it; lords Hatton and Robartes sought the post. The old royalists, and the duke of York in particular, favored Hatton but he failed to gain the seal. Charles chose Robartes to relieve the conflict in Irish affairs between him and Albemarle; probably Charles also wished another Presbyterian to follow the Presbyterian Say, the Anglican royalist Hyde having the great seal. Robartes entered the house of lords as privy seal on May 16, 1661, although the grant of the office did not clear the chancery until June. Clarendon described Robartes as "a Man of more than ordinary Parts, well versed in the Knowledge of the Laws, and esteemed of Integrity not to be corrupted by Money. But then He was a sullen, morose Man, intolerably proud...." He was a good servant to the house of lords, sitting on a large number of committees and representing the house frequently in conferences between the houses. In the house legal advisers assisted Clarendon and Robartes. Judges had once sat in the house of lords but had lost this privilege by the reign of Henry VIII. Their position in relation to the house of lords had remained undefined until June 4, 1660, when the house ordered "that the Lord Chancellor do move his Majesty that he would be pleased to give orders for writs to the Judges, whereby they may attend in the House as Assistants". The chancellor took up this request in the privy council, which decided to direct the judges to attend. To issue writs was deemed improper since the peers themselves did not have writs to the Convention Parliament. The chancellor and king also considered summoning all commoner members of the privy council to sit with the judges, but finally decided against doing so. In addition to Sir Edward Nicholas, the chief secretary, a number of legal assistants

[16]  J. Campbell, *Lives of the Lord Chancellors*, III, pp. 157, 165; E. Chamberlayne, *Angliae Notitia*, p. 131; *L.J.*, XI, pp. 176, 336, 355; B.M., *Add. Ms.* 27,590 fo. 91; J. Oldmixon, *History of England*, p. 473.

were summoned in 1661. Those summoned included the judges, the master of the rolls, the attorney-general, and two serjeants at law. Among this group were such able lawyers as Robert Foster, Harbottle Grimstone, Orlando Bridgman, Jeffrey Palmer, and the great Matthew Hale. Thus the house had a rich supply of legal talent.[17]

The most contested office was that of lord great chamberlain. The award of this office tended to be on the basis of traditional possession in a family or by old patent, as its holder had only honorary functions to perform. As the last holder had been the earl of Lindsey, the house of lords continued his son in the office. However, the earl of Oxford revived an ancient claim to the office in May of 1660. The earl of Derby followed with his claim on December 21. Baron Windsor added another six days later. The earl of Lindsey countered by claiming the earldom of Oxford on December 28. The lords, wisely, postponed from time to time the hearing of the petitions. At Charles's coronation the earl of Lindsey served as lord great chamberlain, but the issue was re-opened in the Cavalier Parliament. The king referred the petitions of the earls of Derby and Oxford back to the house of lords in June of 1661. The lords finally resolved the issue by rejecting both petitions, though Oxford's failed only by virtue of a tie vote.

Among other offices was that of the lord steward, now purely honorary. The marquess of Ormond held this office and sat on the earls' bench by virtue of his English peerage of Brecknock. Burnet described James Butler as "a man every way fitted for a court; of a graceful appearance, a lively wit, and a cheerful temper: a man of great expense, decent even in his vices; for he always kept up the form of religion". Ormond played little role in the house of lords, for he was usually absent, continuing to go "through many transactions in Ireland [undertaken] with more fidelity than success". The lord chamberlain of the house did play an important role in the lords. He was the earl of Manchester. Though disappointed in his hope of gaining the Treasury, he continued, according to Clarendon, "still to perform all good Offices to his old Friends, complied very punc-

---

[17]  B.M., *Add. Ms.* 29,550 fos. 400-401; *H. Mss. C.*, *5th Report*, Appendix, Part I, Duke of Sutherland Mss., pp. 156, 185; T. H. Lister, *Life and Administration of Clarendon*, II, p. 5; Clarendon's *Life*, pp. 1030, 1050; *C.S.P.D.*, 1661-1662, p. 26; *L.J.*, XI, pp. 52, 225; *Pepys' Diary*, II, 72 n.; L. O. Pike, *Constitutional History of the House of Lords*, pp. 247-248; W. D. Macray, ed., *Notes which Passed at Meetings of the Privy Council*, p. 18; E. Timberland, *The History and Proceedings of the House of Lords, from the Restoration in 1660, to the Present Time* (London, 1742), I, pp. 35-36.

tually with all the Obligations and Duties which his Place required, [and] never failed being at Chapel...." Manchester was a third to Clarendon and Robartes in these years in shouldering the burden of most of the official business of the house. By his reconciliation with the old royalists, he smoothed many difficulties from the path of the lords' business.[18]

The formal organization of the house was completed by the clerk of the parliament and the officers of the house, the usher of the black rod, the yeoman usher, the serjeant at arms, and their assistants. The clerk of the parliament was John Browne, a man in whose firm hand the records of the house have come through three centuries. The ordering of entry to and exit from the house of all but members was entrusted to Alexander Thayne, gentleman usher of the black rod. Black rod and his assistants usually apprehended delinquents and presented them before the house, although the lords reserved to themselves the right "to employ what Persons they shall think fit, for the sending for of Delinquents, and keeping them in safe Custody, as they shall see Cause". The lords petitioned the king on May 15, 1661 for two serjeants at arms to maintain order outside the walls of the house proper. The lords had customarily had such officers, but none had been appointed at the restoration. The lords complained of the difficult of entrance and egress through a mob of petitioners, courtiers, and hangers-on. Two days after the request, the lords received the two serjeants. The income of the officers came largely from regular fees from services in the house, and occasional fees such as every peer was expected to pay upon his first sitting in the house of lords. The major regular source of fees was from the private bills, which the house ordered paid before the second reading of any such bill. In 1662 the lords diverted the old 40s. fee on every private bill from the lords' entertainment to the payment of the reading clerk who attended them. As the restoration brought many occasional fees, and private bills were frequent in the early 1660's, the officers of the house fared unusually well.[19]

The functional organization of the house of lords was substantially dissimilar from its formal organization. The house had gained in

[18]   *L.J.*, XI, pp. 24, 220, 226-231, 252, 256, 265, 280-281, 288; *Old Parliamentary History*, XXIII, pp. 70-75; D. Ogg, *Reign of Charles II*, I, p. 181; Gilbert Burnet, *History of His Own Time*, 6 vols. (Oxford, 1823), I, p. 161; Clarendon's *Life*, p. 1005.

[19]   E. Timberland, *The History and Proceedings of the House of Lords*, I, pp. 35-36; *L.J.*, XI, pp. 85-86, 150, 224, 254-257, 462.

efficiency as a result of the Interregnum. This break in continuity served to interrupt the ties of the house to the Middle Ages. The lords in general adopted the habits of the house of commons in voting and procedure. An old house of commons man now occupied the woolsack. The efficient functioning of the house centered in its committees. Only when a committee of the whole house was in session did protracted debate take up the time of all its members. Although committees usually did not meet concurrently with the whole house, the sessions of the house were short, usually from nine or ten in the morning until noon or one in the afternoon. Thus sufficient time was afforded for committee sessions. The custom of referring a bill to committee had become the usual practice toward the end of the sixteenth century. In the mid-seventeenth century all bills originating in the house of lords went through committee at some stage. This was true of most bills sent up from the commons. Sometimes the lords rushed these through on the floor of the house when a session was near its end. As the commons pressed their rights on money bills, the need of a committee stage for this class of legislation declined. All members of the lords might attend, and any peer could speak there concerning a bill, though only members of the committee could vote. The house employed two types of committees, the great standing committees and their sub-committees, and *ad hoc* committees created to draft or study particular bills.[20]

The first of the standing committees was the committee for privileges, organized two days after the Convention Parliament sat. At first it was composed of twenty-seven members, with nine as a quorum. By the close of the Convention Parliament over sixty peers were members of the committee, including the most influential members of the house. The first order to the committee concerned the personnel of the house. "Ordered, That it is referred to the Lords Committees for Privileges, to consider of the different Cases of those Lords that have late come to sit in this House, and those as do not; and also what Assistants that formerly sat in this House are now alive, and capable of being admitted to be Assistants to this House." The committee was the starting place for any matter concerning the membership of the house. Its scope was even larger, as the house indicated when it

[20] R. W. Perceval, "The Origins and Development of the House of Lords", pp. 40-41; J. E. T. Rogers, *A Complete Collection of the Protests of the Lords*, p. v; Henry Elysinge, "The Method of Passing Bills in Parliament", in *Harleian Miscellany*, V, p. 228; B.M., *Hargrave Ms.* 167 fos. 29-30.

directed the committee in May of 1660, "to consider of the Privileges of this House, both in and out of Parliament; and what Order ought to be observed in the passing of Business between both Houses". The order of affairs inside the house was also the business of the committee. It first dealt with the question of the lords choosing their own Speaker. In the Cavalier Parliament the committee swelled to eighty-seven members, nine from the episcopal bench. Attendance on the committee was less important than membership, since much of the committee's work was routine. However, if any important matter did concern the lords, at least one significant vote was apt to occur in that committee. The committee could be overriden, and matters referred to it for action could be withdrawn by the whole house. This happened with the committee's investigation of peers who had abjured the king, which the whole house decided to pass over in silence, although the action elicited a protest from the lord privy seal and Lord Willoughby. More mundane matters also concerned the committee as an order of December 15, 1660, illustrated: "That it is referred to the Committee for Privileges to consider of improving of Seats for the Lords in this House, the better to prevent Disorder in the House when they come to voting, for Want of Seats." More typical of the committee's business was a protest that the Irish Viscount Brouncker had taken his place before English barons at a public function. The outraged lords brought a report from the committee that "Every Peer of England hath, by Right, Precedency in England, before all other Peers and Noblemen whatsoever". The records of the house were also the committee's responsibility. In June of 1660 the lords established a sub-committee to examine the journal book on every Saturday and indicate their approval of its contents by their signatures. In May of 1661 they expanded the role of this sub-committee to include "Consideration of the Customs and Orders of the House, and Privileges of the peers of this Kingdom and Lords of Parliament". Thus the sub-committee became record-keeper and memory to the committee and acquired much of the committee's original function as the committee undertook a greater variety of business.[21]

The second great standing committee of the house of lords was the committee for petitions. This committee served as the center of the lords' judicial functions. This centralization did not immediately take

[21] H.L.R.O., *Minute Book of the Committee for Privileges*, I, pp. 1-2; *Committee Appointment Books*, 1661-1664; *L.J.*, XI, pp. 5, 30, 53, 59, 61, 68, 194, 211, 250-252, 333, 340, 345, 398-399, 422; B.M., *Harleian Ms.* 7158 fo. 208.

place. In June of 1660 the lords required all petitions read before the whole house, and ordered that every peer possess a copy before they were referred to the committee for petitions. Another order barred the committee from exercising exclusive control of petitions; at the same time it laid down rules of procedure.

Ordered, That in all Cases of Petitions read in this House, and referred by their Lordships Order to any Committee, the Party upon whose Petition the Order of Reference is granted do take out the said Order from the Clerks attending in this House, and bring it to that Committee, or the Clerk attending the same, whereby Cognizance is to be taken of such Petition by that Committee; or else the Petitioner is to have no benefit of the Reference.

The large number of petitions coming into the house and its increased business in other areas led to a new order in May of 1661 strengthening the role of the committee. "Ordered ... That the Lords Committees for Petitions shall hereby have the Power to receive and consider of Petitions, and make Report to this House, and to reject such as are not fit and proper for the Cognizance of this House; and also shall have Power to send for Parties and Witnesses, as they shall see cause."

The pressure of numerous petitions also provoked an order "That the Committee for Petitions do dismiss all Private Petitions between Party and Party, which may have Relief in any other Court of Law or Equity". Despite this order few petitions were so dismissed. The committee took its equitable function seriously and applied the concept to its procedures. When a petition involved a case between a peer and a commoner, the committee accorded as a privilege to the commoner the right the peer had to be present at the committee hearings. Unlike the committee for privileges, the committee for petitions was renewed or "revived" at the opening of each session. The lords did this regularly, and renewed automatically the powers and membership of the committee, so that it had more the character of a standing committee. The committee also was assisted by a subcommittee. In July of 1660 the house directed the committee to appoint eight peers, with three a quorum, to review petitions already referred to the committee and determine which were fit to present to the committee, which to the house, and which should be dismissed. This function was later expanded to cover petitions, whether or not they were referred to the committee. So large was the number of petitions presented to the house during the unsettled period from 1660 to 1680 that the sub-committee would have failed if it had been inefficient. Fortunately, five of the original eight members were among the most able men in the house. The young earls of Dorset, Bridgwater, and Portland carried a good portion of the committee work of the lords. Viscount Say and Lord Wharton were old and able workers. However, Dorset was the only one of the five who remained on the expanded sub-committee of November, 1660. The addition of Baron Robartes and the earls of Lindsey and Bolingbroke kept a core of at least four able men at work on the processing of petitions.[22]

Most petitions to the lords either asked for special redress which, the petitioner said, the courts could not provide, or appealed the decisions of the courts. However, the committee was from time to time called upon to deal with less common petitions. One group involved disputes within noble families. In June of 1660 the marquess of Winchester and his son, Lord St. John, were in conflict over property ownership, and on petition from Lord St. John the matter went to the committee for petitions. The committee struggled with the two haughty Paulets until they despairingly asked the chancellor to move the king "That He would be pleased to use His Wisdom and Mediation, that so a Reconciliation may be made between the said Marquis and his son, and a Determination of all Differences between them". The king's luck was not notably better; the dispute remained under discussion in the spring of 1662, and had drawn in four more members of the Paulet clan. As difficult a task in another regard was the flood of petitions for restitution that came to the committee in the wake of the Interregnum. The plight of many ministers was particularly moving. The committee for petitions could do little in this regard to improve on the provisions made in the general legislation of the restoration settlement. Less tolerable but not less trying were petitions for revenge that accompanied those for restitution. Notable among them was the request of the countess dowager of Derby for satisfaction in kind upon her husband's "murderers". The committee was relieved of this plea when proceedings on the act of indemnity caused the countess's petition to be transferred to the special committee for that bill.[23]

---

[22]  *L.J.*, XI, pp. 43, 52, 69, 81, 184, 251, 258, 333, 359; H.L.R.O., *Committee Appointment Books,* 1661-1664; *Order Books of the Committee for Petitions,* I, p. iv.

[23]  *L.J.*, XI, pp. 55-58, 67, 73, 401, 408, 436; H.L.R.O., *Order Books of the Committee for Petitions,* I, p. iv.

Every bill passed through a committee, as a rule; usually the lords approved a special committee for each individual bill. Although the number of committees was thus large, the number of peers involved composed but a small part of the house. This can be seen from a sample of seventy-one committees in the first three sessions of the Cavalier Parliament of which fifty-one committees included bishops, who did not come in until the start of the second session. The seventy-one committees represent about half of the committees in the three sessions; they examined about 80 per cent of all public bills considered and about 60 per cent of all private bills concerning peers, as well as some private bills of general interest. Four peers sat on fifty or more committees, whose size ranged considerably with an average membership usually in the mid-twenties. Twelve peers, including one bishop, sat on forty or more committees. Twenty peers, including two bishops, sat on thirty or more committees, and thirty-three peers sat on twenty or more committees. Thus of 140 peers, temporal and spiritual, who sat on at least one committee, less than a quarter of them actually bore most of the committee work of the house. Most active was the thirty-eight year old John Egerton, earl of Bridgwater, who participated in sixty-seven of a possible seventy-one committees. One of the four committees he did not sit on concerned him and the only significant committee he did not sit on was concerning the act restoring the temporal power of the bishops. Jerome Weston, earl of Portland, was second in committee service, with fifty-six committees to his credit. The forty-seven year old earl of Anglesey and twenty-seven year old earl of Bolingbroke both sat on at least fifty committees. Of the prominent members of the house, Baron Robartes led with forty-seven committees, followed by Ashley on forty-two. The earl of Manchester sat on thirty. John Cosin, bishop of Durham, led the episcopal bench with forty-three committee assignments, followed by Humphrey Henchman, bishop of Salisbury, with thirty-seven. Gilbert Sheldon, of London, sat on twenty-seven. The most active peers were generally young. Of those who sat on thirty or more committees, ten were under fifty, nine older, none above sixty-nine. Six were not yet forty. This group bore the greater burden of the business of the house of lords.[24]

The house as a corporation exercised tight control over its business. This was assumed to start with regulation of its own members. The

[24] See Appendix A for a table of peers and their committee service.

lords determined their own membership against outside challenges; for example, from the commons' objection to the right of bishops to sit in the Danby impeachement of 1679. But this unchecked control of membership could be a disability to the individual peer. The house, like the commons, held the right to commit a member to custody if he infringed upon the rules or traditions of the house. In such cases the lords asserted the principle that the law courts had no jurisdiction. The house determined what qualifications it expected of its members. The lords determined what oaths with regard to religion would be required of members until the time of the test act. The house could further challenge a member. They subjected Viscount Hereford to scrutiny when rumor said that Charles I had challenged his right to his title; they considered the question whether the viscount had been disloyal in past years. As usual, the Roman Catholic peers were the most harassed. All of them acknowledged the temporal authority of the king over them, but they were still favorite objects of criticism, in an age when "No Popery" was perhaps the most popular public outcry.[25]

The house also regulated the seating and behavior of its members. Rules required them to be in regular attendance, and fixed a fine of 5 s. a day for the benefit of the poor if they were absent without a "just Excuse". Excuses were fairly freely granted and were of two kinds. More common was the excuse for a specific purpose, but the house also issued to one or another of the more infirm members "Liberty to be absent from his Attendance on this House as often as he finds Occasion, in respect of his Indisposition of Health and Lameness". The lords took polls shortly after a new parliament opened, and often after a new session. Here they either renewed or cancelled all excuses and set up the roll of membership for the session. The house also regulated the lords' attendants and assistants. Of the servants of individual peers, only gentlemen attendants were permitted as near as the painted chamber, where footmen, lackeys, and other attendants were barred. The gentlemen had to remain uncovered whenever a peer was in that room. The black rod alone of the non-clerical officers of the house was permitted to stay within the doors of the chamber. The yeoman usher had the privilege of unrestricted entry,

---

[25] Bodley, *Rawlinson Mss.* A 138 fos. 1-21; A 168 fo. 285; B.M., *Add. Ms.* 15,574 fos. 65-67; D. Ogg, *Reign of Charles II*, II, pp. 460-461; E. Chamberlayne, *Angliae Notitia*, p. 258; H.L.R.O., *Minute Book of the Committee for Privileges*, I, p. 16; *L.J.*, XI, pp. 58, 61, *C.S.P.D.*, 1660-1661, p. 217.

but only to deliver messages and depart at once. The house determined the duties and fees and servants of the house.[26]

The house regulated its times of sitting and the times and places of committee meetings. At first meetings began at nine in the morning but on June 7, 1660, the house adjourned until ten the following day, which hour then became the usual meeting time. Sessions seldom ran long into the afternoon. The commons on one occasion pressed the lords to meet regularly in the afternoon as well as in morning sessions but the lords refused. They replied that they would hold such sessions only on "emergent occasions" but not otherwise, as it would too much handicap the business of their committees. The house was generally sensitive of its committees' work, and often declined the commons' wish for special meetings. At the end of sessions, however, afternoon sittings did frequently occur. Such minor matters as the form of prayers to be read in the house were dealt with, and the house provided "That no Penalty, Prejudice, or Reflection, shall be upon any that are not present at Prayers". Over its records the house held strict control. It guarded the privacy of its meetings by restricting the information entered in the journal. The motions of the house were recorded but not the movers; no numbers reveal the size of votes which passed or rejected bills. Not a word of debate appears in official records. Their impersonality is nearly complete. The lords further discouraged much comment upon their activities and had sufficient power to make reporters conscious of the wisdom of silence. Thus the interspersing of diaries or memorials rarely adds to the formality of the public records.[27] Giavarina, the Venetian resident, complained to the Doge and Senate:

As many acts of parliament have subsequently been made public with sinister interpretations, to prevent this in the future they have passed a resolution ... forbidding any member to talk of what takes place in the assembly, no matter what its nature, under severe penalties, and the printers are also forbidden to print what may come to their knowledge without a special order of parliament, so it will now be very difficult to find out about their decisions.

Both houses published by declarations that part of their wishes they desired to be known, but little more. The lords were the more pro-

---

[26] B.M., *Hargrave Ms.* 167 fos. 5-6; *L.J.*, XI, pp. 8, 111-112, 215, 253, 255, 259.

[27] *L.J.*, XI, pp. 50, 56, 155, 216; J. E. T. Rogers, *A Complete Collection of the Protests of the Lords*, p. xii; Caroline Robbins, "The Repeal of the Triennial Act in 1664", *Huntingdon Library Quarterly* (San Marino), 1949, p. 121.

lific with these in the first years of the restoration. Here, too, the house exercised care. They specified "That no Orders of this House shall be printed and published without special Order of this House". They entrusted the chancellor with the duty of bringing to the house's attention such orders when necessary. Speeches were occasionally authorized for printing, but usually only formal addresses.[28]

Rules covered debate in the house as everything else. Since the lords sitting seldom numbered above a hundred they could and did permit informality in their discussions. Still, the house was careful to read its standing orders at the opening of sessions and to enforce them. No peer was permitted to speak twice to a bill at a single reading, except to explain or clarify some point. In 1661 the house had to insist further that every lord both sit and speak at his place. Peers customarily spoke to the house standing. In May of 1661 the lords also restricted new motions to introduction before noon. The division of the business under debate between public and private matters was more exact than in the commons, which dealt with less private business than the upper house. When pressed, the lords would order all private business suspended until public matters could be completed. These orders could be general, until public business was determined, or could bear specific dates during which time private matters were suspended.[29]

The house directed the flow of bills in two ways. The house assigned specific dates for the introduction of a bill and subsequent dates at each stage of its progress. From time to time the lords placed major pieces of legislation in the category of first business, and gave precedence over any other bills depending in the house. Usually no one spoke at the first reading of a bill, unless to move for the rejection of it. On the second reading every member might speak, though but once substantively. If the bill were to be committed after its second reading, every peer might speak on the motion for commitment. Little debate was expected on a third reading unless the bill had emerged substantially modified from a committee, in which case the amendment needed two readings before being joined to the bill for a third reading. The lords amended bills sent from the commons by interlineating changes between printed lines if space al-

---

[28]  *C.S.P.V.*, 1659-1661, p. 167; *Steele*, I, pp. cvi, 384-388; *L.J.*, XI, pp. 48, 57, 79; B.M., *Add. Ms.* 36,102 fo. 4.

[29]  B.M., *Stowe Ms.* 296 fo. 21; *L.J.*, XI, pp. 29, 95-96, 250, 252, 316, 352; D. Ogg, *Reign of Charles II*, II, p. 466.

lowed; if not, on separate sheets. If the commons approved the amendments, a new printing was struck. For both houses, actual amending of the bill took place in the house of origin; the "amendments" of the other house being technically directions for amending the bill. The rules of the house for voting were brief. A member who stayed through a debate was obliged to vote. The lords still voted in their places, and failure to do so disqualified a vote; this the house decided when such an issue arose on May 21, 1661. In January of 1661 the house supported the old rule of Elizabeth's time of *semper praesumitur pro negante* — when votes are equal, including proxies, the motion or bill is lost. Eventually considerable skill developed in The house for putting close motions so that a tie vote by this rule would bring a desired result. The assent of the lords spiritual was not necessary for the passing of legislation. Bills could receive the royal assent either from the king or by commission. Charles II usually attended to this duty in person, but on May 2, 1662, he sent a commission to pass two bills into law. He commissioned six peers for this purpose — the chancellor, treasurer, privy seal, great chamberlain, duke of Albermarle, and marquess of Dorchester — or any two of them. All six in fact participated in the ceremony.[30]

Although the lords were solicitious of the work of their committees when approached by the commons, the business of the house took automatic precedence over the business of the committees, whether they were standing or *ad hoc*. When the house suspended private business the committee for petitions too would cease work, as its membership usually duplicated in large part the membership of committees being pressed to prepare the public bills for consideration. Under ordinary circumstances, however, the standing committees had precedence over all others. The committee for petitions sat regularly on Wednesday and Friday afternoons, and no other committees were permitted to sit then, except on extraordinary occasions. The minor committees were usually given only a regular place and hour of meeting, and could meet every day or at intervals of several days, unless the house directed otherwise. Duplication of membership made flexibility necessary so that the men most concerned could discharge their duties in the house, on the standing committees, in private committees, and in some instances, attend to the duties of their high offices. The house not only regulated the meeting of private committees, but instructed them in policy, as it did in ordering that whenever a com-

[30] B.M., *Add. Ms.* 36,102 fos. 24, 29-30, 51-52, 57; *L.J.*, XI, pp. 96, 155.

mittee made a saving of the rights of particular persons in a bill, there must be a saving for the right of the king.[31]

The grip of the rules of the house upon debate and the course of bills loosened at only one point. By an order of April 18, 1626, if any lord requested that the lords go into committee of the whole house, it ought not be refused without good reason. Here debate was least restricted. The house in committee of the whole could appoint sub-committees to go into the painted chamber adjacent or elsewhere to work on difficult aspects of a bill. The house did not determine until 1662 that its chairman should be the lord chamberlain when in committee of the whole. The last method available to the conduct of business was a committee of both houses of parliament. This expedient had more an executive than legislative function, and was most mentioned immediately following the restoration. It quickly gave way to the more normal course of business. Relations between the houses were usually restricted to formal occasions, free conferences to settle disputes on legislation, and messages. The lords themselves always sent, and never carried, messages to the commons. When they received messages from the commons, only the Speaker of the lords went to the bar of the house to receive them. The rest of the house remained seated in their places. The functional structure of the house of lords served both its legislative and judicial obligations. It discharged the bulk of its judicial duties either by bill or by the committee for petitions and the house proceeding in a legal way.[32]

The legislative role of the house of lords embraced all bills, but the the house had special responsibility for some. The declining fortunes of the house of lords were most clearly seen in regard to public bills. Almost all of these now entered parliament by way of the house of commons. Those few which did not were usually brought into the lords as deliberate government policy produced by fear of a hostile commons. The lords were left largely to initiate a variety of private bills. Only an act of parliament could grant naturalization, and the preliminary work in discharging this function was left to the lords. There were not many such bills, and about half the persons concerned had either married nobles in exile or were their children born abroad. Such bills received prompt attention, but the house required those who wished to be naturalized to take the oaths of allegiance

---

[31]  L.J., XI, pp. 102, 117, 133, 207, 211, 359, 375, 428, 435.
[32]  B.M., *Hargrave Ms.* 167 fos. 29-30; *H. Mss. C., 7th Report,* Appendix, House of Lords Mss., p. 81; *L.J.,* XI, pp. 30-31.

and supremacy before the second reading of their bills. The period of turmoil which produced the exiles also produced many claims for justice outside the court system. When Charles closed the third session of the Cavalier Parliament he recognized that many such bills had been necessitated by past events, but in the summer of 1662 he felt the need had passed, and urged the lords not to present so many private bills to him again. At the same time, both he and the government saw fit to call upon the lords to initiate bills. The lords had the duty on one occasion to consider a bill to prevent the transportation of money out of England. They promptly addressed themselves to this very pressing problem. Actually, the frequency of private bills threatened to upset the government nearly as much as the loss of wealth. Clarendon complained at length:

The long time spent in Both Houses upon the Act of Uniformity had made the Progress of all other publick Business much the slower; or rather, the Multitude of Private Bills which depend there (and with which former Parliaments had been very rarely troubled), and the Bitterness and Animosities which arose from thence, exceedingly disquieted and discomposed the House; every Man being so much concerned for the Interest of his Friends or Allies, that He was more solicitous for the Dispatch of those, than of any which related to the King and the Publick. . . .

The judges and lawyers also showed concern about this trend. Largely under Clarendon's and the king's pressure, the crush of bills subsided, and with the bills, much of the business of the upper house.[33]

The judicial business of the lords came into the house in two forms — appeals from decrees of law or equity and petitions of original complaint. The house did not hesitate to undertake either form of jurisdiction. Petitions of original complaint were numerous. The lords accepted them initially with little more requirement than that they be signed by the petitioner. While most petitions were on behalf of an individual or few persons, at least one petition of more general significance came before the lords in these years. The commons in 1660 had desired to enforce all the penal laws against the Roman Catholics and had sent a declaration to the lords to this effect. The lords, however, declined to act upon it. Aside from that brief flurry the Catholic question was relatively quiet until the lords proceeded to the reading of the acts of supremacy and allegiance on June 10, 1661. At that time Lord Lexington brought in a petition signed by five

---

[33] L.J., XI, pp. 82, 145-146, 150, 474; Clarendon's Life, p. 1082; J. Thirsk, "The Restoration Land Settlement", p. 221.

Roman Catholics. The petitioners pleaded the loyalty of Englishmen of their faith to the crown in the past two decades, and asked upon that ground, and the promise of the Declaration of Breda, that they be relieved of oaths "so penned as might occasion scruple". On both June 10 and 11 the lords debated this petition in the chamber and concluded with the resolution that "nothing hitherto hath been offered to this house to move their lordships to alter anything in the said oaths". However, the lords re-opened the subject on the 14th, and asked the judges to bring in a list of all the penal statutes involved. On the 21st further recusant petitions asked relief from the sanguinary laws. After a long debate the lords adjourned with nothing settled. On June 28 the house re-affirmed its judgment of the 11th, concerning oaths, but did appoint a committee to examine the sanguinary laws. Three Roman Catholic peers sat on this committee of thirty-three. Upon its report on July 16, the house asked the committee to take up consideration of repeal of all or parts of five sanguinary laws and the writ *de Haeretico comburendo*. Nothing more was heard of the matter. Conflicting testimony concerning its fate exists. Clarendon, in his *Life* attributed its disappearance to a split between the English and Ultramontane parties within the Roman Catholic community, who could not agree on the Pope's temporal authority. Clarendon's biographer, Lister, recorded that a request by the Roman Catholic peers stopped the proceeding. This was caused by a split over immunities for the Jesuits within the Catholic community. Kennet gives a different account in his *Register*, based upon the testimony of the aged Viscount Stafford in his examination during the Popish Plot. Stafford stated that the Catholics had tried to proceed through the legislature to gain relief, but Clarendon had firmly opposed them and defeated their efforts.[34]

If there was an occasional petition of interest, no writ of error that the lords considered was of note. All writs of error in all causes were judged to lie properly before the king and lords only; they could decide the cause themselves or appoint a steward to direct an inquiry. Appeals upon writs of error were frequent, and came into the

---

[34] Sir Matthew Hale, *The Jurisdiction of the Lords House, or Parliament, considered according to the Ancient Records,* Francis Hargrave, ed. (London, 1796), p. xci; *L.J.,* XI, pp. 95, 276-277, 279, 286-287, 291, 310-311; *C.S.P.V.,* 1659-1661, p. 221; H.L.R.O., *Stanford Mss.,* Nos. 20, 21; *H. Mss. C., 7th Report,* Appendix, House of Lords Mss., p. 144; Clarendon's *Life,* pp. 1071-1072; T. H. Lister, *Life and Administration of Clarendon,* II, pp. 199-200; W. Kennet, *Register,* p. 142.

house under the signature of the attorney-general. The committee for privileges assumed responsibility for such appeals once they were in the house, and established procedures concerning such matters as the assignment of costs. In reaching a decision, the lords relied mainly upon the advice of their judicial assistants. An abuse grew up from the appeals by persons taking out writs of error merely to delay or avoid a judgment in a judicial proceeding. Thus the house ordered on December 13, 1661, that a plaintiff must prosecute his writ within eight days of bringing it, or lose the benefit of the writ. An associated complaint concerned the bringing of a writ simply as a vexatious procedure. The lords judged one Woodman, plaintiff, guilty of this practice and ordered him to pay the defendant £ 20 and costs within ten days of February 15, 1662. Harding, plaintiff, suffered the same fate in April of that year. The house gave final acceptance to few writs of error; they exercised sparingly this feature of their judicial function.[35]

In addition to judgment upon petitions and writs of error, and staying proceedings at common law by privilege of parliament, the house had judgment in two other areas. It could proceed against delinquents in capital cases as well as for misdemeanors and it could decide suits long depending in other courts either for the difficulty of the cause or any other delay. No case of the last type came before the house in three years, while the house often proceeded against delinquents in cases of privilege, though never for capital crimes. Beside the legislative and judicial functions of the lords, its executive functions were slight. On two occasions it simply ordered the Westminster justices of the peace to mend the streets about Parliament. The second order concluded that the justices "will answer the contrary at their Perils". Proceedings of this kind were, however, extraordinary. The first three years of the restoration provided the lords with a more active role in the government than they had enjoyed for many years, or would for some time again. Although the commons continued their effort to limit the lords' role, the upper chamber participated equally with the lower house in the major legislation of the restoration settlement.[36]

[35] B.M., *Hargrave Mss.* 110; 115 fos. 60-61; *Stowe Ms.* 375 fo. 5; A. S. Turberville, *The House of Lords in the Reign of William III*, p. 96; *L.J.*, XI, pp. 349, 385-386, 433-434, 439-440, 445.

[36] B.M., *Add. Ms.* 15,087 fo. 3, *Lansdowne Ms.* 506 fos. 1-2; *L.J.*, XI, pp. 140-143, 322; *H. Mss. C.*, *5th Report*, Appendix, Part I, Duke of Sutherland Mss., p. 205.

# LORDS AND COMMONS

In 1660 the house of lords renewed its struggle with the house of commons. The lower house had been the gainer in this conflict for many years, and had temporarily achieved supremacy. The lords were not prepared to submit to this change in their status without a contest. Sir William Holdsworth concluded that "it is largely for this reason that we find more controversies between the two Houses during this period than at any other period in their history". From the moment the Convention Parliament assembled this conflict was latently present, but did not at once rise to upset relations. The houses began with a show of co-operation and joined in committees to deal with the most pressing claims of an unsettled state. The existence of difficulties, though, was acknowledged on May 22, 1660, and a joint committee was appointed for their settlement. The lords assigned several of their best men to this body — Southampton, Manchester, Bridgwater, and Northampton. They also appointed men with strong ties to the lower house, such as Robartes and Say. Unfortunately, the quality of this lordly group was marred by the presence of Buckingham and Northumberland, a pair who combined tactlessness with haughtiness. The committee did not play a prominent role in relations between the houses.[1]

Sufficient avenues of communication were open to the houses without relying upon this special committee. The two houses often used messages, sometimes oral, less frequently written, to transmit information and opinions. In 1660 the committee on privileges reaffirmed the custom of only the Speaker of the house of lords going to the bar to receive messages from the commons. Such messages had the disadvantage of coming "without reasons"; they did not resolve con-

---

[1] W. S. Holdsworth, *History of English Law*, VI, pp. 248-249; H.L.R.O., *Committee Appointment Books*, 1661-1664.

flicts but by capitulation of one house to the position of the other. Hence conferences between the two houses were the usual means of smoothing conflict. The lords emphasized this method in May of 1662, when they complained to the commons regarding a bill the lower house had sent up and which the lords had returned to it amended. The commons had sent the bill again to the lords, agreeing with some but not all the lords' amendments, and further adding some amendments of their own. The lords objected on two grounds. They held in the first place that in cases of such differences between the houses the opinions of the commons should have come in a message, not in bill form. Secondly, the message should be a request for a conference, where reasons are given for differences of opinion. The lords returned the bill to the commons with the request that the proper course of parliament be followed. The lords were particularly jealous of the "proper course" of parliament. On one occasion the commons requested a conference in the painted chamber. The lords replied that this was a breach of their privilege to appoint the time and place of all conferences. The commons apologized, stating that the inclusion of the place had been a mistake, and erased it from their books.[2]

Requests for conferences were about evenly divided between the two houses in the first three years of the restoration. These were usually held in the painted chamber, hence the commons' natural mistake of including the place in their request. The conferences served many uses, the most usual being to reach agreement upon legislation and expedite its passage. The closing days of sessions brought a rise in conferences, which were quicker than a succession of messages for reaching agreement on bills. Each house appointed managers to present its position on an issue and argue its case. These were usually the more prominent public figures in either house, though occasionally an individual primarily concerned with a particular piece of legislation would present it, regardless of his general influence. Hyde, before he was raised to the peerage, was permitted to act as manager for the lords by the house's special approval. By a rule of July 1, 1641, at a conference no lord might speak contrary to the general sense of the house. Occasionally strange things happened in conferences. On July 21, 1661, a printing bill was offered to the solicitor-general at a conference and he declined to receive it. The

[2] B.M., *Hargrave Ms.* 167 fo. 39; *Add. Mss.* 27,590 fo. 12; 36,102 fo. 50; *L.J.*, XI, pp. 274-276, 453.

bill was left on the table in the painted chamber and never "heard of more". The smoothing of the legislative process remained the chief function of the conference, but its secondary role was to aid in the resolution of conflicts between the houses. These conflicts centered on the lords' claims in judicial matters and the commons' claims in financial matters.[3]

That the lords possessed a special role in judicial matters was widely acknowledged at the restoration. The Speaker of the commons referred to this at the close of the first session of the Cavalier Parliament. "Amidst these Noble English Barons are placed the Reverend Judges of the Land, the Sages of the Law; Men so learned and expert in the Customs and Statutes of this Land, that if Wat Tyler, or Jack Cade, or the new Fanatics of this latter Age, had burned our Books, they were able to restore our Laws in Purity and Perfection." The Speaker refrained from praise of the lords themselves, nor did he define the proper judicial functions of the upper chamber. In fact, that jurisdiction was not fixed. Anciently it had been largely an original jurisdiction in grave cases, but by the fifteenth century had become more a jurisdiction in error. Both jurisdictions survived the Tudors, and the lords set about expanding their legal interests in the reign of James I. The house exercised an original jurisdiction in a civil case between Canningham and the Muscovy Company. This practice continued under James's son, and the lords went on to exercise appellate jurisdiction over courts of equity, by ordering further proceedings before them. Under the first two Stuarts the old process of impeachment again became popular. The great revolution checked the progress of the lords in judicial matters, but not their ambitions. They declared that theirs was the chamber "where his Majesty is highest in his royal estate, and where the last resort of judging upon writs of error, and appeals in equity, in all causes and over all persons is undoubtedly fixed and permanently lodged". As if this were not enough, the earl of Anglesey argued that peers were really better judges than those of Wesminster Hall, being *judices nati*. He argued that all other judges were under salary, and even the commons received wages, thus the unpaid peers were the freer judges. The commons disputed much of the lords' claims, and conflict first broke out over the right of the lords to act as a court of the first instance in civil matters. The lords first claimed this power in a case between an individual and a trading

[3] B.M., *Hargrave Ms.* 178 fos. 68-70; *Harleian Ms.* 7158 fos. 127-130; *Stowe Ms.* 296 fo. 23; *Add. Ms.* 36,102 fos. 12, 47-48; *L.J.*, XI, pp. 150, 230, 465.

company; so in a similar case they lost it — in the case of Skinner *vs.* East India Co.[4]

Although this case was largely fought out later in the restoration period, it had its origins in 1660 when the two parties first clashed and the East India Company originally brought the matter of Skinner's attempts to trade within its patent to the attention of the lords. The two parties reported to the lords that they had reached a private agreement and the matter was not then proceeded with. When the case reappeared, Skinner was complainant. Skinner in particular claimed that he could not find justice either in law or chancery. The lords attempted to act as a court of first instance and the company complained to the commons, who argued that the remedy must be provided by statute, involving both houses of parliament. In 1670 the case was simply dropped with neither house prepared to yield its claims. In fact the lords never again attempted this jurisdiction and victory was with the commons. The victory was not particularly notable, for the loss to the lords was slight. Use of this type of jurisdiction by the lords was infrequent; a revitalized chancery had drained off most potential cases. The stand-off with the commons only completed a process well under way.[5]

Despite their setback in Skinner *vs.* East India Co., the lords on the whole held their own in their judicial disputes with the commons. In Shirley *vs.* Fagg, they maintained their claim to supreme appellate jurisdiction and secured the function of hearing appeals from chancery. Although customary usage supported the lords' appellate jurisdiction in equity they had not formally advanced their claim to hear appeals from chancery until the reign of James I. Because the basis of their claim was chiefly customary, the lords encountered strong opposition from the commons. Precedents marshalled by William Prynne on the lords' behalf in darker days served them well on this later occasion. By 1677 the commons had conceded to the lords their full claim in appellate jurisdiction. The lords maintained their

[4] *L.J.*, XI, p. 247, XII, p. 718; W. S. Holdsworth, *History of English Law*, I, p. 176; M. Hale, *The Jurisdiction of the Lords House*, pp. xxii, xxxvii, xliv; R. W. Perceval, "The Origins and Development of the House of Lords", p. 39; A. S. Turberville, "Lords under Charles II", XLV, p. 67.

[5] *L.J.*, XI, pp. 20, 29; H.L.R.O., *Order Books of the Committee for Petitions*, I, pp. 3, 6-7; *H. Mss. C., 7th Report*, Appendix, House of Lords Mss., p. 81; L. O. Pike, *Constitutional History of the House of Lords*, p. 281; A. S. Turberville, *House of Lords in the Reign of William III*, p. 95; W. Holdsworth, *History of English Law*, I, pp. 180-181.

rights in other legal areas. They kept unchallenged their vague but potentially significant claims to jurisdiction in important cases, important either because they concerned the king, or grave questions of public law, or great men, or unprecedented matters. In regard to great men the lords solidified their control of the impeachment proceedings, as in 1663, when they decided upon Bristol's charges against Clarendon, that a peer could not exhibit original charges of treason against another peer. In the numerous restoration impeachment cases the lords either alone or with the king frustrated the commons' frequent quests for convictions. The consideration that the target of the charges by the commons was usually a member of the house of lords was a factor in the reluctance of the upper house to find guilty verdicts. Then, too, there were memories of earlier years, and what unfortunate consequences had flowed from impeachment proceedings in the time of the present king's father. More basically, impeachment was not a satisfactory method of governmental control by the commons and a more comprehensive and less cumbersome solution was needed, but not found, in the restoration period. Between the houses, the lords had the better of the judicial differences. They were less successful in financial disputes.[6]

During the Interregnum the commons had enjoyed an extensive, often exclusive control of finance, which they now were reluctant to give up. At the restoration they began to assert not only their sole right to impose taxation but also the lords' inability to change any bill which in any way involved a charge upon the subject. If the lords were willing to admit the first claim, they certainly opposed the second. Further, the two houses had traditionally voted their own taxes, though in the same bill. After 1663, the commons came to insist that they alone fixed the amount of grants to the crown. The commons' claim in law was no better than that of the lords on appeals from chancery, but like the lords in the latter case, the commons made good their claims. By 1671 they had largely secured their aims. The lords in vain asked for documentary evidence; the commons' response was to challenge the lords' rights to any voice in finance.[7]

---

[6]  D. Ogg, *Reign of Charles II*, II, pp. 469-471; G. N. Clark, *Later Stuarts*, p. 11; W. S. Holdsworth, *History of English Law*, I, pp. 172, 185-186, 189; L. O. Pike, *Constitutional History of the House of Lords*, p. 298; B.M., *Hargrave Ms.* 115 fos. 3-4, 61-64; V. M. R. Goodman, "Appellate Jurisdiction", *Parliamentary Affairs*, VII, 1 (London, 1953), p. 80; A. S. Turberville, "Lords under Charles II", XLV, p. 67.

[7]  B.M., *Stowe Ms.* 300 fo. 1; A. S. Turberville, "Lords under Charles II", pp.

The lords had their own claims in this area. They contended for the right to name committees on money bills. They reviewed government expenditures in May of 1660. Two months later they attempted to amend a poll tax bill over the commons' protests. They made good that amendment in September. In December the commons accepted another amendment to a money bill. In 1661 the lords unsuccessfully tried to initiate a money bill. They tried again in the following year, with no better luck. These bills in themselves were never of consequence. The 1661 bill provided for the repair and cleansing of some Westminster streets. The lords evidently knew well what they were trying to do for they substituted a more carefully drafted bill for their first one of the same title before proceeding with it. This second draft went down to the commons on July 29 and the lower house at once requested a conference. Here they argued that no bill should begin in the lords which levied a tax upon commoners. The lords argued that they in fact had initiated such acts in the fifth and thirty-first years of Elizabeth's reign. The commons would not be moved, so the lords yielded, on grounds that the king was inconvenienced by the bad roads, and hence a bill from the commons was better than no bill at all. They did insist upon a proviso saving their rights, but the commons objected to this as well. To this the lords would not yield and the king continued to be inconvenienced. Several lords did not wish to give way even to the extent of their fellows, and entered a protest. Neither protest nor proviso moved the commons. However, the upper house was persistent, and produced a similar bill in 1665. On this occasion the commons simply voted the action an irregular proceeding and laid the bill aside. So ended the lords' attempts to initiate money bills during the restoration.[8]

The lords, despite their agreement in May 1660 not to raise money bills in their house, had not given up their efforts. They were even more persistent in claiming the right of amending money bills, and

63-64; S. B. Bailey, "Introduction to the House of Lords", *Parliamentary Affairs*, VII, 1 (London, 1953), p. 8; G. N. Clark, *Later Stuarts*, pp. 10-11; W. S. Holdsworth, *History of English Law*, VI, pp. 250-251.

[8] B.M., *Add. Mss.* 22,263 fo. 3; 27,590 fo. 11; John Hatsell, *Precedents and Proceedings in the House of Commons, with Observations*, 4 vols. (Dublin and London, 1786-1796), III, pp. 81-85; A. S. Turberville, "Lords under Charles II", pp. 64-65; *H. Mss. C., 7th Report*, Appendix, House of Lords Mss., p. 145; *L.J.*, XI, pp. 291, 318-319, 322, 326, 328, 650; *C.J.*, VIII, pp. 311, 315; L. O. Pike, *Constitutional History of the House of Lords*, pp. 342-343; H.L.R.O., *Braye Ms.* Lot 112, #62.

more successful at first. In December of 1660, the lords deleted from
the post office bill a proviso exempting members of parliament from
the payment of postage, and the commons agreed. In 1663 the lords
successfully amended three money bills concerning post office profits,
wine licenses, and a grant to loyal and indigent officers. Balanced
against these victories was a defeat sustained in 1662. As with the
initiating power, the lords' downfall was over a highway paving bill.
The lords had dropped two clauses and added another to this measure and the commons protested that this challenged their unique
taxing power. The lords yielded in conference to the lower house, but
fourteen of their members protested on behalf of the upper chamber's
rights in money bills. The protesters included Robartes, Derby, Essex,
and Anglesey. The bill passed without the lords' alterations. This
pattern of events, the lords sometimes amending money bills and
sometimes not, continued for nearly two decades. In the late 1670's
the commons moved to close the matter to their satisfaction and
produced an outburst from Lord Holles, who defended the lords' position in print in 1678. He firmly stated: "This is clear; [precedents]
do prove that in [ancient] times, the lords and the Commons did joyn
in the gift, that the one could not give without the other, except they
had otherwise agreed on it among themselves, and that they would
give separately, as they have sometimes done, and but rarely." The
commons argued against this that, "If it be not so to be understood,
then to Grant signifies only to assent, and to say the Lords grant, is
as much as to say, the Lords assent to what the Commons grant." The
lower house further observed, "They have been possessed of this
power in all Ages, and find not one grant of Tunnage and Poundage,
that is not barely the gift of the Commons." As the commons continued to press their case the lords were moved to vote "That the power
exercised by the House of Peers in making the Amendments and
Abatments in [money bills], was a Fundamental, inherent and undoubted right of the House of Peers, from which they could not
depart." Such votes were unavailing and by 1678 the lords had largely lost the power of amending money bills, although some actions of
the eighteenth century house had much the effect of amendment.
Famous and futile attempts in this area by the peers were made on
into the twentieth century. They were left to choose only between
accepting or rejecting such measures. As L. O. Pike described their
position in financial matters, "The Lords could not be taxed without
their own consent, but they could not direct the course of taxation."

This loss was perhaps the most serious setback the lords sustained in the restoration period, and it was not achieved until the period was well along. In financial as in judicial disputes between the houses, the major cases fell in the decade of the 1670's. While the two houses were often involved in disputes in the 1660's, the outcome was less final. There was far greater pressure for the houses to work together; a state had to be reconstructed in 1660, and this task took precedence over more peculiar interests. The reconstruction was largely completed over the years from 1660 to 1663 in the form of the restoration settlement and fell into two stages, divided by the period between the Convention Parliament and the early sessions of the Cavalier Parliament.[9]

⁹  B.M., *Add. Ms.* 32,455 fo. 22; A. S. Turberville, "Lords under Charles II", p. 65; *L.J.*, XI, pp. 411, 452, 459-460, 467, 469-470; J. E. T. Rogers, *A Complete Collection of the Protests of the Lords,* I, pp. 25-27; Denzil Holles, *The Case Stated of the Jurisdiction of the House of Lords in Point of Impositions* (London, 1676), pp. 1-5, 9, 12, 42; D. Ogg, *Reign of Charles II,* II, p. 472; L. O. Pike, *Constitutional History of the House of Lords,* p. 343.

## X

## THE CONVENTION PARLIAMENT

When the lords assembled at Westminster after eleven years' absence, they naturally set about restoring the traditions and procedures of old. On their first day of meeting, they appointed a committee to order Henry Scobell, who had kept the papers of parliament during much of the Interregnum, to deliver up "all Acts, Records, and Journal Books, and all Papers and Writings whatsoever, that are in his Custody, belonging to the Peers" to John Browne, clerk of the parliament. The committee order gave Scobell fourteen days to deliver the papers to Browne's dwelling. The lords also moved to put their house in order, and to delete proceedings now embarrassing from their records.

The action against the nine peers who had gone to sit in Charles I's council at York in 1642 was a prominent case for removal from the records. All nine had been barred from the house of lords and their privileges of parliament declared forfeit. Of the nine so excluded, four were still living — the earls of Devonshire, Dover, and Monmouth, and Lord Howard of Charlton. On May 4, 1660, the lords declared the act of July 20, 1642, against the nine peers to be "repealed, anulled, and made void". In July, 1660, the house further ordered the subsommittee for the journal books to examine them, "that those things which are derogatory to the Honour of the King, and the Queen, and the Peers, may be reported severally to the House, that the same may be expunged out of the Books". The house also appointed a committee to consider all ordinances passed since the "Lords in Parliament were voted useless" and to report to the chamber those fit for repeal. Having thus obscured the past, the lords paused to celebrate the present in the future. A bill was brought in to make May 29, when Charles II had returned to his capital, a day of perpetual anniversary thanksgiving. The bill quickly passed into law if not into observance. The lords also produced an apology to the king in May of 1660. This may be called the official justification of their behavior in the past two decades. The document of the lords stated: "Your Majesties great and many Sufferings have long affected their Hearts with deep Resentments of Trouble and Sorrow, but the same Power that Usurped and Profaned Your Sceptre, Divested them of their Rights and Privileges, and kept them under such Pressures and Difficulties, as they were rendered uncapable of serving Your Majesty, in order to those Ends, to which their Duty and Allegeance did engage them." Their consciences unburdened, the lords turned to rewarding the prime movers of the restoration.[1]

Monck was the first honored by the upper house, and the most generously treated. On the first day of meeting, the lords voted a message of thanks to Monck and adjourned to carry the message to him in a body. In June of 1660 the commons proposed a grant of £ 10,000 to the general, and the upper house quickly concurred in the grant, which was charged against the monthly assessment. A further £ 10,000 was voted Monck. By the end of June nearly three quarters of these large sums had been paid out, something of a record in this period. On July 13, Monck himself entered the lords as duke of Albemarle, earl of Torrington, and Baron Monck of Potheridge, Beauchamp, and Teyes. His patent was dated July 7. He bore the titles of Albemarle and Beauchamp by virtue of his descent from Margaret, one of the daughters and co-heirs of Richard Beauchamp, earl of Albemarle and Warwick, and who had married the famous warrior Talbot, earl of Shrewsbury. Parliament later secured by acts both the lands and possessions newly granted Albemarle and his new titles as well. Edward Montagu was also honored, though neither so quickly nor so generously as was Monck. On May 9, 1660, both houses voted £ 500 to the admiral. Charles had already awarded him the Garter, and on July 12, the more substantial honors of baron of St. Neots, Viscount Hinchingbrooke, and earl of Sandwich. Fourteen days after the date of the patent, Sandwich entered the upper house. Faithful Ormond was also rewarded with English peerages as baron of Lathony and earl of Brecknock. His patent was dated July 20, and he took his seat below Sandwich on the 27th. Parliament was more bountiful to Sir George Booth. They voted him £ 10,000 in August of 1660. This was followed by the quick passage of a bill to permit

[1] *L.J.*, XI, pp. 3, 13-14, 28, 93, 135, 145; "The Humble Answer of the House of Peers to His Majesties Gracious Letter and Declaration" (London, 1660), bound in *English History Tracts*, Cornell U. L., pp. (2)-(7).

him to sell parts of his estates for debts. He would later join the other three in the upper house as Baron Delamere.[2]

With credit paid where credit was due, the two houses turned to serious business. The legality of proceedings in 1660 caused considerable uneasiness, and the parliamentarians determined to bolster their position as much as possible. The commons proposed a bill for the confirmation and future preservation of the privileges of parliament as well as of the fundamental laws made for the conservation of the lives, liberties, and properties of the subject. The lords were less enthusiastic about this measure, and let it languish in committee. They acted much more promptly on a bill legalizing the Convention Parliament. This bill came up from the commons on May 5, 1660, passed the lords and was sent to the commons with slight changes two days later, and was delivered back to the lords; both houses passed it on May 9, and sent it to the king for approval. Parliament moved with equal dispatch on a bill to continue judicial proceedings in May, 1660. This act was sufficient to keep a legal log jam from developing while the houses turned their attention to the problem of all judicial proceedings which had occurred since a legal government of king, lords, and commons last met in England. Even with frequent calls for haste, this bill required well over a month's time to pass the houses. It was wisely decided at the outset to make the bill one for the confirmation of judicial proceedings, and then to except particular cases from its coverage. By mid-August, after a month's debate, private provisos threatened to clog the bill and the lords directed that all of these be laid aside. The bill raised the greatest concern where it dealt with the land problem, for it would have to pronounce on the legality of all private sales. The bill originally had two clauses dealing with this problem. The first provided that nothing in the act was to be construed to confirm or invalidate sales carried out by the treason trustees. It further provided that anyone liable to suffer serious wrong by the confirmation of fines, recoveries, and other sentences at law dating from the Interregnum might appeal for remedy by a writ of error or some other accepted, normal procedure. To this the lords added a third, protective clause that the failure of persons whose lands had been sold to make such an appeal at law was not to prejudice their right to the land, if they either prosecuted their claim by action at law or by lawful entry within five years of

[2] L.J., XI, pp. 4, 21, 72-73, 77, 90, 107-108, 117, 153, 158, 416, 419; Baker's Chronicle, p. 737; S.R., V, pp. 253, 434.

May 29, 1660. With this salvo added, they passed the bill quickly into law without the great difficulties that beset its companion bill, the act of indemnity and oblivion. In November the lords debated a more general bill confirming English law from Magna Carta on, and they provided an act indemnifying officers in courts of justice as an aid to maintaining ordinary processes. Along with securing and settling legal matters the lords brought in an enfranchisement bill to provide the county and city of Durham with elected knights and burgesses. This bill was not proceeded with after its second reading in the lords, although it later became law.[3]

As pressing as legal affairs was the need for settling military affairs. Until the army was firmly under control, the rest of the restoration settlement had to wait, for unless the army were satisfactorily settled, the restoration itself could be overturned in a moment. The first and obvious step was to legalize Monck's *de facto* position and strengthen his hand on the army as much as possible. In May the houses quickly made him captain-general of all the land forces of the realm. Leaving the army to his care, parliament moved to control the militia, and hold it as an armed counterweight, if necessary. The settlement of the militia was entrusted to a committee of twelve peers, with a bare Presbyterian majority. Manchester, Northumberland, and Lincoln led this group and Buckingham, Oxford, and Craven led the cavaliers. But not until 1661 and the militia act of that year did the shire forces become at all reliable conservative agencies, firmly controlled by crown and county magnates. Fortunately for the settling of the realm Monck was able to discipline and order his troops, for the militia was still a forlorn hope to the parliament in 1660. Parliament did move swiftly to aid the general in his task. It passed an act enabling soldiers soon to be discharged to practice trades. This helped to ensure that a disbanded army would not become the graver threat of a leaderless, unemployed mob all skilled at arms. A series of bills then provided for the paying of troops and their mustering out of service. From May to September a frantic series of assessments, always in arrears, were levied to pay the army and to still its discontent. In spite of the heavy financial strain upon the restored government parliament raised enough funds to pay the roughly £ 40,000 a month the army required in wages alone. The actual disbanding of the army required several acts, which were hurried through parliament in the

[3]  *L.J.*, XI, pp. 14-16, 20, 47-49, 81-82, 89-99, 125-144, 154, 164, 187; J. Thirsk, "The Restoration Land Settlement", *C.J.*, VIII, pp. 123-124.

first two weeks of September. When the first bill providing for the actual disbanding of the troops and garrisons reached the lords, they found several defects. The bill originally provided that the receipts of the poll tax bill be used to pay off the men, but the lords discerned that this revenue would be insufficient. Further, if the money did not come in quickly, it would be necessary to throw the army upon free quarters after fourteen days unless parliament made provision for their continued pay in ranks until discharged. The upper house also observed that there was no provision for disbanding the navy, or the forces in Ireland, or two hospitals of maimed soldiers. The commons duly provided for the disbanding of twenty-five ships only. However, to do this and provide for the maimed soldiers and for continuing wages when necessary the lower house saw need of another money bill. These provisions were thus left for a later measure in the haste to pass the main disbanding bill. Parliament passed this bill on September 9, and turned promptly to a second bill to raise £ 140,000 toward the disbanding. So rapidly did the upper house move, that this bill received three readings on September 10. However, some matters concerning garrisons were overlooked in the hasty passage of the second act, and a third measure was brought in to cover its defects. All three bills and the "soldiers-in-trades" bill became laws on September 13. The four bills had gone through the lords in six days, clear indication of the haste parliament felt toward the subject of the army, which was both a latent threat to their security and a present drain upon the scanty revenues of the government. If the laws were not legal masterpieces they were an important and successful part of the restoration settlement. They removed the burden of a standing army from the shoulders of Englishmen.[4]

The money for maintaining the army until its disbanding came from an assessment of £ 70,000 a month for three months, passed in May of 1660. However, this act was not sufficient to begin with, and, in addition, suffered the fate of most restoration money bills of having a series of occasional and incidental expenses charged against it, such as the grant of moneys to Monck. In August parliament was driven to secure a loan of £ 100,000 from the City of London and its merchants upon the security of the poll bill. The London officials were unhappy about the security of the poll, "being so unequal". However, they were more uneasy about the army. Along with loans, efforts were

---

[4] *L.J.*, XI, pp. 9-10, 31-32, 115, 159-171; D. Ogg, *Reign of Charles II*, I, pp. 151, 252; *C.J.*, VIII, p. 158.

made to collect arrears on past assessments, including one levied by the reconvened Rump in 1659. A new assessment at the usual rate of £ 70,000 a month was passed in December of 1660 which was to be applied to both army and navy arrears, but after a dispute between the houses the navy was relegated to consideration only after the army had first been fully provided for, as the commons desired.[5]

With the armed forces provided for, parliament could turn its attention to supplying the royal necessities. The first step in this process was to secure the royal demesne. On May 10, 1660, all wastes upon the king's lands and woods were ordered stopped; on July 16 the lords ordered that all the king's lands should be restored to him. They provided for Henrietta Maria at the same time. In September the houses voted Charles £ 70,000 for his personal use and "present Supply". Parliament had granted the traditional tunnage and poundage to the king for his life on July 28. They acted so quickly in this matter — perhaps to offset an earlier, less pleasant memory concerning these duties — that they were unable to enact a new set of rates. The present bill served thus as a testament of loyalty and a stop-gap measure until an elaborate bill with an extensive table of rates could be passed later by parliament. Following the tunnage and poundage act was a bill to prevent frauds and concealments in the customs, which became law in September. Thus the Convention Parliament promptly granted to the king part of his traditional revenues. Later it would make some innovations concerning another part of his income.[6]

Parliament dealt with a variety of economic measures at this time. In July the lords had instructed the legal assistants to prepare a bill regulating usury to a maximum level of six per cent a year. The bill was then introduced in the commons and passed into law. That such an interest rate was successfully enforced at this time is doubtful. Vastly more important was the bill for encouraging and increasing shipping and navigation, which became law in September 1660. Yet neither of these bills drew the attention in the lords that centered around the post office bill. Lord Stanhope opened the matter on May 14 with his petition. He argued that by a patent in 1608 James I had granted to his father and to him the office of master of the posts and messengers. He had held this office until April of 1637 when, he maintained, the council had deceived him into an alleged surrender of his patent. Edmond Prideaux, a parliamentary commissioner, gained

---

[5] *L.J.*, XI, pp. 34-45, 125-129, 216-217, 223, 225, 231.
[6] *Ibid.*, pp. 21, 54, 70-72, 93-94, 105, 108, 164, 166.

the profits of the office during the "late distractions". Stanhope requested both restoration to the office and recompense from Prideaux's executors. In his behalf, Stanhope produced a string of witnesses in May and June. However, the postal service under Stanhope had been undistinguished but very good indeed during the Protectorate. Thus on September 12 the two houses ruled that the postal service should remain in the hands of the people then employed until a formal decision could be made in November. At that time Stanhope was granted £ 4,000 in consideration of his surrender of his patent and parliament went on to draw up a bill regulating the post office. This produced a brief division between the houses over the matter of free postage for any member of parliament. The lords won their point and members had to pay postage. The bill passed into law without further difficulty.[7]

The Convention Parliament, in its economic legislation, found time to modernize the royal revenues and secure a measure of improvement. This step forward, the most important economic measure of the restoration settlement, concerned the excise. The measure had been an innovation of Pym's in 1643. The two houses showed no sign in 1660 of discarding the revenue because of its originator. Indeed, parliament had not sat a month before it was issuing declarations to quicken payment of the excise. In June the two houses ordered the excise continued beyond the expiration of the law providing for it until a new act could be drafted. On July 28 an unusual act was passed continuing the excise until August 20, less than a month. Two days before that date, August 18, the two houses passed an act of little longer duration, continuing the excise until December 25, 1660. At this point the long ambition of Clarendon to abolish military tenures, with their incidents and reliefs, wardships and marriages, became mixed with the proceedings for continuing the excise. The problem of tenures was an old one, but the passage of time had continued to simplify the medieval complexity regarding land, honor, and service. By the fifteenth century the only surviving serjeanties had become honorary. However, the Tudors had complicated matters with the court of wards, which they used for the extraction of money from and the exercise of personal control over a good portion of the landed classes. The court of wards had levied what amounted

---

[7]   *Ibid.*, pp. 26, 28, 35, 74-75, 97, 142, 145, 158, 160, 170, 222; *H. Mss. C.*, *7th Report*, Appendix, House of Lords Mss., p. 82; *Cal. Tr. Bks.*, 1660-1667, p. 81; *Old Parliamentary History*, XXIII, p. 63.

to death and succession duties upon this particular group. The Inter-regnum had seen the suppression of the court of wards and liveries and Clarendon proposed the court's final abolition and that the king be indemnified by an annual charge of £ 100,000 upon the land which would be relieved. However, members of the commons suggested use of the excise as the source of indemnification rather than a land tax. The courtiers and proprietors took up this cause with fervor. The flagrant injustice of the substitution raised considerable opposition to the landed classes' attempt to spread their burden over the whole English population, but the excise-men prevailed in the lower house by the slim margin of 151 to 149. The commons then softened the attitude of the lords, hardly unfavorable to begin with, by generous consideration for the peers who received revenues from the court of wards. There was still a brief flurry in the upper chamber. A newsletter for December 20, 1660, credited the lords with opposing the two bills for abolishing tenures and supplying the king from the excise. This is certainly in error, but there was reason for the writer's mistake. The passage of the tenures bill did provoke a recorded dissent from Viscount Stafford. The lords had also provided several alterations which required a conference on the 21st to resolve. On December 24, Charles gave his assent to the two measures. "An Act for taking away the Court of Wards and Liveries, and Tenures *in Capite*, and by Knights Service, and Purveyance, and for settling a Revenue upon His Majesty in Lieu thereof" became 12 Car. II, *cap.* 24. It was accompanied by "An Act for a Grant of certain Impositions upon Beer and Ale, and other Liquor, for the Increase of His Majesty's Revenues, during His life". By the two acts Charles was to be secured an income of £ 100,000 a year at the first. For the crown the exchange was in the long run financially advantageous. However, it had another side. Added to the enforced sale of the fee-farms, the acts completed the severance of the monarchy from the land, and from its basis, which since ancient times and by tradition had rested on a territorial base. But the crown had not yet become only an office in popular concept; Charles occupied something of a vacuum, covered over by the great skill with which he handled his contracting and cloudy prerogative. Despite this skill the statute book bore testimony to the rising power of the landed classes. They had benefited most from the exchange. While their major tenures to the crown had been converted into free and common socage, no such benefit was extended to inferior tenures, and those who held of copyhold were still largely at the mercy of the landed magnates. The act itself was poorly drafted, and permitted some anomalies to continue, but did largely establish free and common socage as the overriding tenure. A salvo was also provided for the lords, that the act in no way infringed or hurt their titles of honor, their parallel right to sit in parliament, and their privileges as peers. The passage of the bills was argued as a victory of the landed over the moneyed class, but Sir George Clark believes that "this conflict of interests was almost fictitious. The more carefully society is analysed, the more clearly it appears that there was constant association and interchange between the two." The tenures and excise proceedings were a great victory for this ruling class in its widest sense. Its security in the land and its independence of the monarchy were substantially increased. If the crown lost power it came to gain revenue. The losers were really the commons of England, who paid for the land owners' power whenever they drank their ale.[8]

The tenures and excise victory did not moderate the ambitions of the landed, who were coming to look upon the restoration settlement as being particularly their settlement. They attempted to carry through the lords a bill entitled "An Act for vacating of all such Deeds and Evidences as were passed by any Person whatsoever ... for adhering to His late Majesty". The government managed to cast out the bill on its first reading, but not without stirring a protest. The mood of the new parliament remained high, and they found time to attend to the memory of old enemies. In December the houses ordered the bodies of Cromwell, Ireton, Bradshaw, and Pride exhumed and carried to Tyburn to be hanged by the common executioner. The house of lords proceeded on into dangerous territory. If they had not succeeded in overturning all land conveyances during the Interregnum by a general act, the high fliers would attempt to do it by establishing a precedent with a private act. The case they chose was that of Sir Edward Powell and his wife, who claimed force and fraud in the loss of their lands. The bill presented in the lords was directed at vacating the fines, the legal bases of the title to the land. Thus the bill could be

---

[8]  B.M., *Harleian Ms.* 7158 fo. 96; *Hargrave Ms.* 178 fo. 105; *L.J.*, XI, pp. 40-41, 72, 105, 133-134, 216, 219-226; T. A. Spalding, *House of Lords*, pp. 65-66; A. W. B. Simpson, *Introduction to the History of the Land Law* (Oxford, 1960), pp. 9, 22-23; J. Campbell, *Lives of the Lord Chancellors*, III, pp. 87-88; *H. Mss. C.*, *5th Report*, Appendix, Part I, Duke of Sutherland Mss., p. 201; D. Ogg, *Reign of Charles II*, I, pp. 159-161; *S.R.*, V, p. 260; G. N. Clark, *Later Stuarts*, p. 36.

used to draw into question all fines procured in the last eighteen years. The horror of this vision provoked a strong protest. Leading the protesters was quite naturally Clarendon. He was joined by almost every respected member of the house. Among the twenty-six signatures on the protest were those of Albemarle, Ormond, Manchester, Say, Capel, Colepeper, Robartes, Willoughby, and Hatton. Still the lords carried the bill through three readings and the house of commons had to come to the lord chancellor's rescue and kill the bill. The high-fliers tried the bill again in 1661, passed it over a protest of ten lords, and saw it die in the commons. On the matter of lands, the lords were proving more difficult to the government than were the commons. The upper house proceeded to give the earl of Lauderdale a highly favorable order in his dispute with John Ireton over lands Lauderdale claimed to have been unlawfully expelled from. Rather than allow Lauderdale to proceed at law, as was generally provided, the lords gave him possession, and left Ireton to proceed at law.[9]

If the lords were unreasonable regarding land, they were perhaps more reasonable than the commons on the subject of religion. Here the Convention commons possessed a sufficiently strong Presbyterian group to enable them to pass a bill for the confirming and restoring of ministers in livings. Unfortunately for the Laudians, the case was much more one of confirming than restoring. The house of lords in 1660 had not yet developed rigid lines on the subject of religion, but already there was emerging a majority for the religion of Charles I and Laud, yet sympathetic to government direction. Thus while the bill remained Presbyterian in character, the lords still managed to win several provisos for the Anglicans. Admitted to livings were Anglicans who had been sequestered, and had in the past been presented to livings by lawful patrons, but denied admission by the triers "without lawful cause". Those Anglicans presented under the Great Seal between May 1 and September 9, 1660, were confirmed, as well as those lately presented by patrons who were peers. All incumbents not affected by these displacements were confirmed in their livings. Only two political disqualifications obtained: clergy who petitioned for the trial of Charles I, or had openly opposed the restoration were excluded. Despite these moderating measures of the lords, three of the peers protested because they felt the bill outrageous to their sensibilities. Not unexpectedly they were led by Derby, who was joined

---

[9]   L.J., XI, pp. 190, 195, 205, 208-209, 312, 343-344; J. E. T. Rogers, A Complete Collection of the Protests of the Lords, I, pp. xliv-xlv, pp. 18-21.

by Bolingbroke and Hereford. To carry this story into the Cavalier Parliament, quite the opposite situation occurred. The commons wished to reverse the Presbyterian act of the Convention, and again the government had to call upon the lords to moderate the final settlement. The issue was fought out over a bill entitled "An Act for confirming Three Acts therein mentioned, with additions and alterations in the last". That last act was the Presbyterian measure. It came to the lords transformed into a ruthless purge of all non-Anglicans. Clarendon had no desire to proceed in this way. He still hoped to avoid punitive measures against moderate men of religion who could not bring themselves to accept a narrowly defined Anglicanism. Thus he and Charles mustered a diverse group of peers loyal to government authority, Roman Catholic, and Non-conformist peers to restore the Convention bill to its original form. Even the lords followed the government ungraciously, and only after a hot and prolonged debate. The house as a whole deserves little credit for tolerance.[10]

Tolerance had been the keynote of Charles's address to the people of England in his Declaration of Breda. It had held out the promise for understanding of differing beliefs and opinions and forgetfulness for past offenses. However, it left to parliament the responsibility of carrying out the program of indemnity for the loyal and oblivion for the offenses of the disloyal. Parliament had been selective in favoring the loyal, but suddenly showed itself more comprehensive in surveying the disloyal. Its motive was not a spirit of tolerance. The commons initiated proceedings by citing for arrest sixty-seven alleged judges of Charles I. This successfully excited the lords, who reserved all judicial proceedings to themselves. This dispute, only the first in what was to be a proceeding filled with conflicts, appeared settled by the lords. A draft proclamation against the regicides was phrased that upon complaint of the house of commons the house of lords ordered that the regicides named should be secured, and their estates with them. The issuance of this proclamation on May 18, 1660, signified the opening of a long process which would not come to a conclusion until 1663. Its central motive, despite camouflage, looked

---

[10] *L.J.*, XI, pp. 158, 160-168, 373, 376, 473; J. Campbell, *Lives of the Lord Chancellors*, III, pp. 173-174; Robert S. Bosher, *The Making of the Restoration Settlement* (London, 1951), pp. 179, 240-243; *Old Parliamentary History*, XXII, p. 475; W. D. Christie, *Life of Shaftesbury*, pp. 262-263. Christie incorrectly states that Clarendon's effort to check the high-fliers failed. *L.J.*, XI, p. 376 is clear and precise in stating the opposite.

much like revenge. The main issue was fought out over the act of indemnity and oblivion.[11]

Of the 73 persons listed at one time or another as regicides, twenty-five were already dead by 1660, nineteen more had fled England, and the remaining twenty-nine were taken into custody. The proclamation of May 18 had listed 66 names, specifically excluding Matthew Tomlinson, as the commons had requested. However, the commons were now outraged. In sending the proclamation to the lords they had intended that the upper house should join with them in issuing the proclamation. Instead, the lords had issued the proclamation in their own name, merely "upon complaint" of the commons. On the 19th the lords presented the lower house with the *fait accompli* in a conference. The earl of Manchester informed them that their proposal would "intrench upon the ancient Privileges of this House; Judicature in Parliament being solely in the Lords House...". The commons reacted slowly, not asking for a conference until the 22nd. In the conference the commons maintained that the order was not a judicial, but extraordinary one, for dealing with a "notorious and transcendent Crime". They further contended that they did not recognize the lords' judicature "so largely as they assert it", but declined to press this issue, as not being in question. They added: "The Lords, we conceive, intrench upon the Commons Privileges. ..." Manchester replied mildly for the lords "that they did, with equal Kindness, entertain the Apprehensions of a Tenderness for a good Understanding betwixt the Two Houses, ...". The lower house as a whole was less certain it desired a good understanding, but was unable to determine how to proceed, and the matter was talked to death in committee.[12]

This inauspicious beginning did not augur well for the forthcoming act of indemnity. There were already forces attempting to divine the attitude of the lords. Albemarle was reported to be eager to punish the regicides, but the testimony was Ludlow's. Northumberland hoped that past misfortunes would not be stirred, and was against questioning those concerned in the royal execution. Some regicides attempted to secure the support of peers in their behalf. Ludlow wrote

[11] *New Parliamentary History*, IV, p. 49; *L.J.*, XI, p. 32; *Somers' Tracts*, 1st Collection, IV, pp. 519-520; *C.S.P.V.*, 1659-1661, p. 157.
[12] J. Lingard, *History of England*, IX, pp. 12-13; *H. Mss. C.*, 5th Report, Appendix, Part I, Duke of Sutherland Mss., p. 150; *L.J.*, XI, pp. 32-34, 36-39; *Old Parliamentary History*, XXII, pp. 299-302; *New Parliamentary History*, IV, pp. 50-52; *C.J.*, VIII, p. 41.

that Lord Stourton secured the support of the earl of Lichfield for him, in exchange for Stourton's support of Fleetwood, which Lichfield desired. Such proceedings probably involved only a few peers. Northampton rejected Ludlow's overtures and branded him a great enemy of the king. Certainly the prevailing current in the house showed no clemency. The commons had excepted from mercy to the extent of their lives only a few of the most noted regicides, and on July 11, 1660, sent the bill up to the lords. Eight days later the lords formed a committee of thirty peers to start proceedings on the bill. Facing them was a mass of provisos that exceeded seventy in number, and ranged from special provisions for executing individuals who had once done someone injury to provisos for indemnification for past sufferings. The business of sorting through these papers hardly began before a new voice made itself heard on the general subject of indemnity and oblivion.[13]

The earl of Bristol, in keeping with his ostentatious character, had printed his speech of July 20. That day Lord Robartes had made the first report from the committee, which proposed that all who signed the death warrant of Charles I should be excepted from mercy. Bristol opened his address by questioning the method of proceeding: "My Lords, you have here before you in this Bill of Indemnity, the most important business that perhaps the House of Peers hath at any time had in deliberation. ... Punishing and securing are certainly the two principal ends of this bill ... but whether the means of attaining those ends have been sufficiently lighted upon by the House of Commons in this bill — that I suppose is the present question...." Bristol proposed that a committee be appointed to draw up a bill considering only vengeance for Charles I's death, which should be passed immediately. All other claims should appear in a separate bill. He continued in an excited vein:

My Lords, I profess unto you that I find myself set on fire, when I think that the blood of so many virtuous and meritorious peers, and persons, and others of all ranks, so cruelly and impiously shed, should cry so loud for vengeance, and not find it from us. ... But when I consider that these are mischiefs only to the sufferers, and that to insist upon a remedy might, perhaps, expose the public to an irreparable inconvenience; I thank God

---

[13]  Ludlow's *Memoirs*, II, pp. 267-268, 282, 287; J. Oldmixon, *History of England*, pp. 466-474; L. Echard, *History of England*, III, p. 10; D. Ogg, *Reign of Charles II*, I, p. 154; H.L.R.O., *Papers relating to the Act of Indemnity and Act for the Confirmation of Judicial Proceedings*, fos. 76-77; H. Mss. C., *7th Report*, Appendix, House of Lords Mss., pp. 95-98.

I find in an instant all my resentments calmed and submitted to my primary duty.

My Lords, we have here in our view, a Kingdom tossed and roling still with the effects of past tempests; and though, God be thanked, the storm is miraculously ceased, we cannot say that the danger is, until we get into still water....

The effect of Bristol's speech was both to pour oil on troubled waters, and then set a match to the oil. On the one hand he wisely counselled that public security required a quick settlement. But in preaching this, he managed to extend the scope of those who should be considered proper subjects for vengeance. The lords chose to ignore his first advice, but took up his second point with a willing spirit.[14]

Yet Bristol's voice in the long run was not crucial to the bill as it finally emerged. The primary influence was of king and chancellor, whose attitudes may properly be examined now. In the week following Bristol's speech, the lords continued to list more and more persons fit for punishment. On July 27, Charles finally decided to enter the upper chamber and make a plea for mercy. He reminded the peers of his pledge in the Declaration of Breda, to grant pardon to all those who come in upon it "excepting only such persons as shall hereafter be excepted by parliament". He urged that those excepted should be the regicides only. He argued that he had resolved that the murderers of his father must be punished, but no others. There is no doubt of his sincerity in this wish. In January of 1660, when he still sought to return to his throne, Charles had provided in secret instructions to his commissioners in London that he would honor pardons they granted to all persons, regicides alone excepted. He also argued from political wisdom acquired in a hard school: "My Lords, If you do not join with Me in extinguishing this Fear, which keeps the Hearts of Men awake, and apprehensive of Safety and Security, you keep Me from performing My Promise; which if I had not made, I am persuaded neither I nor you had been now here." The lords sadly lacked their king's great political sensitivity. A full two weeks after Charles's speech, Giavarina wrote, "the Upper House spent all last week over the Bill, excepting new persons and making several amendments, but it does not yet seem to be ready for the king's assent." Charles's best ally was his chancellor. Even Ludlow grudgingly acknowledged that Clarendon could not be counted high for ven-

14 Ludlow's *Memoirs*, II, p. 286; *Old Parliamentary History*, XXII, p. 388; *C.S.P.D.*, 1660-1661, p. 126; *Somers' Tracts*, 2d. Collection, III, pp. 12-14; K. Feiling, *History of the Tory Party*, p. 79.

geance. In fact, he drafted royal addresses pressing clemency and dispatch upon parliament, which still exist among his papers in the Bodleian library. In his own behalf he recorded in his *Life* only that to the degree that he aided in the bill's passage, he did so because the bill had stalled all other parliamentary business. Certainly for several months the bill dominated all proceedings in parliament.[15]

A brief chronology of the early proceedings on the bill gives weight to Clarendon's complaint. The bill, along with the bill for confirmation of judicial proceedings, had come into the lords from the commons on July 11, and passed its first reading the following day. There is then a five day gap before the second reading on July 17. At this point it became clear that the lords proposed to treat the bill in an extraordinary way. They ordered, "That the Consideration of this Bill is referred to the Committee of the whole House; to be proceeded in on Thursday Morning next, the First Business", that is, on the 19th. Both that day and the 20th the lords debated in committee of the whole house, Bristol producing his speech on the second day. On the 21st documents concerning Charles I's execution were sent up from the commons. On the 23rd the lords ordered all regicides absolutely excepted from the act. The following day the lords ordered all private business suspended until the bill be dispatched. Steady debate followed until the king's speech on July 27. So it continued, with a second order on August 3, that no private business should intervene until the bill of indemnity was completed. On the 20th of August Giavarina reported, "Parliament moves so slowly that it affords no material for comment. Both Houses continue to dispute over the Bill of Indemnity ... and these disputes have prevented the decision of any other business." By the 24th the commons requested the lords to sit in afternoon sessions in an effort to speed the bill. The lords agreed to do so. By this point both houses had exchanged their versions of the bill, and conferences between them dominated parliamentary activity.[16]

The lords had been long at the bill, but some justification could be made that they were thorough in collecting evidence and summoning

[15] W. S. Holdsworth, *History of the English Law*, VI, p. 169; *Baker's Chronicle*, p. 738; *New Parliamentary History*, IV, pp. 88-90; M. Coate, ed., *Mordaunt Letter Book*, p. 157; *L.J.*, XI, pp. 108-109; *C.S.P.V.*, 1659-1661, pp. 182-183; *Ludlow's Memoirs*, II, p. 294; J. Campbell, *Lives of the Lord Chancellors*, III, pp. 169-170, 169-170 n.; *Clarendon's Life*, p. 1032.
[16] *L.J.*, XI, pp. 87-110, 117-122, 140, 143-144; *New Parliamentary History*, IV, pp. 84-87, 93; *C.S.P.V.*, 1659-1661, p. 184.

witnesses in an effort to determine the events of the royal execution. Slowly they began to focus their attention. By August 8 no further public provisos might be offered to the bill; private provisos had been closed in July. On the 9th the upper house ordered that no further addition or exception might be made save in the case of Irish affairs. On August 11, the lords' version went down to the commons. It was a much more stern measure than the bill the commons had sent up. They had excepted seven regicides for life on May 14, and added three more on June 8. Twenty more were excepted for penalties not extending to loss of life. The upper house had greatly increased the number to suffer penalties in both categories. The two houses clashed upon their different versions. The first dispute involved the proclamation, which the two houses had requested of the king, calling upon all the regicides to surrender themselves into custody under pain of being excepted for life and estate. Nineteen surrendered in consequence of this proclamation. The commons had accordingly excepted only those regicides who had not come in within the fourteen day limit the proclamation provided. Eleven defaulters were listed by the lower house before the bill was sent to the lords. The upper house maintained that no judge of the martyr king should be spared, not even those who had taken advantage of the proclamation. The commons argued back that the faith of parliament was involved and the lives of the nineteen should not be demanded. The commons threatened proceedings by separate bills for separate cases, with an indication that they could thus block the lords' wishes in this case. The lords responded that the proclamation had only the character of a summons, and conferred only the right of a trial, and the chance of acquittal or pardon. On August 25 the two houses came to a compromise. The nineteen would have to stand trial for their lives, but an act of parliament would be required for their execution. As the commons had already indicated that they were not inclined to approve a separate bill for executing this group, the effect of the compromise was to spare their lives.[17]

The next point of contention concerned only one person, Matthew Tomlinson. The commons had indicated that they desired Tomlinson

---

[17] *L.J.*, XI, pp. 52, 104-105, 120, 122-123; T. H. Lister, *Life and Administration of Clarendon*, II, pp. 15-17, 20-21; W. D. Christie, *Life of Shaftesbury*, I, p. 236; *New Parliamentary History*, IV, pp. 64, 110-111; E. Timberland, *History and Proceedings of the House of Lords*, I, p. 11; Clarendon's *Life*, p. 1031; *C.S.P.V.*, 1659-1661, p. 190; *Old Parliamentary History*, XXII, pp. 419-421, 424-430, 449-451.

pardoned by the bill. He had been Charles I's keeper before his death, and the king had indicated that Tomlinson had behaved most properly to him before his execution. The commons had accepted Tomlinson's moving change of heart, but in the lords it was charged, particularly by the earl of Lichfield, that Tomlinson should have aided Charles to escape, and for this failure his life should be forfeit. The earl of Bristol was of different opinion, and he and Lichfield came close to a duel over their difference of opinion. A motion in the lords finally declared that Tomlinson should be removed from the list of regicides, and the motion passed in the affirmative. Lichfield and Lord Maynard entered their protest to this decision of July 23. Nor did they let the matter rest. On August 1 Tomlinson's omission from the list of regicides was again raised, but again the house resolved that he should remain free of penalties.[18]

The lords also proposed to except totally Francis Hacker, Sir Henry Vane, Sir Arthur Haselrig, John Lambert, and Daniel Axtell, as men too dangerous to live, though not regicides. The earl of Lincoln entered his protest at this expansion of those to suffer, but according to the *Old Parliamentary History* he was alone. Certainly only he signed a protest. The five were accordingly excepted in the lords' version of the bill. The commons would accept only the exclusion from mercy of Hacker, and insisted that the lives of the other four be spared. Still the lords persisted in demanding death for all five. In conference on this point, Clarendon himself replaced Lord Finch as manager for the lords to argue for the death of the remaining four. There is no way of knowing, but possibly Clarendon was willing here to consider judicial murder in behalf of the state, particularly in the cases of Vane and Haselrig, who surely raised unpleasant memories for the chancellor. In any event Haselrig escaped with his life, upon the grounds of the pledge made him by Monck "in the time of the late Troubles". Axtell was not so fortunate; he joined Hacker on the list of totally excepted. The decision left the fate of Vane and Lambert undecided; the house accepted a provision that they be excepted to suffer penalties to be determined in the future.[19]

The upper house showed itself most merciless concerning revenge

[18] B.M., *Add. Ms.* 27,590 fo. 16; Ludlow's *Memoirs,* II, p. 286; *H. Mss. C., 7th Report,* Appendix, House of Lords Mss., p. 123; J. Oldmixon, *History of England,* p. 474; *L.J.,* XI, pp. 103, 113-114.

[19] *New Parliamentary History,* IV, pp. 91, 103-108; *Old Parliamentary History,* XXII, pp. 402-403; *L.J.,* XI, pp. 114, 136, 143; B.M., *Add. Mss.* 27,590 fos. 58-60; 32,455 fo. 93; *C.J.,* VIII, p. 118; *H. Mss. C., 5th Report,* Appendix,

for the deaths of its own members. Not unexpectedly Charlotte, countess dowager of Derby first raised this subject; her husband was one of the four peers executed during the Interregnum. On June 9, 1660, she asked the house of lords to proceed against the judges of her husband by way of exception from the act of indemnity. Her cry was taken up by Lady Elizabeth Capel, "disconsolate widow" of the late Lord Capel. On June 18, she called for "condign punishment" for her husband's judges. Two days later the earl of Holland, Frances Lady Paget, and the other children of the late earl of Holland joined in demanding justice. The lords responded to the cry of the noble bloodhounds. On July 7 they ordered that anyone who had signed warrants for the execution of Lord Capel, the earl of Holland, or the marquess of Hamilton was to be taken into custody and brought before the noble house. The same day the lords summoned alderman Viner of London, who had been high sheriff of Middlesex at the time of the executions, to gain information concerning the judges. Thus, when the bill of indemnity reached the lords, they were already determined to have revenge for the executed peers. The nearest relative in the lords of each of the dead peers was allowed to pick out from the judges one individual whose life would satisfy the life the peer had forfeited. The earl of Derby selected Colonel Thomas Croxton to revenge his father. Lord Paget, for his father-in-law, Holland, picked John Blackwell; Baron Capel named Edmond Waring for his father. The earl of Denbigh was then asked to name a victim for his dead brother-in-law, Hamilton. Denbigh named William Wyberd, who was dead. The lords, upon discovery of this, called upon him to name another, but Denbigh said that since it had so fallen out, he desired to be excused from naming any more. Ludlow said that this action, "tho' seeming to proceed from chance, was generally esteemed to have been voluntary, the Earl of Denbigh being known to be a generous man, and a lover of his country". The lords thus had only three victims to demand, but the commons would have none of it. On August 13 the lower house rejected the proviso for their deaths. In conference three days later the lords praised their own moderation, in demanding only one life for one life. This argument apparently did not much impress the commons. On the 20th they replied "they do not insist upon the shedding of blood upon the account of the death of commoners, and they hope their lordships would not

Part I, Duke of Sutherland Mss., p. 156; L. Echard, *History of England*, III, p. 13; *Baker's Chronicle*, p. 739.

have the sacrifice of the king's blood to be mingled with any other blood". The lords agreed five days later to drop this demand. The earls of Derby and Carnarvon dissented. The commons again proved more merciful than their noble brethren.[20]

The lords went on to consider new penalties, now not extending to life. They listed by name sixteen who were barred for life from holding any public office — civil, ecclesiastical, or military. On this list appeared Blackwell, who at least now escaped with his life. Other notable names were William Lenthall, Oliver St. John, William Sydenham, John Desborough, Charles Fleetwood, and Christopher Pack. Not yet satisfied with an enumerated list, the upper house noted that any person who ever sat on any high court of justice was incapable of bearing office, and liable to further penalties, not extending to life. Rumor exceeded even the heights the lords had achieved. In June rumor said that the earl of Salisbury would be degraded by the house. On July 8, Thomas Gower wrote to Sir Richard Leveson, "the Bill of Indemnity will be finished and sent up to the Lords, who will be very severe if their own words may be believed. ... One of the most active among them told me just now that the Earl of Salisbury and his fellows who dissolved the House of Lords in compliance to the army will be excepted...." Gower was a careful correspondent, and probably such a move was contemplated, but evidently it never emerged onto the floor of the house. Numerous private petitions did. Among peers, the duke of Buckingham, marquess of Newcastle, earl of Berkshire, and four others were allowed provisos. Commoners were accorded this privilege as well — notably Francis Doddington, who was to be permitted to sue for reparations for his great losses. Most of these provisos failed to survive the committees and conferences on the bill in August. One act of mercy the lords permitted themselves; they removed the name of John Thurloe from the bill. On August 25 the two houses found themselves agreed upon the bill and it was ready for the royal assent.[21]

On August 29 Charles II assented to the Act of Free and General

[20] *H. Mss. C., 7th Report*, Appendix, House of Lords Mss., pp. 94-95, 101-102; *L.J.*, XI, pp. 84-85; *Old Parliamentary History*, XXII, pp. 372-373, 403; Ludlow's *Memoirs*, II, pp. 284-285; 285 n.; T. H. Lister, *Life and Administration of Clarendon*, II, pp. 17-18; J. Oldmixon, *History of England*, p. 479; *C.J.*, VIII, pp. 118, 132-133; *New Parliamentary History*, IV, pp. 97-100, 102-103.
[21] *L.J.*, XI, pp. 98, 115, 118-121, 146; *New Parliamentary History*, IV, pp. 91-92; *H. Mss. C., 5th Report*, Appendix, Part I, Duke of Sutherland Mss., pp. 194, 207.

Pardon, Indemnity, and Oblivion, embracing all happenings between January 1, 1638, and June 24, 1660. The act pardoned all political offenses in this period, and then made several exceptions. Paragraph 34 excepted for penalties extending to life fifty-one persons instrumental in the death of Charles I. Forty-nine were named, plus two unknown executioners of the king. Paragraph 35 provided that of these, nineteen regicides, named, who had surrendered upon the proclamation of June 6, 1660, should stand trial, and if found guilty, would be executed only upon passage of an act of parliament to that specific purpose. The act posthumously excepted Oliver Cromwell, Henry Ireton, John Bradshaw, and Thomas Pride. Excepted also was the property of these four and twenty others now dead; their land was forfeited to the crown. Paragraph 38 excepted for penalties not extending to life six men who sat on the high court of justice: William, Lord Mounson, James Challoner, Henry Mildmay, James Harrington, John Phelps, and Robert Wallop. Also excepted for penalties not extending to life was Arthur Haselrig. John Hutchinson and Francis Lassels were barred from any civil or military office, and Lassels must pay the crown own year's full value of his estate. Paragraph 41 excepted for future penalties Henry Vane and John Lambert. Eighteen by name were barred from civil, military, and ecclesiastical office. Finally, anyone who sat on a high court of justice from December 5, 1648, onwards, or who signed a death warrant, was barred from any office, except Richard Ingoldsby and Matthew Tomlinson. The majority of Englishmen could rest more peacefully; the excepted were not so fortunate.[22]

On December 29, 1660, an act of attainder was passed against the regicides excepted for life in the act of indemnity. The act of attainder contained a proviso, inserted by the lords, which forfeited all Cromwell's lands to the crown save those once owned by the marquess of Worcester, which reverted to him. The houses had also asked Charles not to dispose of the lands of those excepted in the act of indemnity until his two brothers had been provided for. Land confiscations of the property of excepted persons continued into 1662. The act of indemnity brought some other changes. It had the effect of canceling certain classes of arrears due the crown. The upper house

[22] L.J., XI, p. 147; S.R., V, pp. 226, 231-233; T. H. Lister, Life and Administration of Clarendon, II, p. 21. Lister mistakenly groups Hutchinson and Lassels, barred from civil and military office, with Lenthall and 17 others, barred from ecclesiastical office as well. Although chance of the two ever occupying ecclesiastical office was slight, they were still not barred by law as were the others.

pointed this out to Charles and he replied that he was aware of the loss he would incur, but relied upon the house of commons to settle a revenue for his well being as they best saw fit. The act also released from prison many persons being held until parliament had made known its wishes in the act. On September 6, the lords ordered this category of prisoners released. A more temperate climate set in, characterized by attempts to secure mercy. The earl of Dover and Lord Hunsdon petitioned that the blood of William Heveningham be preserved from attaint. Haselrig, who had been spared execution by Monck's promise in exchange for his inactivity during the restoration, now died in the Tower. Both houses sent to the king on July 23, 1661, a petition to restore his lands to his family. Earlier, Henry Vane and John Lambert petitioned the houses for mercy. The two houses accordingly petitioned the king in their behalf. The suit of parliament was less important than the carriage of the two at their trial. Lambert sufficiently humbled himself to live out his life in the Channel Islands. The haughty Vane was not forgiven. He was beheaded on Tower Hill, June 14, 1662.[23]

Thirteen other lives were paid as the price of the act of indemnity. In September of 1660, a commission of thirty-four was entrusted with the trial of the regicides. The commission excited attention by the number of its members who had once opposed the Stuart cause. Commissioners in this category included Monck, Sandwich, Manchester, Say, Robartes, Holles, Annesley, Cooper, Morice, and Grimstone. There were few prominent royalists on the commission, notably Hyde, Ormond, and Southampton. Twenty-eight individuals came before the commission, and all were found guilty. Ten were executed at once, and the other eighteen, though condemned, never had sentence carried out against them. Harrison, Carew, Scot, Clement, Jones, Scroop, Cook, and Hugh Peter were executed at Charing Cross; Hacker and Axtell, at Tyburn. In 1661 the commons brought in a bill for the execution of the nineteen regicides who had come in on proclamation. This bill was killed by the king and chancellor as the privy council notes reveal. Clarendon commented to Charles, "Would it not be better that the bill should sleep in the houses and not be brought to you?" Charles replied, "I must confess that I am

[23] L.J., XI, pp. 112, 154, 156-159, 163, 210, 235, 318; S.R., V, p. 290; J. Oldmixon, History of England, p. 475; T. H. Lister, Life and Administration of Clarendon, II, p. 115; Baker's Chronicle, pp. 739-740; B.M., Egerton Ms. 2618 fo. 71; W. Kennet, History of England, III, p. 256.

weary of hanging except upon new offenses." The chancellor asked, "Shall I move it here in the Privy Council, that we may take care that it comes not to you?" The king wrote, "By all means, for you know that I cannot pardon them." The blood-letting which was successfully stemmed in 1661 broke out again the following year. The commons opened the matter of the regicides in early 1662 and the lords proceeded to call in several of the regicides for questioning, but did not pass the bill and the matter appeared to drop. Then, almost abruptly on April 19, Corbet, Okey, and Barkstead, delivered up from the continent by George Downing, were executed at Tyburn. Vane's death two months later closed this severe aspect of the restoration settlement.[24]

The act of indemnity nearly completed the business of the Convention Parliament. A few bills for the commonweal remained on the calendar. Charles had called upon the house of lords to prepare a bill to support the work of draining the great level of the Fens in Lincolnshire, often referred to as the Lincoln level. This extensive project for salvaging land from the sea, diking, draining, and irrigation had survived the civil wars in perilous condition, despite occasional progress during the period. The lords took up the bill, and were joined by the commons in passing it into law, at the close of the first session of the Convention Parliament. In the second session the lords prepared and passed a second Fens bill, dealing with the Lindsey level, also in Lincoln. They sent it down to the commons, but it never came to discussion there. The commons did join with the lords in passing a bill for the nominating of commissioners of sewers. The commissioners were responsible for regulating the drainage of towns in coastal areas and along tidal rivers. Not until 1667 did London come under their jurisdiction but their function was already important. Charles assented to the bill establishing the commissioners, first instituted by his grandfather, on July 8, 1660. Another measure reminiscent of James I passed the lords. It prohibited the planting of tobacco within the kingdom of England. The commons dropped the measure.[25]

[24] J. Oldmixon, *History of England*, pp. 477-478; W. D. Christie, *Life of Shaftesbury*, I, pp. 243-244; T. H. Lister, *Life and Administration of Clarendon*, II, pp. 55-56, 116; W. Kennet, *History of England*, III, pp. 242, 256; W. D. Macray, ed., *Notes which passed at Meetings of the Privy Council*, p. 29; *L.J.*, XI, pp. 375-378, 380-381.

[25] *L.J.*, XI, pp. 91-95, 102, 104, 148-153, 160, 168, 193-194, 201; *H. Mss. C.*, 7th Report, Appendix, House of Lords Mss., p. 129, 135.

The Convention was determined in December, 1660. Its record entitled it to consideration as one of the most important of parliaments. The traditions of government which had been interrupted for nearly two decades were re-established. The Convention peacefully disbanded a standing army. It largely restored order to the realm. This was particularly true of judicial affairs, where most proceedings of the recent past were confirmed, and the government continued to afford justice during this difficult period of adjustment. The effect upon land-holding of confirmation of judicial proceedings was most notable. There was no vast exodus of dispossessed to trouble the countryside. If it did not do perfect justice, it did preserve the interest of general security with the sanctity of private transactions in law. In connection with this, the last of feudal tenures were eliminated in general throughout England, and the burdensome court of wards abolished. The landed classes had benefited here, by rejecting a land tax in favor of the excise as compensation for the loss of feudal and court fees. Though prompted by self-interest, the exchange was still a wise economic measure. The land was in no condition to bear a new tax in 1660. The excise could be better absorbed by the country and better collected by the government, to whom it promised a steady and increasing revenue. The house of lords had shown itself to good effect in the bills confirming and restoring ministers. Its influence had been moderating in an area which had seen too little moderation for too many years. The record of the upper house on the act of indemnity was much poorer. Fortunately, the wisdom of king and chancellor and the responsiveness of the commons had prevented the act from exceeding a tolerable, if not admirable, degree of severity. The part of the restoration settlement accomplished by the Convention Parliament was predominently conservative and moderate. At points it was enlightened, thanks to the political wisdom of Charles and his chief minister, Clarendon. The settlement afforded England the chance to pause after a rapid, dizzying, and often brilliant succession of events, a pause which would set the stage for some slow, difficult, and usually undramatic settlements in constitutional affairs, after which England would launch herself on the path of worldwide influence. Such was the distant future. For the present the houses dispersed to the country. Before they assembled again at Westminster, England had a king to crown.

## XI

## BETWEEN PARLIAMENTS:
## THE LORDS AND THE CROWN

The five months between the close of the Convention Parliament and the opening of the Cavalier Parliament was a time of evident festivity. England had a king again, and planned to honor him in a glittering coronation ceremony. Before this occurred, Charles himself bestowed honors upon his servants. The coronation honors had long been rumored. Hyde, Ormond, and Northumberland had all been reported as candidates for dukedoms. In fact, the king bestowed no dukedom in these honors, and only one of the three named benefited. On April 20, 1661, Charles promoted three barons to earldoms, created three more earls, and raised six commoners to baronies. The three promotions were Baron Hyde to earl of Clarendon, Lord Capel to earl of Essex, and Lord Brundenell to earl of Cardigan. The three new earls were Arthur Annesley, now earl of Anglesey, Charles Howard as earl of Carlisle, and John Grenville, earl of Bath. Denzil Holles, Horatio Townshend, and John Crewe all received baronies in their names. George Booth was styled Lord Delamere and Anthony Ashley Cooper became Lord Ashley. These eleven were introduced into the house of lords on May 11. They were followed three days later by Frederick, Lord Cornwallis. The new earl of Anglesey had two claims for Charles's favor. He had aided the Stuart cause in Ireland and had served in the process of restoration as president of the council. An able politician of low church inclination, he was a valuable addition to the upper house. John Grenville was a man of longer royalist service. He had held the Scilly Isles for the Stuarts from 1649 to 1651. Chiefly through Grenville Charles had made contact with Monck. For his services he was originally promised the barony of Bideford in 1659. As the royal fortunes rose, so did Grenville's. After he had delivered the Declaration of Breda in England, Charles promised him an earldom, £ 3,000 a year, and the payment of his and his father's debts. Oldmixon, no friend, has left the tale that when Grenville opened the packet of letters containing the declaration, to deliver it, "he found there, like the Cup in Benjamin's Sack", his warrant and the rest. Burnet was no more kind to Bath. He characterized him as a notorious spendthrift, who left his affairs in such disorder that his son committed suicide upon discovery of the chaos and was buried with his father. Bath was also no mean politician, and became one of the most notable of the early borough-mongers. Arthur, Lord Capel, received the viscounty of Maldon and earldom of Essex more for his father's services than his own. Brudenell gained the earldom of Cardigan when Charles honored a pledge of his father's. Clarendon did not take these proceedings very well. He recorded:

And it was not long before the day for the coronation was appointed, when the king had appointed to make some barons, and raise some who were barons to higher degrees of honour; most of whom were men not very grateful, because they had been faulty, though they had afterwards redeemed what was past, by having performed very signal services to his majesty and were able to do him more: upon which the king had resolved to confer these honours upon them, and in truth had promised it to them, or to some of their friends, before he came from beyond the seas.

Such a person was Charles Howard, old Cromwellian, now earl of Carlisle. Of less certain category was Anthony Ashley Cooper. He had tacked from party to party without belonging to any, finally coming down rather late on the Stuart side. Yet of the nine new creations of Charles II, he would prove by far the most distinguished. As the first earl of Shaftesbury he would make a major contribution to the evolution of the constitution and the development of party politics. Another able choice was Denzil Holles. Burnet described him as "a man of great courage, and of as great pride: he was counted for many years the head of the presbyterian party. He was faithful and firm to his side, and never changed through the whole course of his life." The remaining four barons were of much less note. Crewe and Booth gained rewards for tenacious rather than able service to Charles. Townshend and Cornwallis are best known for their eighteenth century descendants. Still, of the three promotions, Clarendon's was fully merited; of the nine new creations, the additions of Ashley, Holles, and Anglesey were meritorious. This was better than average and positively distinguished for a Stuart.

Pepys attended the creation of the peers.

Then ... to White Hall; and in the Banqueting-house saw the King create my Lord Chancellor and several others, Earls, and Mr. Crew and several others, Barons: the first being led up by Heralds and five old Earls to the King, and there the patent is read, and the King puts on his vest, and sword, and coronet, and gives him the patent. And then he kisseth the King's hand, and rises and stands covered before the king. And the same for the Barons, only he is led up by three of the old Barons, and are girt with swords before they go to the king.

The five earls assisted, one by bearing the mantle of the new earl, one the sword, one his cap and coronet, and two on either side of the nominee. The barons were provided with only surcoat, Pepys's "vest", and mantle, which one baron carried, while two proceeded on either side of the new baron. A mixed group of earls officiated, and Clarendon had four old parliamentarians, led by Northumberland, assist him. Carlisle, on the other hand, had three prominent royalists. A banquet followed the ceremonies.[1]

Shortly after this ceremony, the Venetian resident wrote the Doge and Senate that the chancellor, now earl of Clarendon, "is the one who does everything at the moment in England". This was on the whole England's fortune. Edward Hyde was not without shortcomings. Burnet allows, "He was a good chancellor, only a little too rough. . . ." As a minister he had "too magisterial a way". His haughty manner, combined with personal conservatism and a lack of sympathy with young men, even if genuine royalists, finally led Charles to be rid of his services. But by the time he left, he had made a great contribution by the weight he attached to the continuity of national life. Sir George Clark described Clarendon as having "conferred on the country one imperishable service: he had worked continuously and successfully to identify the royal cause with the cause of legality, and the Restoration therefore stood, as he stood, not for absolution and arbitrary power, but for the common law, for the historic institutions of the country, including parliament, for regularity and precedent and good order".[2]

Clarendon was by nature a careful person, and feared display as

---

[1] B.M.,*Add. Ms.* 28,792 fos. 22-24; *H. Mss. C.,* 5th *Report*, Appendix, Part I, Duke of Sutherland Mss., p. 158; D. Ogg, *Reign of Charles II*, I, p. 181; A. S. Turberville, "Lords under Charles II", XLV, pp. 403-404; D. Underdown, *Royalist Conspiracy*, p. 300; J. Price, "The Mystery and Method of His Majesty's Happy Restauration, . . .", in Baron Maserès, *Tracts*, II, p. 791; J. Oldmixon, *History of England*, p. 462; G. Burnet, *History of His Own Time*, I, pp. 166-169; Clarendon's *Life*, p. 1018; *L.J.*, XI, pp. 250, 253; *Pepys' Diary*, II, 14-15.

[2] *C.S.P.V.*, 1659-1661, p. 305; G. Burnet, *History of His Own Time*, I, pp. 160-161; K. Feiling, *History of the Tory Party*, pp. 104, 117; G. N. Clark, *Later Stuarts*, p. 2.

courting popular hostility, and hence a threat to power. On several occasions he declined grants of land or money for fear of the attention they would bring. He himself attributed his acceptance of an earldom to the insistence of his royal son-in-law, the duke of York. Servant of two Stuart kings, Clarendon would be grandfather of two Stuart queens. His character and office caused him to be a lonely man, and to stand in isolation. Thus he greatly depended upon the royal favor, which at first was generously given. Charles wrote to Sir Alan Apsley:

... t'is not to be wondered at, that at the same time that I have so many enemies ... those that are faithful to me should have some. And t'is from some of those who are not much my friends that the report comes that the Chancellor should have lost my favour. The truth of it is, I look upon the spreaders of that lie as more my enemies than his, for he will always be found an honest man, and I should deserve the name of a very unjust master if I should reward him so ill that hath served me so faithfully. Therefore I do conjure you to let as many as you can of my friends know the falsehood and malice of that report, and I shall take it as a service.

So Charles wrote on the eve of his restoration. Late in 1661 he was writing warmly to Clarendon, "Have a care of the game about Cornbury that I may have good sport next year when I come thither." Beyond the king, Clarendon's allies were chiefly Southampton, Ormond, and Nicholas. In 1662 Ormond went to attend to Irish affairs. In October of that year Nicholas gave way to Henry Bennet, no friend of Clarendon, as chief secretary of state. Upon Clarendon's banishment in 1667, only five peers protested against the action. The young earl of Strafford bravely cited seven objections, which applied as much to the proceedings against his father as against Hyde. Baron Colepeper also protested, perhaps out of memory of his father's close relations with the fallen minister. Barons Berkeley and Lexington did likewise, but most notable was Lord Holles. No friend of Clarendon, this doughty Presbyterian earned Burnet's laurels for courage in protesting an injustice. Such efforts could not save Clarendon, for when he lost control of parliament, Charles with sure political instinct threw him to the wolves.[3]

[3]   Clarendon's *Life*, pp. 1016-1018; L. Echard, *History of England*, III, p. 5; A. Bryant, ed., *Letters, Speeches and Declarations of Charles II*, p. 89; *Clarendon S.P.*, III, p. 735; W. D. Macray, ed., *Notes which passed at Meetings of the Privy Council*, p. 37; J. Campbell, *Lives of the Lord Chancellors*, III, p. 157; K. Feiling, *History of the Tory Party*, p. 115; J. E. T. Rogers, *Complete Collection of the Protests of the Lords*, I, pp. 37-38.

Deeply as Clarendon believed in parliaments, they always gave him trouble. He wrote of their financial vision: "Parliaments do seldom make their Computations right, but reckon what they give to be much more than is ever received, and what They are to pay to be much less than in Truth They owe." A cantankerous commons was to be expected, but neither king nor minister expected the lords to prove as independent as they showed themselves to be. Pepys reported on November 13, 1661: "And so on foot to my Lord Crew's ... with whom I had great talk: and he tells me in good earnest that he does believe the Parliament (which comes to sit again the next week), will be troublesome to the Court and Clergy, which God forbid! But they see things carried so by my Lord Chancellor and some others, that get money themselves, that they will not endure it." Clarendon had organized the commons by communicating his wishes to selected influential members, who in turn held separate meetings of their friends, and in this decentralized manner Clarendon continued without at first attracting undue attention. As these members were consistently royalists, often high-fliers, his ability to moderate the extremists in the house was all the more notable. As Hyde's friends passed from the scene, and Charles became restless, the royalist majority began to break into cabals. Young royalists in the commons wished greater organization, and approached the king. They made contact with Charles, and had found a sensitive ear by 1663. Clarendon wrote of that period:

To this time [1663], the king had been content to refer the conduct of his affairs in the parliament to the chancellor and the treasurer; who had every day conference with some select persons of the House of Commons, who had always served the king.

During the last four years of his administration Clarendon's influence in the lower house waned. Still he remained the center of the royalist party; rumor said he maintained at least 178 placemen in the commons in 1665. Placemen there were, but they were not Clarendon's. Charles more and more passed him by, and left him exposed to his enemies.[4]

Clarendon's enemies launched their attacks upon him from two directions, depending upon the house in which they sat. Clarendon never had an assistant of great ability in the commons. In fact the

---

[4] B.M., *Lansdowne Ms.* 805 fos. 83-89; Clarendon's *Life*, pp. 1074, 1093; G. N. Clark, *Later Stuarts*, p. 10; *Pepys' Diary*, II, p. 128; J. Lingard, *History of England*, IX, p. 25-26; K. Feiling, *History of the Tory Party*, pp. 104, 116.

restoration period is characterized by the lack of a great commoner. The most able members were consistently promoted into the lords. This left Hyde with a relatively vulnerable position in the lower house, one so difficult to control that its own officers had difficulty in requiring the members to use the aisles, and not to climb over the forms. The commons did possess enemies of the chancellor. In the Convention Parliament, this opposition was based on what survived of the once formidable Presbyterian party. What strength it retained was centered in the house of commons, for the great Presbyterian magnates had largely caved in when their attempt to limit admission to the house of lords collapsed. Several of them were then variously honored in efforts by the government to neutralize their influence, if not to gain some of them over outright. Of the Presbyterian cabal in early 1660, only two received no spoils at the restoration. These two were the earl of Bedford and Philip, Lord Wharton. Bedford accepted his fate and was quiet, but such was not the case with Wharton, who in earlier years had shown a much more Independent outlook than the position he had come to by 1660. In any case, it was he who acted as party manager for the Presbyterians in the Convention Parliament. The government evidently was sufficiently concerned by Wharton's activity to attempt to except him from the act of indemnity. Not only did this prove impossible, but Wharton himself was soon active on the lords' committee for the uniformity bill in the Cavalier Parliament, where he struggled to modify its severity. But Wharton was largely isolated in the upper house in his efforts, and his party in the lower house was devastated by the elections to the Cavalier Parliament. Clarendon rather easily survived the challenge to his policy and power from this direction. Rather it was to be from the old cavalier ranks that there emerged the movement which would eventually bring down the chancellor. It was not really a new struggle; it dated back to the opening sessions of the Long Parliament. Hyde had never favored an unrestrained prerogative nor did he support the high-fliers who gave semi-divine status to kingship and who made much of the cult of the martyr king. Many of these types had risked all and lost much for the Stuarts in the civil wars. These were the men, now entering the house of commons, who railed most bitterly of indemnity for the king's enemies and oblivion for his friends. Their struggle with Clarendon then embraced the issues of both wealth and political power. Clarendon and those he represented, the old royalist magnates, had emerged in 1660 not

only in control of the royalist party but also rather well provided for
in the economic aspects of the restoration settlement. Yet Clarendon
always had one great point of weakness; he needed the king's support. And this support was Clarendon's only so long as Charles believed that Clarendon was necessary to him. Thus the frustrated
royalists in the commons waited for their opportunity. They were a
mixed group of men, some long enemies of Clarendon, others rising
opportunists. But they were all united in that Clarendon stood as a
block to their political future. The Coventry brothers and young
George Savile opposed him. Most dangerous was Henry Bennet.
Bennet was a cavalier, and a rake thoroughly at home in the king's
pleasures. He was also a diligent worker, and one of the few men in
England who could handle foreign affairs. Bennet was particularly
the king's man; a modern opportunist and as such distasteful to
Clarendon. Therein lay his danger. When Charles tired of Clarendon's
sermons on morality, Bennet was his best agent against the chancellor
for he could be trusted and was able, as well as being agreeable.
Hyde has left little record of his thoughts on Bennet, largely that he
was pro-Spanish, and probably a Roman Catholic. While Bennet
pressed in the commons, a larger group opposed Clarendon from the
lords. Like their allies in the commons, they were royalists. While
Presbyterians and Roman Catholics largely had opposed Clarendon's
coming to power in 1660, they soon found him more agreeable than
the Anglican high-fliers. Burnet even states that Clarendon lost the
support of cavaliers by his use of and favor toward such men as Manchester, Holles, and Anglesey. The opponents of the chancellor in the
upper house were of two groups, personal rivals for power and cavalier
rank and file who objected to his leadership and policies. Albemarle,
Buckingham, Bristol, and later Bennet as earl of Arlington led the
first group; among the second were Bath, Byron, Lucas, and
Northampton. The feuds with Bristol and Buckingham stretched back
to civil war and Cromwellian times; for others, such as Lord Berkeley
of Stratton, the cause of differences was Clarendon's rise after the
restoration, particularly his daughter's marriage to the duke of York.
Bristol tipped the hand of the opponents by attempting impeachment proceedings against Clarendon in 1663; he failed miserably.
Against this array of enemies, the keystone of Clarendon's defense
was the king. As Mr. George Montagu told Pepys, "That my Lord
Chancellor is much envied, and that many great men, such as the
Duke of Buckingham and my Lord of Bristol, do endeavour to under-

mine him, and that he believes it will not be done; for that the King (though he loves him not in the way of a companion, as he does these young gallants that can answer him in his pleasures), yet he cannot be without him, for his policy and service." In 1667 Charles was in no position to defend Clarendon after a military fiasco more his fault, and that of his new advisors, than Clarendon's. Moreover, Clarendon's declining ability to handle parliament sealed his fate. His enemies distinguished themselves by calling for his impeachment on a general charge of treason, as in the case of Strafford. When the house of lords would not have this, they recorded themselves for posterity by signing a protest at this decision. Twenty-six called for impeachment. Buckingham, Albemarle, Bristol, and Arlington headed the group. The "little royalist" group was well represented by Norwich, Bath, Northampton, and Berkshire from the earl's bench, joined by barons Gerard, Byron, Lucas, and Berkeley of Stratton. Three bishops were represented – Durham, Hereford, and St. Davids. Powis and Teynham from among the Roman Catholics joined Bristol. Pembroke and Dover were the only notable old parliamentarians who wished to proceed harshly against the chancellor. Clarendon's fall was the signal for his enemies to attempt government by cabal and the period from 1667 to about 1672, when Danby and Shaftesbury emerged, was one of great unrest. Clarendon had become old, and his solutions had fallen behind the problems English government faced. But none of his detractors were statesmen enough to replace him. He had many accomplishments; among them his restoration of an ordered government acceptable to the people in the form of the monarchy, yet without absolutism, which is sufficient reason to secure his memory. Much as he desired responsible government, his definition of it differed from that emerging in the restoration period – the role of parties as forming a governing majority and quasi-constitutional opposition.[5]

[5]    B.M., *Add. Ms.* 35,865 fo. 42; *C.J.,* VIII, p. 264; G. N. Clark, *Later Stuarts,* p. 56; A. S. Turberville, "Lords under Charles II", XLIV, pp. 406-407; K. Feiling, *History of the Tory Party,* pp. 114-116; Clarendon's *Life,* pp. 1006-1007, 1010-1011, 1094; J. Campbell, *Lives of the Lord Chancellors,* III, p. 166; G. Burnet, *History of His Own Time,* I, p. 167; D. Ogg, *Reign of Charles II,* I, pp. 205-206; *Pepys' Diary,* II, p. 67; J. E. T. Rogers, *A Complete Collection of the Protests of the Lords,* I, pp. 35-36; Caroline Robbins, "The Repeal of the Triennial Act in 1664", pp. 139-140. G. F. Trevallyn Jones, "The Composition and Leadership of the Presbyterian Party in the Convention". *E.H.R.,* LXXIX, #311 (April, 1964), pp. 312-318.

Party divisions did not manifest themselves in the early years of the restoration in a form recognizable to the modern observer, nor did they yet appear openly even in the form Danby and Shaftesbury created in the 1670's and 1680's. New lines of party and interest were beginning to form after the upheaval of 1640-1660. The political divisions of that period rapidly lost significance, and new political factions tended to grow out of personal and group attitudes toward the restoration settlement. Roger North identified the noble components of the court party of this later period as a triple alliance of the bishops, the cavalier peers, and the Roman Catholic lords. Not one of these three groups in the house of lords can be said to have voted as a block loyal to the government during Clarendon's administration.

The initial division in the upper house, over which the entry problem was so bitterly disputed, was the jealousy between the cavalier and Presbyterian components of the royalist party of 1660 whose union had made the restoration possible. Their differences hung over the early 1660's. As Feiling observed, "Resentment at the favour shown to the old enemy rankled in every Cavalier heart." But the Presbyterians felt slighted as well, as an anonymous letter of 1660 stated: "The Court and royal party [grudge] at every favour to the Presbyterians, and they on the other side [think] they have not enough."

At first, the Presbyterians' arch-devil was Clarendon. As he himself wrote, "The Chancellor was a man very much in the prejudice of the presbyterian party, as in truth he was...". However, the government's relatively moderate course, and its refusal in general to stir up sleeping dogs from the past, substantially modified the initial cavalier-Presbyterian division. Men like Manchester and Holles became dependable supporters of the government, while such undoubted cavaliers as Buckingham and Bristol went into opposition. Unfortunately, the opposition was one of the most irresponsible in English history. Its two most prominent early members were as often at each other's throats as at Clarendon's. A letter revealed: "Yesterday there passed some hot and high words in the Lords House betwixt the Duke of Buckingham and Earl of Bristol, by reason the Earl of Bristol did set higher value on the Marquis of Newcastle's actings and sufferings for the King than of the Duke's; in so much as it amounted to a challenge as some say....". Charles confined the two peacocks to their quarters.

Bristol, though a Roman Catholic, usually stood apart from the other recusant lords. He became a convert to that faith only in 1659, when he was in Spain. The only policy he consistently pursued was one of animosity toward Clarendon, whom he blamed for his exclusion from office and royal service. Parties in the lords were further confused by a French interest, a carry-over from the Louvre party of Henrietta Maria. The earl of St. Albans and Lord Loughborough constituted its core, with the earl of Carlisle and his wife intriguing on its periphery. On the whole, the upper chamber submitted less to organization in a party way than the lower house. However, for the early years of the restoration, at least till 1663, the government could usually muster a majority in the lords as well as in the commons.[6]

Clarendon's problems of management were not all in parliament; his own family presented him with a startling development. Clarendon's daughter, Anne Hyde, had been secretly contracted for by the duke of York on November 24, 1659, at Breda. She was pregnant by him in the summer of 1660, but at this time he seems to have had second thoughts about marrying her. However, Anne Hyde was not easily put off, and a crisis quickly developed. Clarendon denied in his *Life* any knowledge of the early stages of the affair, a statement Oldmixon scorns. Giavarina reported that Clarendon was ready to take the case of his daughter before parliament, but Giavarina is the only source for this doubtful version of the events. Pepys had a delightful account of a marriage promise signed in blood and then stolen from the lady's closet. Lord Berkeley of Stratton swore, then didn't swear, the child was his. According to the Venetian resident, if Hyde became a duke the marriage would join two nearly equal families. So went the speculation, which necessitated public action. It appears that the two parties were married privately at Worcester House on September 3, 1660, by Dr. Joseph Crowther, according to the rites of the Church of England. On February 18, 1661, the duke publicly owned his marriage. Pepys, who was about a month late in learning of the secret marriage, commented, "The Duke of York matched to

---

[6] A. S. Turberville, "Lords under Charles II", p. 62; K. Feiling, *History of the Tory Party*, p. 103; *H. Mss. C.*, 5th Report, Appendix, Part I, Duke of Sutherland Mss., pp. 155, 158, 177, 184; Clarendon's *Life*, pp. 993, 1040; Richard Lodge, *From the Restoration to the Death of William III*, vol. VIII in the *Political History of England* (London, 1910), p. 65; T. Carte, ed., *Duke of Ormonde's Papers*, II, p. 341; D. Underdown, *Royalist Conspiracy*, p. 235.

my Lord Chancellor's daughter, which do not please many." Two notable queens of England were products of the marriage.[7]

To move forward in time, a second royal marriage was being contemplated. Ever since Charles II returned to England his bachelor status had demanded prompt consideration of a royal match, to secure the succession. Several groups had candidates. A Catholic party wished an Italian princess with Spanish approval. The French party inclined toward a Portuguese match. Many Protestants urged a north European marriage. The earl of Bristol was the most active advocate of an Italian match, and Clarendon seems to have successfully fooled him into a personal trip to inspect prospective brides, while keeping close watch on his activities. In the end, the decision seemed to rest with Charles alone, and he chose the Portuguese princess, Katherine of Braganza. He announced his choice to parliament on May 8, 1661, as an accomplished fact, with no request for their approval. In later years Clarendon's enemies charged him with selecting a barren queen, to ensure that his descendants would sit on the throne. The Anglican historian, Echard, falls the other way in Clarendon's defense, that he opposed the marriage upon information that Katherine could not bear children. In fact, poor Clarendon had the task of reconciling the queen to Charles's mistresses, and had evidently not much more to say in the matter.[8]

On April 23, 1661, Archbishop Juxon placed the crown upon the head of Charles II. This festive occasion did not call forth good behavior by the peerage. Summons had gone out to them in February to give attendance upon their sovereign lord at his coronation. The summons set off a series of disputes for the rights to particular honorary offices. The dispute for the office of lord high chamberlain of England flared again between the earls of Lindsey and Oxford. Lindsey gained the post for the coronation, with a saving of rights for Oxford. The earl of Northumberland, for the trustees of the duke of Norfolk during his infirmity, contended for the butlership and the office of bearing the spurs and redeeming the sword. The earl of Pembroke gained the right to bear the spurs while the earl of Shrewsbury carried the sword. The earl of Manchester was named to redeem it. The lords Abergavenny and Maynard contended for the of-

---

[7]  J. Oldmixon, *History of England*, p. 453; *Pepys' Diary*, I, pp. 237, 290; *C.S.P.V.*, 1659-1661, pp. 210, 228-229; W. Kennet, *Register*, pp. 247, 381-382.
[8]   *C.S.P.V.*, 1659-1661, pp. 262-263; *Clarendon S.P.*, III, p. viii; *L.J.*, XI, p. 241; L. Echard, *History of England*, IV, p. 83.

fice of chief larderer and caterer, which the latter secured. The sharpest dispute came over precedence. Ormond's eldest son, the earl of Ossory in Ireland, claimed precedency over Lord Percy, the earl of Northumberland's eldest son. Ossory claimed the place of a duke's eldest son. Percy contended that as the dukedom was Irish, Ossory must take his place as an earl's eldest son, according to Ormond's English title of earl of Brecknock. As Northumberland was of much older creation than Brecknock, this gave Percy precedence. Charles upheld Percy's claim, but from the matter came embittered relations between the two great houses. Shortly after the coronation Charles granted to barons the right to wear a coronet. Elizabeth had given this privilege to viscounts, and Charles completed the extension of this insignia to the lowest order of nobility.[9]

Parallel to the coronation festivities there were meeting at the Savoy clerics of differing persuasion from highest Anglican to broadest Presbyterian. In synod, opening on April 5, 1661, these divines contended for possession of the Church of England. Attempts to arrive at a formula that would share the household of God between the two groups failed to make headway. The old bishops, who relied on the cult of their martyred king, were in no humor to make concessions to those whose co-operation had made their return possible. As the historian of the restoration religious settlement commented, "The Establishment had reverted to its original ownership. Anglicans were in possession of the house; it only remained to regulate the household." Yet the house would not appear to be of old until the last door was unbolted to the repossessing owners; they still had to gain entry into the lords. Pepys sagaciously noted at the coronation, "The Bishops come next after Barons, which is the higher place; which makes me think that the next Parliament they will be called to the House of Lords." [10]

Nine of the old bishops were still living in 1660. Premier among them was William Juxon, bishop of London, whom Charles now translated to Canterbury. The grand old man, lord treasurer in 1640, and the attendant of Charles I at his execution, was too old to serve as more than a figurehead. Another survivor, Accepted Frewen, was moved from Coventry and Lichfield to York, on Octo-

[9]  C.S.P.D., 1660-1661, pp. 500, 506, 584; B.M., Add. Ms. 34,217 fos. 71-72; Clarendon's Life, pp. 1048-1049; Pepys' Diary, II, 19 n.
[10]  D. Ogg, Reign of Charles II, I, p. 199; R. S. Bosher, Making of the Restoration Settlement, p. 218; Pepys' Diary, II, p. 16.

ber 4, 1660. Pepys, who witnessed the ceremony, commented: "Here I saw the Bishops. ... But, Lord! at their going out, how people did most of them look upon them as strange creatures, and few with any kind of love or respect." Bishops had not been seen in England for some time. To make their dignity better known, more prelates were speedily consecrated. On October 28, 1660, Frewen officiated at the consecration of five bishops, including Gilbert Sheldon of London and George Morley of Worcester. On December 2, seven more were elevated to sees, among them John Cosin of Durham. Four more consecrations on January 13, 1661, filled the episcopal bench, except for Frewen's old see. Upon Sheldon and Morley, who was translated to Winchester in 1661, fell the task of guiding through the church legislation of the next four years. Their high Anglicanism met little opposition on the episcopal bench, which held only one Presbyterian, Reynolds of Norwich, though several others had been offered sees. Sheldon was a man of great power, a politician as much as a clergyman, and his influence dominated the Church from 1660 until 1677; he spent the last fourteen years at Canterbury. Morley was not a poor second. Clarendon called him "the best man alive", and he served as chief speaker for the Laudians at the Savoy Conference. Seth Ward, Sheldon's closest ally, waged relentless war on dissenters from his see at Salisbury. These three had strong support from Cosin at Durham, Gunning at Ely, Brian Duppa, and Humphrey Henchman. The more moderate Henry King at Chichester was not less able. The episcopal bench was unquestionably talented.[11]

While the general belief was that the bishops would be restored to the Cavalier Parliament, they had to wait until its second session for their entry, for the statute of 1642 still needed repeal. Their return was intended to strengthen not only Church but government. Sheldon, in a letter to Cosin, made it clear that their parliamentary duties were to have precedence over their pastoral duties. Further, a proxy did not constitute meeting one's parliamentary duties. Thus twenty-three of the twenty-six prelates took their seats promptly on November 20, 1661. If the government had looked to the house of lords, strengthened by the bishops, to protect its religious interests

[11] B.M., *Add. Ms.* 28,792 fos. 14-15; *Pepys' Diary*, I, p. 236; J. Oldmixon, *History of England*, p. 487; K. Feiling, *History of the Tory Party*, p. 136; R. Lodge, *From the Restoration to the Death of William III*, pp. 15-16; W. Kennet, *Register*, pp. 300-302, 323; L. Echard, *History of England*, III, p. 32; *Somers' Tracts*, 1st Collection, IV, pp. 360-362.

in the Cavalier Parliament as it had in the Convention Parliament, the elections of 1661 altered its calculations. With such force had the cult of king and Church swept the country, aided by government promptings, that the new commons would fly far higher than the lords. In fact the government was quite outdone, if not quite undone. It would have to call upon the lords to protect the Church settlement from the Laudians rather than from the Latitudinarians. While the lords still boasted liberal and moderate peers, they now had strange brethren in the other house. Macaulay called the newly elected lower house "more zealous for royalty than the King, more zealous for episcopacy than the bishops". Lord John Campbell said of the Cavalier house of commons, at the outset, that it greatly exceeded the lords "in the desire to fix the Church on the narrowest foundation, and to persecute all who should not rigidly conform to its doctrines and discipline". To this body the second part of the restoration settlement was entrusted.[12]

[12]    *H. Mss. C., 5th Report,* Appendix, Part I, Duke of Sutherland Mss., p. 202; R. S. Bosher, *Making of the Restoration Settlement,* pp. 211-212, 237; J. Campbell, *Lives of the Lord Chancellors,* III, p. 178.

XII

## THE CAVALIER PARLIAMENT

The Cavalier Parliament distinguished itself as the second longest parliament in English history. For its accomplishments: "The Legislative record of the first five sessions of the Cavalier parliament reveals a violent reaction not only from the many utopian and revolutionary ideas of the interregnum, but also from the comparatively moderate traditional policies of 1640-41." The parliament had hardly assembled in May before the commons sent the proposal to the lords that the Solemn League and Covenant be burned by the common hangman. The lords agreed. They were also proceeding with a regard for past events. On May 13 a bill for reversing the attainder of the earl of Strafford passed its first reading in the upper house. On the 21st a major debate, "with great heat on both sides", developed on the question whether the attainder should be nullified or repealed. Repeal was finally favored by a margin of five votes, if an anonymous letter can be trusted. However, this was the last time the bill was considered on the floor of the house in the first session. It was not revived until the third session; the lords passed it on February 17, 1662, and the commons gave their unanimous consent ten days later. The caution of the lords' proceedings was notable. The upper house was showing considerable concern for the propriety of legal proceedings. In June of 1661 the house ordered the attorney-general to prepare a bill to declare the Long Parliament determined. The need for such a measure was not pressing, but the action was characteristic of the temper of the peers.[1]

The concern of the upper house with legality carried it in some strange directions. In January of 1662 it had taken up consideration of rescinding acts made during the Long Parliament, a proceeding

[1] C. Robbins, "The Repeal of the Triennial Act in 1664", p. 121; *L.J.*, XI, pp. 252, 254, 260-261, 273, 368, 381, 387, 472; *H. Mss. C.*, *5th Report*, Appendix, Part I, Duke of Sutherland Mss., p. 196; *C.J.*, III, p. 374; *S.R.*, V, p. 424.

which produced "long Debate". A large committee was finally appointed and charged with preparing a bill to repeal all acts of the Long Parliament, with the proviso that the bill provide clauses reinacting such acts as the committee felt merited continuance. As if this were not disturbing enough, the committee reported to the house that it believed there was need for a court similar to the star chamber. They asked the house who should sit on this court, what its jurisdiction should be, and what procedures should govern its operation. The house declined to offer any opinions upon the resurrection of this controversial agency of government, and told the committee to proceed as it saw fit. The committee numbered fifty members, or better than half a normal house at that time. Whatever the views of the committee were then, the house evidently had other second thoughts; there is no further record of the matter.[2]

But the star chamber was not the only agency of an old era to reappear in the records of the Cavalier Parliament. In July of 1661 two petitions from Yorkshire came before the king and privy council; they called for reinstitution of the council of the north. The lords examined the petition and appointed a committee to review the records from Charles I's reign which led to the abandonment of the court. They drafted a bill providing for the erection of a court, and establishment of a president and council of the north. Charles and Clarendon went so far as to contemplate the appointment of the earl of Strafford as president of the council, but in the ensuing inquiries Charles learned that the earl was "not at all beloved in that country". The proceedings in the lords also took a new turn. After a second reading on January 25, 1662, a long debate developed; the earl of Northumberland and the duke of Buckingham had exchanged sharp words. Clarendon as Speaker ordered them both to end their arguments, but Buckingham persisted. The house then proceeded to "reprehend" him. The bill died in this debate. Thus on two occasions agencies with ill-starred associations had come under consideration in the lords, though only once at their own initiative. In both cases the house judiciously decided not to proceed further with them. The house did join the commons in seeking an act to confirm the public acts of the Convention Parliament. The upper house had for the present maintained its balance when visited by ghosts from the past.[3]

[2]  L.J., XI, pp. 369, 370, 375, 378, 382; T. H. Lister, *Life and Administration of Clarendon*, II, pp. 112-113.
[3]  Bodley, *Rawlinson Ms.* A 162 fos. 1-4; B.M., *Harleian Ms.* 7158 fo. 139;

The lords persisted in a moderate course when confronted by the first bill in the group of laws usually called the Clarendon code. In July of 1661 the commons had passed the corporation bill, to ensure the good-affection of all town officials. The bill required them to take the oaths of allegiance and supremacy, an oath renouncing armed opposition to the king, and renouncing the legality of the Solemn League and Covenant. Any new officials must receive the sacrament according to the form of the Church of England once a year. The bill appointed commissioners to enforce the provisions, and gave them such latitude that they could at their own discretion remove officials for the public safety. The commons proposed to appoint as commissioners only sturdy high churchmen. The lords attempted amendments to give the crown and government control over these commissioners; indeed these amendments if adopted would have required the renewal of borough charters. However, the commons rejected all the lords' amendments and the lords insisted only on provisos whose effect was to put off further consideration of the bill until the second session of parliament. The delay did not lead to a more moderate measure. The upper house yielded to the commons' wishes, though its decision stirred some protest. Lord Ashley spoke against the bill, and the earl of Bolingbroke entered his protest to it. Bolingbroke particularly objected to the provision which allowed commissioners power to dismiss corporation officers if they deemed it expedient for the public safety. This he felt to be contrary to the guarantees of Magna Carta and the traditional proceedings of trials by oath. The bill became law on December 20, 1661.[4]

The commons had bested both king and lords in the corporation act proceedings. However, its passage was challenged from the lower house. William Prynne directed two pamphlets or "Summary Reasons" against the bill. Prynne found the bill contrary to the act of indemnity by infringing upon corporation officials in a discriminatory manner. The bill would further invalidate the grants and patents anciently given the corporations as well as numerous acts of parliament confirming them. It violated the privileges of parliament by

---

L.J., XI, pp. 294, 296-298, 302-303, 310, 370-371; H. Mss. C., 7th Report, Appendix, House of Lords Mss., p. 154; W. D. Macray, ed., Notes which passed at Meetings of the Privy Council, p. 49.
[4] L.J., XI, pp. 313-322, 346-353, 358; K. Feiling, History of the Tory Party, p. 111; J. E. T. Rogers, Complete Collection of the Protests of the Lords, I, pp. 21-22; W. D. Christie, Life of Shaftesbury, I, pp. 260-261.

giving commissioners control over peers and members of parliament who were also municipal officers. It transgressed, said Prynne, the sacred provision of Magna Carta: "That no Freeman shall be disseised or put out of his Freehold, Franchises, Liberties, free Customes, Lands or Tenements, nor put to answer for the same, unless he be brought to answer by due process of law, ...." He concluded his argument with the statement that the act was unnecessary, because the corporations were loyal; if some should not be, he asserted authority to take legal action was available without this act. The commons declared his anonymous pamphlets to be libels, totally illegal, false, scandalous, and seditious. They ordered the author sought. At this point Prynne revealed himself and sought the pardon of the house. After a "humble submission to, and concurrence with the censure and judgment of the house", the house pardoned his "offence".[5]

The commons were now very much in a mood to impose restrictions. They produced a bill in 1661 to license printing. The lords successfully blocked this bill in a dispute over the legality of the searching of peers' houses for unlicensed materials. In 1662 a modified bill was brought in, which after some amendment by the upper house, passed into law. Parliament also passed an act "for securing and preserving His Majesty's Person and Government against all treasonable and seditious Practices and Attempts". This bill passed the lords unanimously. Parliament was assuming an increasingly repressive attitude. An act against tumultuous petitioning passed the upper house the day after the bill securing the king's person.[6]

The Cavalier Parliament also passed some measures of sound legal benefit. In this regard the record of the upper house was better than that of the commons. The two houses joined to pass an act for preventing vexations and delays in suits at law. The lords also took up a bill for settling the jurisdiction of the court of admiralty, but this measure was allowed to die after its second reading. The lords did

[5] W. Prynne, "Summary Reasons humbly rendered ... against the new intended Bill for Governing and Reforming Corporations" (London, 1661), B.M., 190 g. 12(165); "Summary Reasons humbly tendered ... against the new intended Bill for Governing and Reforming Corporations" (London, 1661), B.M., C. 112 h. 4(92); "Votes and Resolves of the Commons House of Parliament", B.M., 190 g. 12(253); *C.S.P.V.*, 1661-1664, pp. 25-26.
[6] *L.J.*, XI, pp. 252-267, 324-325, 366, 393, 396, 435, 439, 469; A. Amos, *The English Constitution in the Reign of Charles the Second*, p. 241; *C.S.P.V.*, 1661-1664, p. 32.

better in rejecting another bill the commons originated. This proposed that royalists be relieved from all interest above three per cent on debts contracted before the civil wars. This partisan measure received no support in the upper house. Some adjustments in local government boundaries concluded the more technically legal work of the first three sessions of the Cavalier Parliament. For example, a bill proposed to move two hundreds from the jurisdiction of the city of Gloucester and return them to the county. This brought a protest from the earl of Bolingbroke who argued that the change would vacate a grant to the city made under the great seal of England. Bolingbroke's concern was singular, for local officials had sought passage of the act. The chief bills concerning legal affairs of the Cavalier Parliament — that is, the corporation and licensing acts — hardly compared favorably with the work of the Convention Parliament in passing the act confirming judicial proceedings and the act of indemnity. The new parliament did not improve its record when it turned its attention to military affairs.[7]

In truth, military affairs had become far less pressing in 1661 than they had been during the previous year. Parliament passed an act regulating the navy, as well as an act for preventing "theft and rapine" on the northern border of the kingdom. The lords wished to include the county palatine of Durham within the scope of the latter bill, but yielded to the commons' desire that it be kept separate. A third bill raised some constitutional debate. This was the militia act of 1662, which provided that the sole right of the militia should rest in the king, along with its ordering and disposal. An oath provided in the bill required the lord lieutenant and other officers to swear to the unlawfulness of taking up arms against the king or "against those that are Commissioned by him". The constitutionalists received this last phrase as potentially dangerous and wished it to read "lawfully Commissioned". The earl of Southampton led the constitutionalists in the house of lords; the earl of Anglesey opposed him. Anglesey held that the amendment was unnecessary, since a commission was not a commission if it were not lawful. Southampton felt this might be well enough understood within parliament, but not by most people. To this the reply was that parliament's understanding of it would quickly spread over the country. Accordingly the constitutionalists failed to

[7] L.J., XI, pp. 339-342, 347, 358, 374-381, 389, 408, 415-416; T. H. Lister, Life and Administration of Clarendon, II, 114 n.; J. E. T. Rogers, A Complete Collection of the Protests of the Lords, I, pp. 24-25.

secure insertion of the word. The point at issue was not a grave one, but its outcome was another indication of the direction in which parliament was moving. The balance between the interests of the state and the interests of the individual was tilting more and more in favor of the state. More unfortunate yet, the character of the state as the Cavalier Parliament was defining it placed narrow limits upon personal liberties, particularly of conscience.[8]

In one way, at least, the Cavalier Parliament in its early sessions resembled most parliaments. Finance was a central feature of much of its time and its legislation. One grant gave relief to loyal and indigent officers who had served the royal cause; the sum of £ 300,000 allocated for this purpose was indeed quite generous. The act provided for commissioners to try the merits of petitioners and award grants. The earl of Bolingbroke objected, somewhat technically, that this gave commissioners what belonged to the king alone — the control of dispensing money. Before enactment the bill suffered a reduction to £ 60,000, but Bolingbroke's argument did not attract support. At the same time parliament provided funds for carriages for the Royal Navy and Ordnance. These two acts were the only ones dealing with military and naval administration; only one act was passed which concerned the king in his particular estate. This enabled him to make leases of lands in the Duchy of Cornwall. Two bills were primarily regulatory in intent. The first was to prevent the melting of silver coins of the realm and the second proposed the enclosure of lands once used as public highways.[9]

Parliament devoted increasing attention to bills concerning foreign trade. Three bills on this subject became law. One provided beneficial arrangements for the importation of madder, an important dye-stuff, and regulation of its purity. A second bill barred the importation of foreign wool-cards, card-wire, or iron-wire, in response to petitions for protection. The last bill dealt with the prevention of frauds and regulating abuses in the customs, not a particularly hopeful task in this part of the seventeenth century. Better results could be hoped for in domestic economic measures. One promising arrangement to which parliament gave its blessing was a group of agreements between Thomas Bushell and two parties of miners in Somerset and

[8] *L.J.*, XI, pp. 305-306, 309, 314, 317, 437, 446, 466; L. Echard, *History of England*, III, p. 80.
[9] *L.J.*, XI, pp. 289, 297, 306, 334-358, 400, 405; J. E. T. Rogers, *Complete Collection of the Protests of the Lords*, I, p. 25.

Derbyshire. Bushell would provide capital and the miners labor in attempting to recover the drowned and deserted works of Row Pitts and Dove-Gange in the respective counties. A proposal to grant a glass bottle monopoly did not fare as well, and died after its second reading in the lords. Two counties received regulating acts. The making of woolen stuffs in Norwich and Norfolk was the object of the first bill, the manufacture of woolens in Yorkshire of the second. An additional act concerning merchant assurances also passed. Although both houses approved a bill for a register of sales and pawns to cover London and Westminster pawnbrokers, the king vetoed the measure, without offering explanations in his speech.[10]

Parliament passed two acts to ease the lot of local officers. The first provided safeguards against unnecessary charges upon sheriffs, and an easement in passing their accounts. The second bill was for the relief of collectors of public moneys. A bill for relief of the poor also passed; in general it restricted the poor within parish boundaries. Workhouses were provided in the London and Westminster area, including Surrey. London and Westminster finally received an omnibus streets bill, embracing building and repair, cleaning and regulating, and ordering of hackney cabs. Another bill concerning London gave the bishop of London authority to lease tenements recently erected on his property. Other bills dealt with problems arising outside the metropolis; for example, one provided for the repair of Dover harbor. The adventurers engaged in the draining of the great level of the Fens, led by the earl of Bedford, complained that their work, authorized by the Convention Parliament, was being hindered. The house of lords issued a strict prohibition against such abuses, and parliament passed an act confirming the acts of the Convention Parliament for the draining of the Fens. The economic measures of the first three sessions of the Cavalier Parliament were thus numerous and varied. Yet the legislation of 1661 and 1662 which would be long remembered was in religious affairs.[11]

When the Cavalier Parliament opened in May of 1661, the house of commons agitated for the repeal of the act barring the bishops from the house of lords. Heneage Finch, one of the most dependable Anglicans and a close friend of Clarendon, drafted the repealing bill.

[10] L.J., XI, pp. 361-378, 384-407, 412-432, 436-444, 459, 473.
[11] L.J., XI, pp. 258, 355, 374, 390, 398-401, 405-426, 434-443, 461-464, 476-478; H. Mss. C., 7th Report, Appendix, House of Lords Mss., p. 165; S.R., V, pp. 351-357.

This bill, "An Act for Repeal of an Act of Parliament Entituled an Act for disinabling all persons in Holy Orders to exercise any Temporall Jurisdiction or Authority", received its first reading in the commons on June 1. Pepys reported that Prynne leveled several assaults at the bill in the commons, but the bill received no notable check there, and passed its third reading on June 13. While the commons' passage was fairly smooth, Edward Gower "thought the Lords will scarce pass it with so little difficulty: some do not stick to say they will oppose it there". Clarendon reported that the upper house had little business to occupy it at this date, and could devote almost unlimited time and attention to the measure. Presbyterian opposition was surely to be expected; they had no love for bishops, and their position was supported by a statute of the realm. They would hardly give up twenty-six votes in the lords without a struggle. The Roman Catholic peers were no better inclined. Clarendon related that when the bill reached the lords it met with obstruction. Both nonconformist and recusant peers assaulted it, most particularly the earl of Bristol. Some years later Clarendon stated that Bristol never forgave him for rallying to the bill's defense and carrying it through the upper house. Yet the *Lords' Journals* do not suggest a great struggle. The bill was sent up to the lords on June 13 and passed its first reading on the next day. On the 15th the house heard a second reading and sent the bill to committee. On the 18th the lords went into committee of the whole house to discuss the bill, which was then given its third reading in essentially unaltered form. On the next day the commons indicated their agreement with some slight changes made to the bill by the lords' committee. Nowhere does the phrase "after long Debate", so commonly used by John Browne, appear. The bill evidently received little or no debate at the second reading, but went directly to committee. The committee held it only two days. The only debate acknowledged by the official records was in committee of the whole house on June 18. Yet the bill emerged unaltered from this session. The commons took thirteen days to pass the measure, the lords four. If Bristol or anyone else "held up" the bill, the pause was remarkably short; few bills ever went through the lords so rapidly. The only dissent entered was that of the Catholic Viscount Stafford. Yet Clarendon's version has long been the accepted one, although probably the royalist historian had confused events in the passage of the act with his defence of the religious settlement in parliament in 1663. Campbell's view concerning the bishops seems most probable: "There was a general feeling that for the dignity of the assembly of which they had ever formed a constituent part, and for the honour and protection of the church, they should again exercise their parliamentary functions along with the hereditary nobility."[12]

On November 20, 1661, at the opening of the second session of the Cavalier Parliament, twenty-three of the lords spiritual took their places in the upper house. After two decades, the house of lords again sat as it had in more halcyon days. Frewen of York led the episcopal delegation, for Canterbury was too old and ill to venture into the lords. The addition of the bishops added substantially to the votes the crown and government could depend on in the upper chamber, at least upon all but religious issues. The majority of the bishops steadily opposed Charles's attempts at religious moderation, despite royal threats. In all other matters they usually were obedient servants.[13]

The bishops did not so much lead as join in the general religious intolerance of the Cavalier Parliament. In May of 1661 a group of Quakers had petitioned the upper house, affirming their loyalty but asking that their beliefs, practices, and freedom be not impaired. The lords appointed a committee to study the petition with the directive "To consider a proper Remedy to cure the Distempers of these People, and to report the same to this House." The committee reported in three days. They recommended that the lords reject Quaker requests to give affirmations in place of oaths, not to doff hats to any man, and not to pay tithes. The general question of their adherence to the rites of the Church of England, and in particular non-observance of fasts, abstinence, and holy days was left to the whole house to debate. The house ordered the attorney-general to prepare a proclamation for the suppressing of Quakers. No further proceedings took place until the bishops had returned to the upper house. A bill was then brought in

[12] B.M., *Egerton Ms.* 2043 fo. 11; *Harleian Ms.* 7158 fo. 96; *Hargrave Ms.* 178 fo. 105; *S.R.,* V, p. 306; *Pepys' Diary,* II, p. 43; *H. Mss. C., Le Flemyng Mss.,* p. 25; *5th Report,* Appendix, Part I, Duke of Sutherland Mss., p. 203; Clarendon's *Life,* p. 1070; J. Campbell, *Lives of the Lord Chancellors,* III, pp. 172-173, 179; T. H. Lister, *Life and Administration of Clarendon,* II, p. 111; *L.J.,* XI, pp. 278-279, 281, 283-284; A. S. Turberville, "Lords under Charles II", p. 402; J. Lingard, *History of England,* IX, p. 33; D. Ogg, *Reign of Charles II,* I, p. 198; W. S. Holdsworth, *History of English Law,* VI, p. 165. Lingard states that the hard core of the Presbyterians alone joined Stafford in voting against the bill. Ranke, in his *History of England* (III, p. 370), states that Charles personally opposed the measure "because he foresaw that the bishops would oppose his schemes of toleration in the House".

[13] *L.J.,* XI, p. 352; A. S. Turberville, "Lords under Charles II", XLIV, p. 402, XLV, pp. 61-62; D. Ogg, *Reign of Charles II,* II, p. 466.

for preventing dangers arising from the Quakers. Under this title the commons had included action against all who scrupled at oaths. The lords rejected this extension of the bill's provisions; they wished to forbid meetings of ten or more Quakers, and to punish every offense. The commons insisted upon the broader scope concerning oaths, and desired meetings of five or more forbidden, though planning to punish every third offense. The lords yielded; they accepted a bill of greater scope as proposed by the commons. On May 2, 1662, the bill became law.[14]

The problem of the Quakers was only a small part of the great question of uniformity that concerned such persons as Clarendon, Sheldon, Morley, Cosin, and Henchman. Uniformity also concerned the commons. In July of 1661 they sent a bill of uniformity to the house of lords, where it was ignored. This sudden death was surely the work of the government. Most probably, Clarendon wished the bishops to take their seats in the upper house before the house considered an uniformity bill. In 1662 the lords took up in earnest a proposal for restoring uniformity to public prayers and the administration of sacraments. The lords committed the bill to a committee of thirty-six, eight of these bishops, and another twelve of undoubted Anglican sympathy. Only five distinctly non-Anglican members balanced the twenty. Unlike the bill restoring the bishops' temporal authority, the progress of the uniformity bill was hard. The lords debated the bill without break from March thirteenth to nineteenth. Attendance on March 12 was 78 members, on March 20 it was 79. On the six days of debate between these two dates attendance averaged nearly ninety-one peers, and never slipped lower than eighty-seven. The bill under consideration in the lords provided that all clergymen should, under pain of deprivation from all preferment, subscribe to a declaration of assent to everything contained in a revised Book of Common Prayer, including Psalter and form of Ordination. This Prayer Book must be used in all places of public worship. In addition anyone entrusted with the cure of souls must receive episcopal ordination, except only some French and Dutch ministers. Southampton and Ashley raised their voices against the bill in the lords, though without success. But the lords were moderate beside the commons. They demanded renunciation of the Covenant and of the lawfulness of bearing arms against the king, of all clerical incumbents, heads and fellows of colleges, professors, schoolmasters, and tutors. The

[14] *L.J.*, XI, pp. 267-269, 273, 338, 340, 353, 365, 372, 389-397, 442-443.

Prayer Book itself became an object of controversy. It had been revised by the Savoy Conference, where the earl of Northumberland had appeared to plead for the use of the Elizabethan Prayer Book. Spurned by the Conference, he carried his battle into the lords. Debate on the Prayer Book continued from February 25 to March 15, but in the end the decision was to retain the Savoy version. Moderating attempts continued in the upper house. Clarendon brought in a proviso in the king's name that Charles might be allowed to make provision for clergy deprived of their livings by the bill of uniformity. The lords added it to the bill, and passed it on April 8, 1662. The commons now worked on the bill with a vengeance. Clarendon and the duke of York had managed, during debate in the lords, to insert another royal proviso allowing Charles to grant a dispensation to ministers who scrupled at certain ceremonies. The commons rejected this. The lords' proviso, granting a minister who was turned out of his benefice by the proposed act a fifth of his income upon the king's signification of his good behavior, also failed in the lower house. Elizabeth, and more recently, the Long Parliament had both allowed the fifth in similar circumstances; not so the Cavalier commons, in spite of the lords' pressing arguments. The commons rejected pleas regarding the Declaration of Breda; "tender consciences" said the commons, were not "schismatical consciences". The unity of the lords suffered a shock through the independent position taken by Bristol, whose antipathy toward Clarendon was unrestrained. When Clarendon tried to carry through the proviso allowing Charles to dispense ministers who scrupled at surplice and sign of the cross, Bristol rose to claim that Charles wished no such thing. In the struggle the crucial clause demanding the "assent and consent" of all clergy to all parts of the Book of Common Prayer, so critical in forcing conscientious ministers to abandon their cures, received little attention, or so Clarendon related in his *Life*. On May 2, 1662, the bill became law. Clarendon wrote: "The chancellor was one of those, who would have been glad that the act had not been clogged with many of those clauses which he foresaw might produce some inconveniences; but when it was passed, he thought it absolutely necessary to see obedience paid to it without any connivance." The bill in part avenged the martyr king. The Cavalier Parliament had laid a burden upon the nation's religious life, and its political life as well, whose effect would endure for generations.[15]

[15]  *L.J.*, XI, pp. 364, 366, 383, 393, 396, 400-413, 421-427, 441-442, 446-451;

Charles, for one, had no intention of seeing "obedience paid" to the act of uniformity. In December of 1662, he issued a royal declaration of toleration, but parliament held him captive on the religious issue, and would not hear of dispensation for nonconformists and recusants. The king therefore determined upon an act of parliament to resolve his difficulties. Clarendon was ill and out of the house. Charles's allies in this task produced a bill giving the crown power to dispense with the act of uniformity. In February, 1663, a bill was presented to the house of lords which bore the clear imprint of the king's continuing struggle for religious moderation in the face of parliament's high Anglican fervor. From the outset the royal effort had little chance of success, for even if it should survive the house of lords, it was almost certain to meet defeat in the house of commons, which in religious matters had continued to impose its will upon the religious moderates. Not even attempts at comprehension, or a broadening of the base of Anglicanism to resemble the Church of Elizabeth's time, had managed to make headway against the strength of the narrow Anglicanism which had gripped the majority of the lower house, and was supported by the most powerful of the bishops in the upper house. In fact the royal bill died swiftly and violently. Dispute over religious policy remained the particular curse of seventeenth century England and vastly complicated the course of constitutional and political growth.[16]

The first three sessions of the Cavalier Parliament did not equal the Convention Parliament in the quality of its legislation. The moderate and constitutional course of 1660 had not been followed in 1661 and 1662. The bishops had been restored to their temporal authority and the old constitution thereby honored. However, the overriding character of the major legislation was one of harshness. The first two statutes of the Clarendon code, the corporation act and the act of

---

R. S. Bosher, *Making of the Restoration Settlement*, pp. 244, 250-252; J. Old-mixon, *History of England*, p. 507; T. H. Lister, *Life and Administration of Clarendon*, II, pp. 184-186; Clarendon's *Life*, pp. 1077-1079, 1081; W. D. Christie, *Life of Shaftesbury*, I, pp. 260-261; D. Ogg, *Reign of Charles II*, I, p. 200; K. Feiling, *History of the Tory Party*, p. 130; *H. Mss. C.*, 7th Report, Appendix, House of Lords Mss., pp. 162-163; J. Campbell, *Lives of the Lord Chancellors*, IV, p. 180; R. Lodge, *From the Restoration to the Death of William III*, p. 65; *C.S.P.D.*, 1661-1662, p. 324; *S.R.*, V, pp. 364-370; *C.S.P.V.*, 1661-1664, pp. 124-125.

[16] B.M., *Stowe Ms. 304*; D. Ogg, *Reign of Charles II*, I, p. 204; A. S. Turberville, "Lords under Charles II", XLIV, p. 407; J. Campbell, *Lives of the Lord Chancellors*, III, p. 186; Bodley, *Rawlinson Ms. A 162* fos. 52-53.

uniformity, breathed this spirit. The Quakers had become the objects of an harsh and oppressive bill. Acts for the security of the king's person and against tumultuous petitioning had been passed. Finally, there had been a dangerous flirtation with the old "prerogative" courts. The changed tone of the legislation reflected a changed commons; the lords continued to be men of mixed outlook. The addition of the bishops stiffened the Anglicanism of the upper house; yet, it was also virtually the only place in England where the voice of nonconformist and recusant legally might be raised. In all the religious bills the lords had taken a decidedly more moderate line than the commons. The nobles had twice rejected revival of the agencies of Charles I's government. But the upper house had lost to the commons in virtually every point of disagreement over religion. This weakness did not appear on issues where all the lords were in agreement, such as those concerning the judicial rights of their chamber. The lords, by virtue of their diversity, were more moderate than the commons in religion. Any proposal of theirs on matters of religious policy was of necessity a compromise measure, and as such less apt to run to extremes. But this became a disadvantage, because whole-hearted support was lacking when the house fought for its proposals, hence the frequent capitulations to the commons.

By the end of 1662 there had been five sessions of parliament. All the major acts of the restoration settlement had become law, except three. In 1664 parliament would pass the conventicle act and the triennial act replacing the famous one of the Long Parliament; in 1665 it would add the five-mile act to the Clarendon code. As hereditary legislators, the lords could claim to have discharged their traditional duties well. They had played an active, and occasionally distinguished, part in the settlement. Their activity in itself was a victory, for it had not been expected of them. The upper house had shown great powers of recovery upon its return from the grave. The moderation of its policies had increased its stature in many parts of the realm. Extinct in 1659, the house of lords was very much alive three years later. This was the legacy of the restoration peers to the great eighteenth and nineteenth century houses that followed them.

# CONCLUSION: THE RESTORED HOUSE OF LORDS

"By the end of 1662 the Restoration settlement in England had been practically completed. Church, State, and social organization had been re-erected on the old foundations." In each element of this restoration, the position of the house of lords was significant. The church did not stand on its old foundations until the bishops enjoyed again their temporal power as spiritual lords of parliament. So too, what Keith Feiling called a "rake's progress of political theology", the Clarendon code, was no more extreme because the upper house attempted to act as a moderating force in the church settlement, and at least was not usually an active partner of the commons in the work of persecution. As late as 1665, when the commons were still hot upon the nonconformists, the house of lords, led by Earle, bishop of Salisbury, sought to check their aggression in the drafting of the five mile act. In the early years of the restoration era, the upper house alone afforded political expression to groups outside the Anglican communion.[1]

The restoration of the state was complete only upon the restoration of the upper house. The role that the lords proceeded to play in the government of the state was notably more vigorous than anyone writing in 1659 would have predicted. A. S. Turberville has summed up this aspect of the lords' return: "It is clear that the house of lords emerged from the testing time of the Restoration a much stronger body than might have been anticipated in 1660. The house succeeded in re-establishing itself as an ... integral part of the mechanism of the state. Conscious that it must make an effort to secure its position, in its corporate capacity it let slip no opportunity of doing so." In this process the upper house not only had considerable success in defending its own judicial role in the constitution, but also gave the com-

---

[1] R. Lodge, *From the Restoration to the Death of William III*, p. 23; K. Feiling, *History of the Tory Party*, p. 131.

mons a good fight over their financial claims. Both as a corporate body and as a group of distinguished individuals the lords furnished the government with services which might have been called indispensable, had not the Puritan Revolution shown otherwise. The vitality of the lords in the next two centuries bears testimony to the determination with which the house re-entered upon its duties in 1660.[2]

The social organization, like church and state, regained its old structure only with the return of the peers to their old eminence. The tenacity of the peerage in preserving much of their landed estates during the years of disruption, and their thoroughness in securing their economic position during the restoration, afforded them a position of power in the shires. This position, added to the strong position the house of lords had regained at Westminster, was of major political and constitutional importance. The first major evidence of this appeared in the Glorious Revolution. As Sir George Clark observed, James II was not brought down, and William III brought in, by a popular uprising, but by the work of men of political experience, wealth, and territorial influence. Of the seven signatories of the invitation to William III, four were peers: Danby, Lumley, Shrewsbury, and Devonshire. The fifth was the bishop of London, a spiritual lord. The sixth and seventh were members of the great noble houses of Russell and Sidney. The character of English political life for the three generations following the Glorious Revolution had its roots in the estates of the great Whig magnates. While the house of lords was becoming more a second chamber, a body which acted as a check upon the house of commons, it exchanged this loss of evident co-ordinate power for the no less significant control of the great eighteenth century borough-mongers over the membership of the house of commons. Even the surrender of claims to the co-ordinate power came slowly. In the 1660's the upper house had by no means abandoned such power to the commons. By the surprising force of its return to the political life of the nation, the house of lords assured that the constitution was what they believed it ought to be — "Of King, Lords, and Commons".[3]

[2]  A. S. Turberville, "The Lords under Charles II", XLV, p. 74.
[3]  G. N. Clark, Later Stuarts, p. 133; W. S. Holdsworth, History of English Law, VI, p. 248.

# APPENDIX A

## COMMITTEE SERVICE OF PEERS

Committee Service in the first three sessions of the Cavalier Parliament, 1661-1662, based on 71 selected committees (51 for bishops).

| Number of Committees: | Name of Peer: |
|---|---|
| 67 | John Egerton, earl of Bridgwater |
| 56 | Jerome Weston, earl of Portland |
| 51 | Arthur Annesley, earl of Anglesey |
| 50 | Oliver St. John, earl of Bolingbroke |
| 48 | William, Baron Craven |
| | John, Baron Lucas |
| 47 | John, Baron Robartes |
| 43 | Richard Sackville, earl of Dorset |
| | John Cosin, bishop of Durham |
| 42 | James Compton, earl of Northampton |
| | Robert Sutton, Baron Lexington |
| | Anthony Ashley Cooper, Baron Ashley |
| 39 | Charles Stanley, earl of Derby |
| 38 | Charles, Baron Howard of Charlton |
| 36 | Henry Mordaunt, earl of Peterborough |
| | Humphrey Henchman, bishop of Salisbury |
| 33 | John Carey, Baron Hunsdon |
| 31 | William Howard, Viscount Stafford |
| 30 | Edward Montagu, earl of Manchester |
| | Denzil, Baron Holles |
| 29 | George Digby, earl of Bristol |
| | Henry King, bishop of Chichester |
| | Richard, Baron Byron |
| 27 | Gilbert Sheldon, bishop of London |
| | Warwick, Baron Mohun |
| | John, Baron Berkeley of Stratton |
| 26 | George Morley, bishop of Worcester |
| | William, Baron Paget |
| 24 | Henry, Baron Arundell |
| 22 | Philip, Baron Wharton |
| | John, Baron Crewe |
| 21 | John Gauden, bishop of Exeter |

| *Number of Committees:* | *Name of Peer:* |
|---|---|
| 20 | William, Baron Grey of Warke |
| 19 | Edward Reynolds, bishop of Norwich |
| 18 | James Butler, earl of Brecknock, marquess of Ormond (I) |
| | John Grenville, earl of Bath |
| | Charles Howard, earl of Carlisle |
| | George, Baron Berkeley of Berkeley |
| 17 | Thomas Wriothesley, earl of Southampton |
| | George Villiers, duke of Buckingham |
| | Henry Pierrepont, marquess of Dorchester |
| | John Neville, Baron Abergavenny |
| | William Brydges, Baron Chandos |
| | Frederick, Baron Cornwallis |
| 16 | Theophilus Fiennes, earl of Lincoln |
| | William Lucy, bishop of St. David's |
| | John, Baron Belasyse |
| | Francis, Baron Newport |
| 15 | William Russell, earl of Bedford |
| | William Wentworth, earl of Strafford |
| | Robert Skinner, bishop of Oxford |
| 14 | Mountjoy Blount, earl of Newport |
| | Benjamin Laney, bishop of Peterborough |
| | Thomas, Baron Windsor |
| 13 | Charles Stuart, duke of Richmond |
| | Thomas Howard, earl of Berkshire |
| | Thomas Belasyse, Viscount Fauconberg |
| | Christopher, Baron Hatton |
| 12 | George Monck, duke of Albermarle |
| | Montagu Bertie, earl of Lindsey |
| | George, Baron Eure |
| 11 | John Paulet, marquess of Winchester |
| | Algernon Percy, earl of Northumberland |
| | Philip Stanhope, earl of Chesterfield |
| | Nicholas Leke, earl of Scarsdale |
| | Matthew Wren, bishop of Ely |
| | Richard Sterne, bishop of Carlisle |
| | William, Baron Widdrington |
| 10 | Baptist Noel, Viscount Campden |
| | Accepted Frewen, archbishop of York |
| | John Hacket, bishop of Coventry and Lichfield |
| | Francis, Baron Seymour |
| | Richard, Baron Vaughan |
| 9 | Philip Herbert, earl of Pembroke |
| | Thomas Wentworth, earl of Cleveland |
| | Robert Sanderson, bishop of Lincoln |
| | Horatio, Baron Townshend |

| *Number of Committees:* | *Name of Peer:* |
|---|---|
| 8 | Basil Fielding, earl of Denbigh |
| | Nicholas Monck, bishop of Hereford |
| | William, Baron Sandys |
| | Thomas, Baron Wentworth |
| | Francis, Baron Willoughby of Parham |
| | Charles, Baron Gerard of Brandon |
| | George Booth, Baron Delamere |
| 7 | John Holles, earl of Clare |
| | Arthur Capel, earl of Essex |
| | William Roberts, bishop of Bangor |
| | Edward, Baron Howard of Escrick |
| | Richard Boyle, Baron Clifford, earl of Orrery (I |
| 6 | William Fiennes, Viscount Say and Sele |
| | George Griffith, bishop of St. Asaph |
| | Christopher Roper, Baron Teynham |
| | Edward, Baron Montagu |
| | Thomas, Baron Colepeper |
| 5 | James Stuart, duke of York and Albany |
| | James Howard, earl of Suffolk |
| | John Cecil, earl of Exeter |
| | Charles Rich, earl of Warwick |
| | James Ley, earl of Marlborough |
| | Hugh Lloyd, bishop of Landaff |
| | Edward, Baron Herbert of Cherbury |
| 4 | William Cecil, earl of Salisbury |
| | Thomas Savage, Earl Rivers |
| | John Tufton, earl of Thanet |
| | John, Viscount Mordaunt |
| | Charles West, Baron DeLaWarr |
| | Thomas, Baron Coventry |
| | William, Baron Petre |
| | Marmaduke, Baron Langdale |
| 3 | William Cavendish, earl of Devonshire |
| | Lionel Cranfield, earl of Middlesex |
| | Henry Jermain, earl of St. Albans |
| | Leicester Devereux, Viscount Hereford |
| | Robert Greville, Baron Brooke |
| | Edward Watson, Baron Rockingham |
| | William, Baron Crofts |
| 2 | Edward Somerset, marquess of Worcester |
| | Francis Talbot, earl of Shrewsbury |
| | Aubrey de Vere, earl of Oxford |
| | Mildmay Fane, earl of Westmorland |
| | Henry Grey, earl of Stamford |
| | Edward, Viscount Conway |
| | Brian Walton, bishop of Chester |

*Number of Committees:*          *Name of Peer:*

William Nicholson, bishop of Gloucester
John, Baron Poulett
William, Baron Maynard
Francis Lennard, Baron Dacre
Humble, Baron Ward
1          Prince Rupert, duke of Cumberland
Philip Sidney, earl of Leicester
Charles Howard, earl of Nottingham
Charles Dormer, earl of Carnarvon
Francis Browne, Viscount Montagu
William Pierce, bishop of Bath and Wells
John Warner, bishop of Rochester
Gilbert Ironside, bishop of Bristol
Conyers, Baron Darcy
William, Baron Stourton
Henry Hastings, Baron Loughborough

### Peers not participating on the Selected Committees

| | |
|---|---|
| Edward Hyde, earl of Clarendon | Presiding Officer of the House |
| William Juxon, archbishop of Canterbury | Ill |
| Thomas Howard, duke of Norfolk | Insane at Padua |
| William Seymour, duke of Somerset | Minor |
| William Cavendish, marquess of Newcastle | In Retirement |
| Anthony Grey, earl of Kent | Minor |
| John Manners, earl of Rutland | Ill |
| Theophilus Hastings, earl of Huntingdon | Minor |
| Robert Rich, earl of Holland | |
| John Sheffield, earl of Mulgrave | Minor |
| Henry Carey, earl of Dover | Aged and Ill |
| Heneage Finch, earl of Winchilsea | At Constantinople |
| Robert Spencer, earl of Sunderland | Minor |
| James Savile, earl of Sussex | Minor |
| George Goring, earl of Norwich | |
| John Wilmot, earl of Rochester | Minor |
| Edward Montagu, earl of Sandwich | On Foreign Assignment |
| Thomas Brudenell, earl of Cardigan | |
| Brian Duppa, bishop of Winchester | Ill |
| James Tuchet, Baron Audley | |
| Thomas Parker, Baron Morley | |
| Edward, Baron Vaux | Ill |
| Thomas, Baron Cromwell | |
| Dudley, Baron North | |
| Charles, Baron Gerard of Bromley | |
| Charles, Baron Stanhope | |

John, Baron Lovelace
Thomas, Baron Bruce
Thomas, Baron Leigh                      Ill
Charles Smyth, Baron Carrington
Issac, Baron Astley
Charles Kirkhoven, Baron Wotton          Abroad
Herbert Percy, Baron Powis

# APPENDIX B

## LORDS LIEUTENANT IN 1661

| Shire: | Lord Lieutenant: | Commons' Seats: |
|---|---|---|
| **The West Country:** | | |
| Cornwall | Earl of Bath | 44 |
| Devonshire | Duke of Albemarle | 26 |
| Somerset | Earl of Brecknock (Ormond) | 18 |
| Dorsetshire | Duke of Richmond | 20 |
| **The Marches toward Wales:** | | |
| Gloucestershire | Lord Herbert of Raglan | 8 |
| Monmouthshire | — | 3 |
| Herefordshire | Lord Herbert of Raglan | 8 |
| Worcestershire | Baron Windsor (+ Earl of Southampton, 1662) | 9 |
| Shropshire | Baron Newport | 12 |
| Staffordshire | Baron Brooke | 10 |
| Lancashire | Earl of Derby | 14 |
| Cheshire | Earl of Derby | 4 |
| **Southern and Eastern England:** | | |
| Hampshire | Earl of Southampton | 26 |
| Wiltshire | Earl of Southampton | 34 |
| Berkshire | Baron Lovelace | 9 |
| Oxfordshire | Earl of Clarendon | 9 |
| Buckinghamshire | Earl of Bridgwater | 14 |
| Bedfordshire | Earl of Cleveland | 4 |
| Hertfordshire | Earl of Essex | 6 |
| Middlesex | Earls of Dorset and Berkshire | 8 |
| Surrey | Viscount Mordaunt | 14 |
| Sussex | Earl of Northumberland | 28 |
| Kent | Earl of Southampton (1662) | 18 |
| Essex | Earl of Oxford | 8 |
| Cambridgeshire | Earl of Suffolk | 6 |
| Suffolk | Earl of Suffolk | 16 |

| *Shire:* | *Lord Lieutenant:* | *Commons' Seats:* |
|---|---|---|
| Norfolk | Earl of Southampton (Baron Townshend in 1662) | 12 |
| Huntingdonshire | Earl of Manchester | 4 |

**Central England:**

| | | |
|---|---|---|
| Northamptonshire | Earls of Exeter and Westmorland | 9 |
| Warwickshire | Earl of Northampton | 6 |
| Leicestershire | Baron Loughborough | 4 |
| Rutland | Viscount Campden | 2 |
| Lincolnshire | Earl of Lindsey | 12 |
| Derbyshire | Earl of Devonshire | 4 |
| Nottinghamshire | Marquess of Newcastle | 8 |

**Northern England:**

| | | |
|---|---|---|
| Yorkshire | | 30 |
| West Riding | Duke of Buckingham | |
| East Riding | Baron Belasyse | |
| North Riding | Viscount Fauconberg | |
| Durham | Viscount Fauconberg | 4 |
| Westmorland | Earl of Carlisle | 4 |
| Cumberland | Earl of Carlisle | 6 |
| Northumberland | Earl of Northumberland | 8 |

# GENERAL INDEX

(Peers have been indexed by title rather than by name, as they are usually identified in the text by title. A cross reference is provided for any peer identified by name in the text.)